Transformation, Development, and
Regionalization in Greater Asia | 16

The Series

Transformation, Development, and
Regionalization in Greater Asia

is edited by

Prof. Dr. Christoph Schuck
Department of Philosophy and Political Science
TU Dortmund University, Germany

Matthias Heise, M.A.
Department of Philosophy and Political Science
TU Dortmund University, Germany

Julia Dumin (ed.)

South Korea
after the 2017 Impeachment

Implications for Politics, Society, and Democracy

 **Nomos**

The Deutsche Nationalbibliothek lists this publication in the
Deutsche Nationalbibliografie; detailed bibliographic data
are available on the Internet at http://dnb.d-nb.de

ISBN   978-3-8487-8170-6 (Print)
        978-3-7489-2630-6 (ePDF)

British Library Cataloguing-in-Publication Data
A catalogue record for this book is available from the British Library.

ISBN   978-3-8487-8170-6 (Print)
        978-3-7489-2630-6 (ePDF)

Library of Congress Cataloging-in-Publication Data
Dumin, Julia
South Korea after the 2017 Impeachment
Implications for Politics, Society, and Democracy
Julia Dumin (ed.)
177 pp.
Includes bibliographic references.

ISBN   978-3-8487-8170-6 (Print)
        978-3-7489-2630-6 (ePDF)

Onlineversion
Nomos eLibrary

1st Edition 2022
© Nomos Verlagsgesellschaft, Baden-Baden, Germany 2022. Overall responsibility
for manufacturing (printing and production) lies with Nomos Verlagsgesellschaft mbH
& Co. KG.

Acknowledgements

This book was developed in the context of the international conference "South Korea after the 2017 Impeachment: Implications for Democratic Consolidation" conducted at TU Dortmund University in November 2019. For both to be made possible and successful, I am greatly indebted to several people and institutions. First and foremost, I would like to extend my gratitude towards the Faculty of Humanities and Theology of TU Dortmund University and particularly to Prof. Christoph Schuck, Professor of Political Science and Dean of the Faculty, for awarding to me the extraordinary opportunity to organize a conference and subsequently publish a book on a topic from the very core of my research interests. I would also like to thank Prof. Christian Neuhäuser, Professor of Political Philosophy, for taking the time to officially open the conference and extending a welcome address to the participants. Many thanks also go the participants of the conference for their contribution to the success of the conference as well as the subsequent book project. The academic exchange in this context proved to be very fruitful and inspiring and was very much appreciated on my part. Specifically regarding the book project, I would also like to thank the reviewers of this book for their valuable comments and suggestions on the individual chapters, as well as the editors of the book series, Prof. Christoph Schuck and Matthias Heise, for extending to me the much-appreciated opportunity of joining their series with this book. Last, but definitely not least, my heartfelt thanks go to Rika Althoff and Karin König for their great organizational support during the conference, to Rika Althoff for her attentive proofreading of the entire book, to the faculty staff, particularly Maria Möllenberg-Hemker and Julia Pferdekämper, for their support and advice with the preparation and administrative processing of the conference, to Nomos, specifically Beate Bernstein and Eduard Schwarzenberger, for their editorial support throughout the publication process, and to all my colleagues at the Department of Philosophy and Political Science for their ongoing support and advice during this project and for letting me benefit from their experience and knowledge. Without the support of all the above-mentioned, the publication of this book would not have been possible.

Dortmund, February 2022   Julia Dumin

Table of Contents

Introduction: Conceptualizing South Korea's Impeachment Case in the Context of Democratization Theory

Julia Dumin

When the Constitutional Court of the Republic of Korea (hereafter: Korea) announced its ruling on the impeachment of the then president Park Geun-hye (*Pak Kŭn-hye*)[1] in March 2017,[2] upholding the National Assembly's December 2016 vote to impeach Park Geun-hye, it finalized Korea's first case of presidential impeachment that ended with the removal from office of the incumbent.[3] Apart from the fact that presidential impeachments that result in removal from office remain a rather rare phenomenon to occur, not only in Korea but also globally,[4] the procedure gained international attention mainly through the public protests that preceded the impeachment, the so-called candlelight vigil (*ch'otpuljiphoe*). While this candlelight vigil was not the first to have been used as an instrument to express public dissatisfaction about politics in Korea,[5] its scope was exceptional.[6] It was probably also in the context of international events like the

---

1 Throughout this volume, the McCune-Reischauer method of romanization is used to transcribe Korean terms. In cases where a different spelling is of common use, this spelling is introduced with an additional mention of the McCune-Reischauer transcription at its first appearance in every chapter.

2 A translated version of the ruling is available at http://search.ccourt.go.kr/xmlFile/0 /010400/2017 /pdf/e2016n1_1.pdf [Accessed January 3, 2022].

3 Mosler, H. B. (2017). The Institution of Presidential Impeachment in South Korea, 1992-2017. *Verfassung und Recht in Übersee/Law and Politics in Africa, Asia and Latin America*, 50 (2), 111-134, p. 112. In 2004, the only other instance where an incumbent was impeached by the National Assembly, then president Roh Moo-hyun's (*No Mu-hyŏn*) impeachment was overturned by the Constitutional Court. Ibid.

4 Ginsburg, T., Huq, A., and Landau, D. (2021). The Comparative Constitutional Law of Presidential Impeachment. *The University of Chicago Law Review*, 88 (1), 81-164, p. 119.

5 Kim, S.-C. (2017). South Korea's Candlelight Protests. *East Asia Forum*, February 7, 2017, [online]. Available at: https://www.eastasiaforum.org/2017/02/07/south-korea s-candlelight-protests/ [Accessed January 31, 2022].

6 Lee, S. J. (2017). A Democratic Breakthrough in South Korea? *Carnegie Endowment for International Peace*, March 24, 2017, [online]. Available at: https://carnegieen dowment.org/2017/03/24/democratic-breakthrough-in-south-korea-pub-68394 [Accessed January 30, 2022].

protests in the Arab Spring that the absence of violence throughout the candlelight protests became notable.[7] These characteristics then triggered conclusions about what the impeachment and the protests meant for the state of Korean democracy, roughly three decades after its establishment and against the backdrop that Korea has been achieving high scores in various democracy indices since the mid-1990s.[8] While these conclusions were generally on a positive note regarding the impeachment itself (i.e. its legitimacy and constitutionality as well as the nature of the processes surrounding it), minor differences can be observed regarding the outlook on the future of Korean democracy. One of the most emphasized perspectives in this context viewed the impeachment as constituting an example for a well-functioning democratic system because throughout the whole impeachment process and including the overwhelming majority of the actors involved, democratic procedures were respected and adhered to.[9] On a similar note, the rule of law principle was perceived as being strengthened by the unwillingness of the protesters to accept the prevailing of corruption in politics[10] as well as by the consequent criminal prosecution of these cases of corruption.[11] Nevertheless, it was also highlighted that the impeachment accentuated some weaknesses of the Korean democratic system, especially with regard to the partial failure of Korean political

---

7 Kelly, R. (2017). South Korea's Finest Hour: Lessons From the Impeachment. *The Interpreter*, April 11, 2017, [online]. Available at: https://www.lowyinstitute.org/th e-interpreter/south-korea-s-finest-hour-lessons-impeachment [Accessed January 30, 2022].

8 See for example the Bertelsmann Transformation Index, where Korea has been receiving scores between 8.51 and 8.99 (on a scale from 1 to 10, with 10 being the most democratic) between 2006 and 2022, Bertelsmann Stiftung (n.d.). *BTI 2006-2022 Results*, [online]. Available at: https://bti-project.org/en/index/political-t ransformation [Accessed February 23, 2022]; the Freedom House Freedom in the World Index, which has awarded Korea scores between 82 and 84 (on a scale from 0 to 100, with 100 being the most free) between 2017 and 2021, Freedom House (n.d.). *Freedom in the World: South Korea*, [online]. Available at: https://freedomh ouse.org/country/south-korea/freedom-world/2021 [Accessed February 21, 2022]; or the Democracy Matrix, attributing to Korea scores between 0.85 and 0.93 (on a scale from 0 to 1, with 1 being the most democratic) between 1993 and 2020, Lauth, H.-J., Schlenkrich, O., and Lemm, L. (n.d.). *Country Graph South Korea*, [online]. Available at: https://www.democracymatrix.com/online-analysis/country #/South%20Korea/total_index_core [Accessed February 21, 2022].

9 Shin, G.-W. and Moon, R. J. (2017). South Korea After Impeachment. *Journal of Democracy*, 28 (4), 117-131, p. 121. In this context, Kelly specifically emphasizes the fact that the protests did not question the state or democracy. Kelly 2017.

10 Kelly 2017.

11 Lee 2017; Shin and Moon 2017, p. 130.

parties to fulfil their intermediary function[12] and to the power balance between the executive and the legislature.[13] In their outlook, observers were somewhat divided, some seeing the Korean democratic system on a stable way "toward a maturing realization"[14] of democracy, while others emphasized the need for reforms and framed the impeachment as an opportunity for Korea to "restore and renew"[15] its democracy by taking up the impetus the impeachment provided for structural reforms in society, economy, and culture.[16]

The central topics as identified in the academic discourse about the impeachment above can thus be summarized to be the following: 1) adherence to democratic rules and procedures, 2) prevalence of the rule of law principle, 3) the role of political parties as intermediaries between politics and civil society, and 4) checks and balances. The nature of these aspects, combined with the fact that the impeachment of Park Geun-hye coincided with Korean democracy marking its 30th anniversary, suggests that researching the case in a theoretical frame of democratic consolidation theory could provide further insight into the question what these events signify for the state of Korean democracy. Thus, the remainder of this introduction will be structured as follows: First, different conceptions of democratic consolidation will be discussed with the goal of laying the foundation for framing this volume in the context of a theoretical background. On this basis, a short evaluation will follow on why a case of impeachment might prove to be a useful instrument in an analysis of the status of democratic consolidation. Finally, the chapters of this volume, their contents, as well as the connections between them will be summarized and contextualized in the theoretical framework.

---

12 Mobrand, E. (2018). Democracy Is More Than a Political System: Lessons From South Korea's Democratic Transformation. *The Asan Forum*, December 20, 2018, [online]. Available at: https://theasanforum.org/democracy-is-more-than-a-political-system-lessons-from-south-koreas-democratic-transformation/ [Accessed January 30, 2022]; Shin and Moon 2017, pp. 119-120. Supporting this analysis, Shin and Moon also point out that the call for impeachment against Park Geun-hye had not been initiated by political elites, but by actors from the grassroots level, with the former (the opposition parties as well as a Park-critical faction of Park's own party) following suit only after initial hesitation. Ibid., p. 120.

13 Kang, S.-G. (2019). Candlelight Demonstrations and the Presidential Impeachment in South Korea: An Evaluation of the 30 Years of Democracy. *Asian Education and Development Studies*, 8 (3), 256-267, p. 257.

14 Shin and Moon 2017, p. 129.

15 Kang 2019, p. 263.

16 Ibid.; Lee 2017.

While transition research has traditionally been working on finding out more about "how, why, and under which conditions"[17] political systems shift from autocratic to democratic systems, research on democratic consolidation can retrospectively be seen as having emerged as a related, but distinct branch of research ever since O'Donnell, Schmitter, and Whitehead's seminal work "Transitions of Authoritarian Rule" (1986), which founded the splitting of the transition process into three phases: liberalization, democratization, and consolidation.[18] Generally speaking, the term democratic consolidation denotes the situation in which the expectation that the democratic system will persist (as opposed to the expectation that it might relapse into authoritarianism) prevails.[19] Different approaches on how to determine when this state of affairs may be seen as achieved include both minimalist and more inclusive conceptions.[20] One strand of argumentation builds on the perspective that the state of achieved consolidation includes that relevant political actors perceive democratic rules as binding (the "only game in town"[21]) and do not try to act outside of them. Przeworski (1991) added that political actors were not only to adhere to the rules of the democratic game, but also to perceive this to be an advantageous option.[22] Huntington (1991) also put down the only game in town-concept as a basis for his often-cited two turnover-test: If political actors were to perceive democracy as the only game in town, they would not try to handle political disagreement bypassing the democratic

---

17 Pickel, G. (2016). Transitorische Demokratietheorie. In Lembcke, O., Ritzi, C., and Schaal, G. S. (Eds.), *Zeitgenössische Demokratietheorie: Empirische Demokratietheorien*. Wiesbaden: Springer VS, 427-454, p. 427. Quote translated from German by the author.

18 Ibid., p. 438. For this conclusion, Pickel also refers to Beichelt. Beichelt, T. (2001): *Demokratische Konsolidierung im postsozialistischen Europa: Die Rolle der politischen Institutionen*. Wiesbaden: Springer Fachmedien.

19 Schedler, A. (1998). How Should We Study Democratic Consolidation? *Democratization*, 5 (4), 1-19, pp. 2, 10. Schedler points out that, as a part of the "pervasive lack of methodological reflection we can observe in the study of democratic consolidation" (Ibid, p. 2), it is often unclear whose expectations exactly should be taken into account when trying to determine whether a democracy has fully consolidated or not – "we must ask everybody" vs. "we may ask anybody." Ibid., p. 10.

20 Merkel, W. (2010). *Systemtransformation: Eine Einführung in die Theorie und Empirie der Transformationsforschung*. Wiesbaden: VS Verlag für Sozialwissenschaften, p. 110.

21 Przeworski, A. (1991). *Democracy and the Market: Political and Economic Reforms in Eastern Europe and Latin America*. Cambridge: Cambridge University Press, p. 26.

22 Ibid.

system and the "in-system" conflict resolution instruments it provides.[23] With the goal to develop a concept that was both minimalist and not overly reductionist, Linz and Stepan (1996) extended the notion of consolidation as democracy being the only game in town by adding three levels of analysis: a behavioral level focusing on the desired absence of political groups wishing to abolish democracy or seceding from the state in question, an attitudinal level looking at the degree to which citizens believe that democracy remains the best possible system even in time of crisis, and a constitutional level concentrating on adherence by all political actors to the rules given by the polity and the prevailing of the mindset that "violations of these norms are likely to be both ineffective and costly."[24] Another strand of argumentation, which in its implications can be viewed as related to the first one but still setting a different focus, proposes that the most important task of consolidation of a democracy is the successful containment of anti-democratic forces. In this vein, Valenzuela (1992) states that it is vital during the stage of consolidation to "eliminat[e] the institutions, procedures, and expectations that are incompatible with the minimal workings of a democratic regime [...]."[25] Pridham (1995) picks up the notion and expands it by differentiating between negative consolidation, which is achieved as soon as political elites with an anti-democratic system approach "[become] numerically or politically insignificant,"[26] and positive consolidation meaning the "inculcation of

---

23 Huntington, S. (1991). *The Third Wave: Democratization in the Late Twentieth Century*. Norman and London: University of Oklahoma Press, p. 266. The two turnover-test is a suggestion by Huntington as a concrete criterion to measure consolidation: If the governing group elected after transition is being replaced by a group from a different position in the political spectrum in a democratic election and this process is again reversed in another democratic election, this may be seen as evidence that relevant political actors are willing to accept the outcome of democratic elections, and thus, one of the central democratic rules. Ibid., pp. 266-267.
24 Linz, J. J. and Stepan, A. (1996). *Problems of Democratic Transition and Consolidation: Southern Europe, South America, and Post-Communist Europe*. Baltimore and London: The John Hopkins University Press, p. 5.
25 Valenzuela, J. S. (1992). Democratic Consolidation in Post-Transitional Settings: Notion, Process, and Facilitating Conditions. In Mainwaring, S., O'Donnell, G., and Valenzuela, J. S. (Eds.), *Issues in Democratic Consolidation: The New South American Democracies in Comparative Perspective*. Notre Dame: University of Notre Dame Press, 57-104, p. 70.
26 Pridham, G. (1995). The International Context of Democratic Consolidation: Southern Europe in Comparative Perspective. In Gunther, R., Diamandouros, P. N., and Puhle, H.-J. (Eds.), *The Politics of Democratic Consolidation: Southern Europe*

democratic values at both elite and mass levels,"[27] the latter clearly leaving minimalist approaches behind and proposing requirements for democratic consolidation that go well beyond a formal level and extend into the realm of political culture, not only on the political elites' level, but also on the mass citizens' level. This extended notion of consolidation as containment of anti-democratic forces also forms the base for the model of democratic consolidation developed by Merkel (2010).[28] Premising his model on the concept of positive consolidation by Pridham,[29] Merkel proposes four analytic levels for democratic consolidation: 1) the constitutional level, 2) the representative level, 3) the level of integration of potential veto actors, and 4) the civic culture and civil society level. Regarding the constitutional level, analysis is focused on the process of adopting a new constitution in a newly established democratic system on the one hand and the new constitution's empirical legitimation, i.e., its effective appropriateness for tackling the societal and political challenges of the state in question, on the other hand.[30] On the representative level, political parties and non-party associations are at the center of analysis trying to determine if they are able to fulfill their assigned intermediary functions in the political system and if their influence is well-balanced.[31] The third level, integration of potential veto actors, a more traditional focus of democratization research, looks at the behavior of actors who have often been appearing as opposing democratization in past transition processes: the military, paramilitary associations, actors from industry and finance sectors, owners of large estates, radicalized trade unions, or terrorist groups.[32] Finally, on the level of civic culture and civil society, two foci are distinguishable: firstly, the characteristics of the civic culture predominant in the country in question, which should ideally be a mixture of "parochial, subject, and participatory

---

in Comparative Perspective. Baltimore and London: The John Hopkins University Press, 166-203, p. 169.

27 Pridham 1995, p. 169.

28 The first edition of Merkel's volume cited in this chapter was published in 1999. An earlier version of the consolidation model cited in this chapter was published in Merkel, W. (1996). Institutionalisierung und Konsolidierung der Demokratien in Ostmitteleuropa. In Merkel, W., Sandschneider, E., and Segert, D. (Eds.), *Systemwechsel 2: Die Institutionalisierung der Demokratie*. Opladen: Leske + Budrich, 73-112.

29 Merkel 2010, p. 110.

30 Ibid., pp. 113-116.

31 Ibid., pp. 118 and 122.

32 Ibid., p. 122.

political cultures,"[33] with an increasing importance ascribed to participatory political culture as the consolidation of the democratic system in question progresses,[34] and secondly, civil society as a categorization of the form that citizens' behavior towards the state may take, in the context of which Merkel favors a "reflected cooperation"[35] between civil and political society based on a constant self-restriction of both groups.[36]

There are at least two reasons why viewing the topic of the state of consolidation of Korean democracy through the lens of an analysis of the 2017 impeachment and the events surrounding it may prove to be fruitful. Firstly, impeachment can be treated as a shock to the system[37] that tests its resilience. This applies, on the one hand, to the impeachment process itself as it may both question political allegiances and deepen already existing cleavages.[38] Furthermore, if it is successful, it leads to immediate change in the head of the executive, followed by a certain period of a power vacuum after the impeached president has been removed from office and before a new president has been elected. On the other hand, impeachment processes often follow political scandals that can seriously undermine citizens' trust in the integrity of the political system.[39] Secondly, the instrument of impeachment is a strong weapon in the context of a defensive democracy, to be used in cases where "a president threatens and endangers democracy."[40] Thus, used constitutionally (i.e. when a president has committed impeachable wrongdoings),[41] impeachment can possibly serve as an indication for institutional shortfalls that have enabled or even fostered these wrongdoings. In cases where impeachment is politically instrumentalized

---

33 Merkel 2010, pp. 124 and 125. In this context, Merkel also draws on the concept of civic culture developed by Almond and Verba.
34 Ibid., p. 125.
35 Ibid., p. 126. Quote translated from German by the author.
36 Ibid., p. 126.
37 My thanks for the initiation of this train of thought to Hannes B. Mosler.
38 Baumgartner, J. C. (2003). Introduction: Comparative Presidential Impeachment. In Baumgartner, J. C. and Kada, N. (Eds.), *Checking Executive Power: Presidential Impeachment in Comparative Perspective*. Westport: Praeger Publishers, 1-20, p. 1.
39 Rottinghaus, B. (2014). Surviving Scandal: The Institutional and Political Dynamics of National and State Executive Scandals. *PS: Political Science & Politics*, 47 (1), 131-140, p. 138.
40 Mosler 2017, p. 115.
41 This is not to say that "impeachable" or "not impeachable" are categories that can be unambiguously defined. As Baumgartner points out, there are often different opinions about what constitutes an impeachable offence, which, amongst others, renders impeachment not a purely legal, but a very political process. Baumgartner 2003, pp. 4-5.

(i.e. used against a president who has not committed impeachable wrong-doings), however, the impeachment case in question may be viewed as a clear sign that not all political actors completely adhere to democratic rules yet (i.e. viewing democracy as "the only game in town"), and thereby points to a deficient consolidation on the level of relevant political actors' behavior. It becomes clear in this context, however, that a purely legalistic view of impeachment might not suffice: Apart from the question whether an impeachment is right or wrong in a constitutional law sense, it is also highly relevant for an assessment of democratic consolidation how the impeachment process (extending from the first suggestion of impeachment to the rendering of the impeachment ruling by the constitutional court) is handled on the politics level by the political actors involved. In this sense, the importance of founding an analysis of the implications of Korea's 2017 impeachment for the democratic consolidation of its political system on a theory of democratic consolidation that is inclusive enough to be sensitive to aspects on a politics level becomes salient. For this reason, the analytic levels of consolidation developed by Wolfgang Merkel will be used in the following to give an overview of which dimensions of consolidation research the chapters of this volume may contribute to using the 2017 impeachment as a case study.

The first chapter of this volume, "Changing South Korean Politics without Taking Power: The *Presidential Power Trap* Three Years after Impeachment" can thus be contextualized in the realm of the first and fourth levels (and the dynamics between those two levels) of Merkel's consolidation model. In its course, *Hannes B. Mosler* takes a close look at the first three years of the presidency of Park Geun-hye's successor Moon Jae-in (*Mun Chae-in*) in order to assess to what extent the 2017 impeachment resulted in a successful reboot for Korea's political system, curbing systemic weaknesses that might have played a role in the development of the scandal that ultimately triggered the impeachment. For this, the author applies the theoretical concept of the "imperial presidency," coined by Arthur Schlesinger and frequently used, amongst others, to describe the governing conduct of various Korean presidents, which is rooted threefold in the constitutional design, the personal governing style of the president, and in the political culture of the country[42] and is characterized mainly by presi-

---

42 At this point, it becomes clear why also the fourth level of consolidation (civic culture and civil society) is relevant for the theoretical contextualization of this chapter. Specifically to the fourth level Merkel ascribes an important function: If consolidation is well-advanced on this level, it may act as a stabilizing factor towards the other levels if a destabilizing crisis occurs. Merkel 2010, p. 112.

dential decision-making which disregards the voice of other incremental parts of the polity like the legislature and by staffing decisions based on non-merit appointments. Mosler argues that this "presidential power trap," denominating the situation presidents can find themselves in when excessive presidential power leads to heightened expectations directed towards the president, attraction of advantage-taking, and countering reactions by other political actors, can be regarded as a hindrance to democratic consolidation as it might lead to law being violated and the checks and balances of a political system being harmed. Regarding Moon Jae-in's first three years in office, the author finds that, despite Moon's announcements of trying to curb the tendency of excessive use of power in the Korean presidential office, several of the related problems persisted also in his presidency and that thus the 2017 impeachment, even though it was effective in removing Park Geun-hye rightfully from office, did not act as the answer to the systemic problems in Korea's polity. These findings thus also suggest that the 2017 Korean impeachment was an impeachment case that can be viewed as having illustrated institutional shortfalls in Korean democracy.

In her chapter "The Political Role of Courts in the Trials of South Korea's 2016-2017 Impeachment Scandal," which can be viewed as relevant for the analytic dimension of the first level of Merkel's consolidation model, *Justine Guichard* reviews several of the verdicts connected to the 2017 impeachment case given by the Constitutional Court as well as by other courts on various levels of the Korean judicial system. This results in the finding that the Constitutional Court, even though it did eventually uphold the impeachment in a unanimous ruling, left out the public protests and many of its demands from its argumentation in that verdict, despite the popular estimation that these protests were decisive for the initiation of the impeachment in the first place. Other courts that, after the impeachment, rendered the verdicts in the criminal trials against Park Geun-hye and Samsung heir Lee Jae-yong (*Yi Chae-yong*) were found to have failed to refer to government-business collusion as a problem for democracy on a system level, keeping their judgment tied to the misdemeanors of the person of Park Geun-hye specifically. The author argues that, in so doing, the courts, both on the constitutional as well as on the ordinary justice levels, interpreted their role as one of political actors in the sense that the verdicts displayed a distinct understanding of democracy – one that puts a core emphasis on a well-functioning market economy and on keeping mass mobilization in certain limits. Theoretically, this can be contextualized in the area of an empirical legitimation of the constitution, which looks at the ability of the political system to tackle relevant problems in politics and society.

Differing understandings of democracy coming to light through the 2017 impeachment and its surrounding processes is also one of the core themes in the next chapter, "Park Geun-hye's Impeachment: Theorizing a Political Economic Revolt." In the course of this chapter, *Juliette Schwak* argues in favor of interpreting the candlelight demonstrations preceding the 2017 impeachment as a protest against specific aspects of Korea's current political economic order. Tracing the main historical connections, the author shows that this political economic order is strongly shaped by a structural interdependence between the state and the *chaebŏl*, Korea's large business conglomerates, leading to heightened state-business collusion. Against the backdrop of recent developments in the Korean economy, namely high unemployment rates specifically among young, well-trained citizens, growing poverty among the elderly, as well as generally increasing labor precarity, this state-business collusion becomes the subject of criticism voiced by Korean citizens. Interviews conducted by the author also support this perspective of a society in which life opportunities are increasingly dependent on individual family background rather than on meritocratic achievements. Schwak therefore concludes that the candlelight protests, which were mainly a popular outburst of anger about Park Geun-hye's behavior, characterized also by usage of familial connections and privileges, can be viewed as a demand for more equality of opportunity and economic democracy. On a theory level, this chapter can therefore be seen as providing insight into the third and fourth levels in Merkel's democratic consolidation model as well as the interactions between them.

In his chapter "Who Raised a Candle and Why? Ascertaining Participation in the 2016-2017 Candlelight Protest in South Korea," *Youngho Cho* then assesses the composition and motivations of the participants of the candlelight protests in an empirical study analyzing data from surveys amongst both participants and non-participants. Testing several hypotheses derived from democratization theory, he finds that a large part of the protest participants has a middle-class background and college-level education, resides in Seoul and adjacent areas, and identifies as progressive and supporting the then opposition Democratic Party (*Tŏburŏminjudang*). These findings largely support the assumptions made by modernization theory about the triggers of democratization processes to the extent that the protests seemed to be initiated mainly by citizens with rising income and education and therefore equipped with the resources needed for protest initiation. However, Cho also concludes from the analyzed data that these citizens' protests were not mainly driven by a deep-rooted belief in democratic values, but rather by anger about then President Park Geun-hye's actions and failures, as well as about unequal opportunities in Korean society, the former also viewed in part as a manifestation of the latter. Therefore, the author remains critical regarding the description of the candlelight demonstrations as demonstrations for democracy and concludes that a major problem of Korean democracy, namely the low degree of institutionalization of the representative system combined with a very active civil society that misses formal linkages into the representative system, not only persists but has also become even more apparent through the protest. In this context, this chapter contributes to the discussion by shedding light on the second and fourth levels of Merkel's consolidation model, viewed through the lens of the 2017 impeachment and the protests that surrounded it.

In the final chapter, "South Korean Democratic Consolidation: Lessons from the 2017 Impeachment," *Gabriel Jonsson* assesses and puts into theoretical context a relevant selection of evaluations made about the question of what might be the conclusions to be drawn from the 2017 impeachment with regard to the state of democratic consolidation in Korea. In the course of this assessment, the author finds that, on the one hand, the impeachment is generally being viewed as both a positive sign for democracy (as democratic procedures were adhered to throughout the process) and as being legitimate (as reasons for impeachment were in line with the constitution). On the other hand, however, there are also voices of criticism pointing to the weaknesses of Korean democracy, namely the lingering low institutionalization of the party system, and a general imbalance of power, favoring the executive over the legislative branch of the political system. The author concludes that, while democracy in Korea can be regarded as consolidated in the narrow sense that it has become "the only game in town," the core weaknesses of Korean democracy remain largely unabated even after the 2017 impeachment.

Apart from the different foci that the chapters of this volume apply, one theme can be identified as a common finding: The 2017 impeachment raised awareness towards *systemic* problems that were then treated as *individual* shortfalls. In the first chapter, Hannes B. Mosler finds that it were constitutional design, political culture, and the prevailing traditions of interpreting the presidential position by the incumbents that were causing the repeated phenomenon of the imperial president – a fact that the removal from office of one incumbent, Park Geun-hye, by impeachment did not fundamentally change. Justine Guichard finds in her chapter that the Constitutional Court in its impeachment ruling treated corruption as an individual and much less as a systemic problem, which can in turn be interpreted as downplaying the problem to a certain extent. In the third chapter, Juliette Schwak comes to the conclusion that the impeachment did not actually question the Korean interpretation of democracy as primarily a free market economy, which she identifies as the cause of the strong state-business collusion, the strong influence of the *chaebŏl*, and therefore by extension also the persisting inequalities in Korean society that the candlelight protests addressed. Youngho Cho analyzes in his chapter that the candlelight protests were mostly driven by anger at Park Geun-hye and her personal actions, and not so much by expressed belief in democratic values and the wish to change the Korean democracy for the better at a system level. And finally, Gabriel Jonsson finds in the fifth chapter of this volume that an assessment of the Korean political system after the 2017 impeachment suggests that structural weaknesses, also stemming from a Confucian-influenced political culture, remain in large parts. In conclusion, these findings suggest that while an impeachment itself may not act as a solution to systemic problems, it may function as a beacon drawing attention to these systemic problems even if they cannot be addressed in the course of the impeachment case, but need to be tended to in regular legislation periods which are not dominated by the exceptional state of an impending or recently undertaken impeachment. For the Korean case, it has also been shown that the normative role of civil society, ranging from an active, direct, and immediate influence on political decisions to a mediated influence in close collaboration with a strongly institutionalized and integrative representative system, has been a salient theme in the discussion about the lessons of the 2017 impeachment.[43] It can thus be concluded for the Korean case that impeachment might also have functioned as a magnifying glass that brings different normative ideas about democracy and the form of democracy best suited for the country in question to the surface, which may then, after the "dust" of impeachment has settled, be subject to further collective contemplation in politics and society.

---

43 See specifically the chapters by Justine Guichard, Juliette Schwak, and Youngho Cho.

References

Baumgartner, J. C. (2003). Introduction: Comparative Presidential Impeachment. In Baumgartner, J. C. and Kada, N. (Eds.), *Checking Executive Power: Presidential Impeachment in Comparative Perspective*. Westport: Praeger Publishers, 1-20.

Beichelt, T. (2001). *Demokratische Konsolidierung im postsozialistischen Europa: Die Rolle der politischen Institutionen*. Wiesbaden: Springer Fachmedien.

Bertelsmann Stiftung (n.d.). *BTI 2006-2022 Results*, [online]. Available at: https://bti -project.org/en/index/political-transformation [Accessed February 23, 2022].

Freedom House (n.d.). *Freedom in the World: South Korea*, [online]. Available at: https://freedomhouse.org/country/south-korea/freedom-world/2021 [Accessed February 21, 2022].

Ginsburg, T., Huq, A., and Landau, D. (2021). The Comparative Constitutional Law of Presidential Impeachment. *The University of Chicago Law Review*, 88 (1), 81-164.

Huntington, S. (1991). *The Third Wave: Democratization in the Late Twentieth Century*. Norman and London: University of Oklahoma Press.

Kang, S.-G. (2019). Candlelight Demonstrations and the Presidential Impeachment in South Korea: An Evaluation of the 30 Years of Democracy. *Asian Education and Development Studies*, 8 (3), 256-267.

Kelly, R. (2017). South Korea's Finest Hour: Lessons From the Impeachment. *The Interpreter*, April 11, 2017, [online]. Available at: https://www.lowyinstitute.org/the-interpreter/south-korea-s-finest-hour-lessons-impeachment [Accessed January 30, 2022].

Kim, S.-C. (2017). South Korea's Candlelight Protests. *East Asia Forum*, February 7, 2017, [online]. Available at: https://www.eastasiaforum.org/2017/02/07/south-koreas-candlelight-protests/ [Accessed January 31, 2022].

Lauth, H.-J., Schlenkrich, O., and Lemm, L. (n.d.). *Country Graph South Korea*, [online]. Available at: https://www.democracymatrix.com/online-analysis/country#/South%20Korea/total_index_core [Accessed February 21, 2022].

Lee, S. J. (2017). A Democratic Breakthrough in South Korea? *Carnegie Endowment for International Peace*, March 24, 2017, [online]. Available at: https://carnegieendowment.org/2017/03/24/democratic-breakthrough-in-south-korea-pub-68394 [Accessed January 30, 2022].

Linz, J. J. and Stepan, A. (1996). *Problems of Democratic Transition and Consolidation: Southern Europe, South America, and Post-Communist Europe*. Baltimore and London: The John Hopkins University Press.

Merkel, W. (1996). Institutionalisierung und Konsolidierung der Demokratien in Ostmitteleuropa. In Merkel, W., Sandschneider, E., and Segert, D. (Eds.), *Systemwechsel 2: Die Institutionalisierung der Demokratie*. Opladen: Leske + Budrich, 73-112.

Merkel, W. (2010). *Systemtransformation: Eine Einführung in die Theorie und Empirie der Transformationsforschung*. Wiesbaden: VS Verlag für Sozialwissenschaften.

Mobrand, E. (2018). Democracy Is More Than a Political System: Lessons From South Korea's Democratic Transformation. *The Asan Forum*, December 20, 2018, [online]. Available at: https://theasanforum.org/democracy-is-more-than-a-political-system-lessons-from-south-koreas-democratic-transformation/ [Accessed January 30, 2022].

Mosler, H. B. (2017). The Institution of Presidential Impeachment in South Korea, 1992-2017. *Verfassung und Recht in Übersee/Law and Politics in Africa, Asia and Latin America*, 50 (2), 111-134.

Pickel, G. (2016). Transitorische Demokratietheorie. In Lembcke, O., Ritzi, C., and Schaal, G. S. (Eds.), *Zeitgenössische Demokratietheorie: Empirische Demokratietheorien*. Wiesbaden: Springer VS, 427-454.

Pridham, G. (1995). The International Context of Democratic Consolidation: Southern Europe in Comparative Perspective. In Gunther, R., Diamandouros, P. N., and Puhle, H.-J. (Eds.), *The Politics of Democratic Consolidation: Southern Europe in Comparative Perspective*. Baltimore and London: The John Hopkins University Press, 166-203.

Przeworski, A. (1991). *Democracy and the Market: Political and Economic Reforms in Eastern Europe and Latin America*. Cambridge: Cambridge University Press.

Rottinghaus, B. (2014). Surviving Scandal: The Institutional and Political Dynamics of National and State Executive Scandals. *PS: Political Science & Politics*, 47 (1), 131-140.

Schedler, A. (1998). How Should We Study Democratic Consolidation? *Democratization*, 5 (4), 1-19.

Shin, G.-W. and Moon, R. J. (2017). South Korea After Impeachment. *Journal of Democracy*, 28 (4), 117-131.

Valenzuela, J. S. (1992). Democratic Consolidation in Post-Transitional Settings: Notion, Process, and Facilitating Conditions. In Mainwaring, S., O'Donnell, G., and Valenzuela, J. S. (Eds.), *Issues in Democratic Consolidation: The New South American Democracies in Comparative Perspective*. Notre Dame: University of Notre Dame Press, 57-104.

Changing South Korean Politics without Taking Power? The *Presidential Power Trap* Three Years after Impeachment

Hannes B. Mosler

Introduction

The presidential system of government originated in 18th century USA, and from there spread to the rest of the world, including Latin America, Africa, and later Eastern Europe; in Asia, too, some countries adopted the American model. In the US, the founding fathers had designed a new political system, for which they needed a substitute for what had been the king in England. The invented president had to be powerful enough to check the power of Congress, but at the same time had to be balanced so as not to overpower the legislative branch. The institution of presidential impeachment was included in the US Constitution as a last resort, a kind of emergency brake, which has been applied a few times so far. Before Bill Clinton and recently Donald Trump, Richard Nixon had been the most prominent example of impeachment. His extreme excesses and abuses of power led historian Arthur Schlesinger to coin the now-famous term "imperial presidency."[1] Yet, in the aftermath, legal reforms were conducted to curb much of the president's formal powers so as to prevent another "emperor." Nevertheless, signs of excessive power-wielding by US presidents surfaced again at the beginning of the 2000s, and with Trump, the metaphor of the emperor-like president regained much of its earlier prominence. That prompted two US historians, Kruse and Zelizer, to publicly raise the question that resonates with many countries that have adopted a presidential system and experienced presidential impeachments: "Have we had enough of the imperial presidency yet?"[2]

South Korea (hereafter, Korea) is a case in point. Park Geun-hye (*Pak Kŭn-hye*) was not the first Korean president to be called an "imperial

---

1 Schlesinger, A. (1973). *The Imperial Presidency*. Boston: Houghton Mifflin.
2 Kruse, K. M. and Zelizer, J. E. (2019). Have We Had Enough of the Imperial Presidency Yet? *The New York Times*, January 9, 2019. Available at: https://www.ny times.com/2019/01/09/opinion/president-trump-border-wall-weak.html [Accessed January 12, 2020].

president" (*chewangjŏk taet'ongnyŏng*), but her impeachment and ensuing removal from office in 2017 marked a watershed in the contemporary political history of Korea, and internationally, too, represents a rare case of a successful unseating of a corrupt state leader.[3] Against this backdrop, this study explores whether Korea has "had enough of the imperial presidency yet" by examining the president's role and practice after the impeachment. This analysis is based on the thinking that a major event such as an impeachment motion can open a window of opportunity for change as the result of unsettling the equilibrium of the institution of the imperial president. This study's aim is to shed light on in how far incumbent president Moon Jae-in (*Mun Chae-in*) in his first three years in office (2017-2020) was able to implement his explicit election pledge to "share the imperial power of the president as much as possible,"[4] and thus on the extent to which the impeachment might have had stimulating effects on alleviating the imperial president phenomenon in Korea.

To that end, the following section drawing on the existing literature first elaborates on the notion of imperial presidency and the unitary executive theory in the context of the USA and then discusses the characteristics of the Korean variant that is the imperial president (*chewangjŏk taet'ongnyŏng*). The essay goes on to introduce the term "presidential power trap" to better grasp the complexity of the phenomenon at hand in that it more clearly indicates the paradoxical power-limiting effects of the excessive usage of presidential power. These theoretical conceptualizations then serve as a foil against which the succeeding analysis examines the first three years of Moon's presidency focusing on three core topics: organizing the presidential office, operating government, and cooperating with the branches. The chapter concludes by arguing that despite President Moon's pledge and actual attempts, this endeavor of rooting out the bad habit of wielding imperial power has, in many respects, largely failed, and that a partial remedy to the problem is institutional reform.

---

3 Mosler, H. B. (2017). The Institution of Presidential Impeachment in South Korea, 1992-2017. *Verfassung und Recht in Übersee*, 2, 111-134, p. 112.

4 Moon, J.-I. (2017). *Mun Chae-in taet'ongnyŏng yŏnsŏlmunjip 2017-nyŏn 5-7-wŏl [Selected Speeches of President Moon Jae-in of the Republic of Korea, May-July 2017]*. Seoul: Korean Culture and Information Service, p. 9.

1. Theoretical Conceptualizations

When then presidential candidate Moon Jae-in defined the mass demonstrations against President Park Geun-hye (*ch'otpuljiphoe*) as a "candlelight revolution" and pledged to realize a government in the spirit of this "revolution," he set a high bar for his presidency. It is not surprising that many of his ideas resemble those of liberal president Roh Moo-hyun (*No Mu-hyŏn*), for whom he worked as chief of staff at the president's office. This is particularly true regarding his basic governance philosophy, which can be described as changing Korean politics without taking too much power, or, put differently, changing Korean politics by reducing power concentration in the office of the president. Translating the idea of "changing the world without taking power"[5] into the Korean context provides us with three perspectives: first, not taking all the power possible as a president according to the constitution and customs; second, lessening power concentration in the sense of democratic division of powers; and third, in so doing, changing Korean politics by promoting the consolidation of democracy.

In his presidential election manifesto in 2017, Moon pledged to pursue consensual politics (*hyŏpch'i*) vis-à-vis parliament, including the opposition, and emphasized the necessity of jointly agreeing on a candidate for the position of prime minister; operating government mainly based on decision-making through the organ of the cabinet or state council (*kungmuhoeŭi*); putting into practice a prime minister (*ch'aekim ch'ongni*) and ministers (*ch'aekim changgwan*) with real responsibilities; and realizing a government in which the governing party takes responsibility (*ch'aekim innŭn chŏngdangjŏngbu*).[6] One of the central election campaign pledges of President Moon Jae-in to become a better president, which he repeated during his inauguration speech, was to "root out bad habits

---

5 The phrase "changing the world without taking power" was coined by the Marxist author Holloway (Holloway, J. (2002). *Change The World Without Taking Power*. London: Pluto Press) and represents a critique of the previous attempts by revolutionaries of various strands to better society or the world by overthrowing the existing regime and replacing it with a new one. The many attempts the world has seen so far ultimately have not succeeded beyond simply changing the people in power – far from improving the world. That is why the very practice of taking of power falls under question, in the sense of too much power for the wrong purposes. While this essay is not about this Marxist debate, it yet draws on the basic logic of the idea for formulating an ideal of governance for improving and consolidating democracy in Korea.

6 Moon 2017, pp. 112-114.

(*chŏkp'yech'ŏngsan*)," including those of "imperial presidents."[7] The following paragraphs discuss the concept of the imperial presidency as a preparatory step for the analysis that examines possible effects of the impeachment's aftermath on the phenomenon of the excessively powerful president.

1.1 Imperial Presidency and Unitary Executive Theories

Schlesinger's "Imperial Presidency"

> "[U]nless the American democracy figures out how to control the Presidency in war and peace without enfeebling the Presidency across the board, then our system of government will face grave troubles."[8]

US historian Arthur Schlesinger picked up the term imperial presidency, which was popular in the public political discourse in the US during the 1960s; after he used it for the title of his famous book *The Imperial Presidency* in 1973, the catchphrase found fame internationally. Briefly put, in the media and in a somewhat more sophisticated fashion in academia, imperial presidency describes the practice of a president relying on authority that exceeds that provided by the constitution. Most obviously, this leads to a shift toward the executive branch of powers originally constitutionally ascribed to the legislature. In other words, the fundamental idea and practice in liberal democracies of the division of powers and checks and balances is overridden, and presidential power is strengthened to a degree potentially threatening to the basis of a given democracy. The five major problems Schlesinger identified as characteristics of the imperial presidency's phenomenology concern far-reaching emergency rights, presidential secrecy, presidential advisory bodies, appointment rights, and the president's supremacy over congress and political parties.

Having Presidents Johnson and Nixon on his mind, Schlesinger particularly emphasized the presidents' excessive rights regarding foreign policy and war powers in the form of vast emergency laws for domestic usage. "The Imperial Presidency was essentially the creation of foreign policy. A combination of doctrines and emotions [...] had brought about the

---

7 Democratic Party (2017). *Nara-rŭl naradapke. 19-tae taet'ognyŏngsŏn'gŏ tŏburŏminjudang chŏngch'aekkungyakchip [Making the Country Country-Like. The Democratic Party's 19th Presidential Election Manifesto]*. Seoul: Democratic Party, p. 24.
8 Schlesinger 1973, p. x.

unprecedented centralization of decisions over war and peace in the Presidency."[9] The presidency as intended by the founding fathers, that is, the constitutional presidency, was turned into an imperial presidency on the pretext of the extraordinary situation of a crisis in foreign affairs or wars (specifically, WWII, the Korean War, and the Vietnam War) and thus allowed for far-reaching authority bestowed to the president. President Nixon, however, according to Schlesinger, did not stop there but intentionally reformed the presidency by taking the opportunity to translate these emperor-like powers into the domestic realm, too – that is, the Revolutionary Presidency.[10] "With this there came an unprecedented exclusion of the rest of the executive branch, of Congress, of the press and of public opinion in general from these decisions."[11] The notion Schlesinger developed in his book, however, is not limited to extraordinary presidential rights based on a "belief in permanent and universal crisis"[12] but captures a whole variety of power-concentrating manifestations that are subsumed under the term imperial presidency, which can be found in many other presidential systems in the world, too, including Korea.

Regarding presidential secrecy, there are sufficient reasons for certain issues to be dealt with by the executive or the president under the exclusion of the public and even most of the political elites. However, if the line that divides necessary secrecy from unnecessary secrecy is pushed too much, the realm of necessary transparency is transgressed, potentially threatening the basis for reasonable checks and balances against the executive.[13] When it comes to presidential advisory bodies, the most powerful organs are the National Security Council and the Office of Management and Budget, which are organized around the presidents and thus are under their direct command. Depending on the president's personal mode of operation, these core power institutions can lead to a gathering of indifferent aides who do not earn the title of advisors because they are pressured into self-censorship.[14] This involves the danger that the president misuses the additional power and/or overrides the cabinet's influence because these bodies in many cases complement the actual cabinet's responsibilities. The same

---

9 Schlesinger 1973, p. 208.
10 Ibid., pp. 208-277.
11 Ibid., p. 208.
12 Ibid.
13 Ibid., pp. 331-376.
14 Rudalevige, A. (2005). *The New Imperial Presidency. Renewing Presidential Power after Watergate*. Ann Abor: University of Michigan Press, p. 61; Schlesinger 1973, pp. 185-190.

is true for the personnel of the Executive Office of the President, who may decide and act on high-profile issues without accountability to Congress.[15] Presidential appointment discretion is far-reaching. The increasing staff of the strongly growing presidential office are appointed on the basis of loyalty to the individual president and are not subject to external approval or control, for example, by Congress.[16] While core staff and close aides to the president on one hand obviously must be absolutely trustworthy to the president, on the other hand there needs to be a minimum of control because they wield a great amount of power delegated by the president.[17] Similarly, the appointment rights of the president concerning the heads of powerful organs and presidential advisory bodies are to a degree excessive so that checks and balances by the legislature are circumvented at best.[18]

Theorizing the Presidency for Practical Reasons

The excessive expansion of the president's authority under imperial President Nixon that had been dubbed "administrative presidency strategy"[19] was later taken up and cast in a theoretical mold to institutionalize expansive presidential discretion. The result was the birth of the "unitary executive theory," which posits that the US president possesses the sole and unfettered authority to control the entire executive branch, which, in turn, implies that "there must not be any executive responsibilities that either the legislature or the federal judiciary can participate in."[20] In other words, if only the president has complete control over the executive branch, neither Congress nor the courts would be able to execute their constitutionally prescribed function to check and balance the president.[21] While the constitutional law debate has still not been conclusive,[22] it

---

15 Rudalevige 2005, p. 60; Schlesinger 1973, pp. 219-221, 251.
16 Rudalevige 2005, p. 62; Schlesinger 1973, pp. 219-223.
17 Schlesinger 1973, pp. 250-251.
18 Ibid., pp. 245, 252.
19 Waterman, R. W. (2009). The Administrative Presidency, Unilateral Power, and the Unitary Executive Theory. *Presidential Studies Quarterly*, 39 (1), 5-9, p. 5.
20 Crouch, J., Rozell, M. J., and Sollenberger, M. A. (2017). The Law: The Unitary Executive Theory and President Donald J. Trump. *Presidential Studies Quarterly*, 47 (3), 561-573, p. 565.
21 Waterman 2009, p. 8.
22 Fitts, M. A. (1996). The Paradox of Power in the Modern State: Why a Unitary, Centralized Presidency May Not Exhibit Effective or Legitimate Leadership. *University of Pennsylvania Law Review*, 144 (3), 827-902.

seems far-fetched to interpret "[t]he executive Power shall be vested in [the] [p]resident"[23] and "[h]e [...] shall Commission all the Officers of the United States"[24] as providing for "unilateral" power wielding, and thus as grounds for the imperative of an imperial president. It is far more reasonable to suggest that the unitarity of the office was supposed to mean that one person unifies several central political functions, as opposed to, for example, semi-presidential or parliamentary cabinet systems.[25] The development of the strong unitary executive theory began under Ronald Reagan;[26] it was often invoked under George W. Bush,[27] and none of the succeeding presidents surrendered this handy additional "authority, even if they recognize[d] that the authority was illegitimately claimed."[28] Besides Bush, this includes not only Trump, but also Barack Obama.[29]

The Korean Constitution, too, provides that the "[e]xecutive power shall be vested in the [e]xecutive [b]ranch headed by the [p]resident,"[30] and that the "[p]resident shall appoint [...] public officials [...] as prescribed by the Constitution and Act;"[31] there is no comparable movement to use these stipulations for arguing for more power of the president. There are two reasons for this. First, Korea's Constitution clearly establishes that the executive power is vested in the executive branch, not in the unipersonal office of the president. In addition, the president heads the executive branch with the assistance of the prime minister, who, under order of the president, directs the executive ministries.[32] Second, against the backdrop of decades of (military) dictatorship since the last constitutional reform in 1987, the vast majority of scholars, politicians, and the media advocate measures to weaken the president's powers. This discourse is

---

23 Constitution of the United States. Available at: https://www.senate.gov/civics/con stitution_item/constitution.htm [Accessed April 15, 2021], Article II, Section 1.

24 Ibid., Article II, Section 3.

25 Crouch et al. 2017, p. 565; MacKenzie, J. P. (2008). *Absolute Power: How the Unitary Executive Theory Is Undermining the Constitution*. New York: The Century Foundation Press, p. 7.

26 Kelley, C. (2008). The Unitary, or Unilateral Executive? Presidential Power in the Bush Administration. *The American Review of Politics*, 29, 181-196.

27 Waterman 2009, p. 6.

28 MacKenzie 2008, p. 57.

29 Crouch et al. 2017, pp. 566-570.

30 Constitution of the Republic of Korea. Available in English at: https://korea.ass embly.go.kr:447/res/low_01_read.jsp?boardid=1000000035 [Accessed April 15, 2021], Article 66, Section 4.

31 Ibid., Article 78.

32 Ibid., Article 86, Section 2.

conducted mostly under the topos of "power structure debate (*kwŏllyŏk ku-jo nonjaeng*)," pointing to the key issue of how to more effectively implement the separation of powers and check and balance presidential power in particular. However, until now, despite legions of discussions, publications, and presidential pledges to do away the imperial presidency time and again, state leaders have been coming back to the honeypot; they have tapped deeply into the power source and thus have "done much to contribute to its further institutionalization as a commonly accepted feature of the modern presidency."[33] This Janus-faced characteristic of explicitly rejecting the imperial presidency while implicitly practicing a Korean variant of the strong unitary executive theory lies at the heart of Korea's imperial president (*chewangjŏk taet'ongnyŏng*) phenomenon, which will be examined in the following paragraphs.

1.2 The "Imperial President Trap" in Korea

Characteristics of Imperial Presidents

In Korea, the term imperial presidency or imperial president emerges in the media for the first time a year after the publication of Schlesinger's widely read book in a news article that briefly introduces the work; however, the writer restricts himself to briefly introducing the US president's excessive war power only.[34] Scholarly usage of the term begins only at the start of the 2000s.[35] The first account using the label in political science

---

33 Crouch et al. 2017, p. 568.
34 Dong-A Ilbo (1974). Chumokpannŭn miguk-ŭi tu chŏsŏ [Two US-American Books that Receive Attention]. *Dong-A Ilbo*, January 21, 1974, p. 5.
35 E.g., Lim, S. H. (1998). A Paradox of Korean Democracy: 50 Years' Experience of the Imperial Presidency and the Peripheral Legislature. *Korea and World Affairs*, 22 (4), 522-538; Ham, S.-D. (1999). *Taet'ongnyŏnghak [The Korean Presidency]*. Seoul: Nanam; Ham, S.-D. (2002). The Institutional Development of the Blue House in the Park Chung Hee Presidency. *Asian Perspective*, 26 (2), 101-130; Hong, T.-P. (2002). Chewangjŏk taet'ongnyŏngnon: Kŭ t'ŭkching-kwa wŏnin-ŭl chungsim-ŭro [The Concept, Characteristics, and Causes of the Imperial President]. *Kungminyulli Yŏn'gu*, 50, 145-171; Yang, K. (2003). Irŭnba chewangjŏk taet'ongnyŏng nonŭi-e kwanhan sogo [A Study of the Debate on the Imperial Presidency]. *Segyehŏnbŏp Yŏn'gu*, 8, 113-124; Chŏng, C.-S. (2004). *Hŏnbŏp Yŏn'gu [Constitutional Theory]*. Seoul: Pakyŏngsa; Choi, J.-J. (2004). *Minjuhwa ihu-ŭi minjujuŭi [Democracy after Democratization]*. Seoul: Humanitas; Yi, K.-I. (2008).

can be found in 1998, when Lim[36] applies the term; other similar usages did occur, albeit only in the year 2000. Ham presents a first proto-definition when describing the birth of the Korean imperial presidency variant with the *Yusin* Constitution in 1972 when strongman Park Chung-hee (*Pak Chŏng-hŭi*)

> "strongly believed in his presidential authority to act according to his discretion for the public good, without the prescription of the law and sometimes even against it. Therefore, he did greatly broaden the use of presidential power for the public welfare he defined. In other words, he did not care a rap for the mere form and show of power; he cared immensely for the use that could be made of the substance. [...] In fact, the presidential system during this period was a tyranny in the classical sense and [Park Chung-hee] was the tyrant."[37]

Hong for the first time presents an analytical account of the term and relates it systematically to the Korean context.[38] His definition of the imperial president shifts the empirical and dramatic accounts onto a more abstract level when he speaks of the "phenomenon of a president executing political power non-institutionally like a regal power, and who like an emperor reigns over the state and law."[39] Similarly, Yang characterizes the imperial president of Korea as the "phenomenon of the concentration of power in one person, the president, who abuses this power by violating or circumventing the framework or purpose of the executing power as established by the constitution and legal statutes."[40] Characteristic manifestations of an imperial president in Korea can be divided into the president's one-sided decision-making and the privatization of political powers.[41]

As in the case of Schlesinger's imperial presidency in the US, the Korean presidential office, too, is at the center of the phenomenon's manifestation. Though the overly strong growing presidential office is not a new phenomenon, as was pointed out by other scholars such as Ham,[42] recently, debate and literature on the topic speaks of a "Blue House government

---

Chewangjŏk taet'ongyŏng-ŭi kiwŏn [The Origin of the Imperial Presidency]. *Hwanghaemunhwa*, 60, 117-138.

36 Lim 1998.
37 Ham 2002, p. 2.
38 Hong 2002.
39 Ibid., p. 149.
40 Yang 2003, p. 113.
41 Hong 2002, pp. 149-152.
42 Ham 1999, 2002.

(*ch'ŏngwadae chŏngbu*)" to point to the core of the problems regarding Korea's presidency. The term was coined by Pak Sang-hun in the eponymously titled book, where he describes the phenomenon as follows:

> "Blue House government indicates the degenerated conduct by the democratic government of a presidential system. This can be defined as a kind of arbitrary ruling system, in which the president operates the government while concentrating power in the random organization of the Blue House that assists him. [...] Another face of the Blue House government is that accountability-centered organs such parliament and parties, the cabinet etc. become sub-partners to the Blue House."[43]

Regarding the former, imperial presidents, while formally involving exchanges with their advisors, actually one-sidedly and self-righteously decide on important policies; they tend to disregard citizens' consent or opinion as well as the concept of the National Assembly as an equal power representing the people. While displaying an attitude as if they were the owner of the country, imperial presidents tend to promote politics favorable to themselves or the powerful elites surrounding them. Even the advisors to the presidents tend to tell the presidents only what they want to hear, or keep silent in the first place, which in the end leads to crucially restricting free exchange of opinions. Even in the general society of Korea, there is a tacit understanding that what the president says is supreme law. This has the effect of producing an atmosphere in which relatives and close aides come to wield strong influence on the president and thus become instrumental in important decisions. In turn, this means open doors to despotism by those close to the president to a degree that even the presidents themselves cannot easily control. In addition, this dynamic has repercussions on the division of powers, for obvious reasons. Checks and balances between the powers are crucially weakened due to the excessively one-sided decision-making by the president or executive. The balanced relationship between equal partners – the executive and the legislature – shifts into a principal-agent relationship with the powerful executive on the one side and the junior partner of the legislature on the other. The judicature's independence is encroached upon, and it cannot fulfill its role as an autonomous arbitrator any further. This is also true regarding the president's power in relation to sub-organs of the administration itself,

---

43 Pak, S.-H. (2018). *Ch'ŏngwadae chŏngbu [Blue House Government]*. Seoul: Humanitas, pp. 61-62.

wherein the ministers do not execute their duties based on independent views and policies but wait for orders from the president.[44] The president not only decides on details in administrational procedures but also, by abusing power, intervenes in the autonomous realm of civil society and citizens' private lives.

> "An imperial president relies rather on legitimacy than on legality for securing power, which is why the will overtakes the norms, and thus makes one concerned that positive law and institutions will be hollowed out."[45]

The privatization of public political powers (*sayonghwa* or *sa'inhwa*) is the core building block for wielding these powers by the president despite constitutional rules and the principle of division of powers – they serve as a means to achieve personal aims, or those of the president's family members, relatives, or close aides. Based on wide-ranging personnel appointment discretion, presidents tend to appoint to powerful government agencies staff who belong to personal circles such as people who studied at the same school or university, come from the same hometown or region, or belong to other communities the president has a respective close connection and/or attachment to. This appointment practice must not necessarily, but often does, have the effect of degenerating the officialdom's morals, and it promotes conflict about bias and unfairness. Another major effect is corruption, when the president or those close to the president misuse the power to accumulate wealth in return. Also, the threat of weakening the principle of the rule of law, and the danger of the practice of rule by men, become more likely, which, for obvious reasons, is a serious issue regarding democracy. One of the most obvious forms of this phenomenon is the president using his influence on powerful government agencies such as the prosecution, the tax office, or the police to carry out unreasonable decisions or pressure political opponents by relying on the top decision-makers whom the president appointed. Finally, imperial presidents tend to avoid taking responsibility for their decisions by sacrificing prime ministers, ministers, or presidential secretaries like shedding ballast.

Meanwhile, a central characteristic of the imperial president is powerlessness. While this might sound paradoxical at first glance, this seeming contradiction can be easily explained as the result of too much power. President Nixon was well-known for empowering himself to more author-

---

44 Chŏng 2004, p. 190.
45 Ibid., pp. 190-191.

ity than appropriate; however, the very fact that, in a US president's first-ever resignation, he stepped down before he could be impeached for his involvement in the Watergate scandal demonstrates that the president, in fact, was not as limitlessly powerful as the allusion to pre-modern forms of absolutist government suggests.[46] In particular, when it comes to conflict resolution by, and public assessment of, the president, the "individuality, centrality, and visibility of the 'personal unitary presidency' [...] can be a disadvantage."[47] The same is true for Korean presidents, as discussed below in more detail.

Causes of Imperial Presidencies

When it comes to the causes for the phenomenon of imperial presidency, there are three overlapping and mutually influencing dimensions that have to be taken into account to explain the roots of the problem: political institutions of the system, the sitting president's personality, and political culture. Regarding presidentialism, Linz has famously argued that presidential government systems per se have bad traits such as competing legitimacy claims, hostility towards the opposition, disproportional monopolization of the electorate mandate, and populism.[48] In other words, the presidential system induces presidents to individually exploit a given system for building an imperial presidency. Mainwaring and Shugart[49] critically appraised Linz's critique of presidential systems and argued that it is not presidentialism itself, but rather how the government system is *institutionally* designed, that makes the difference between successful and unsuccessful cases, in terms of stabilizing governments and furthering democratization.[50] They found that a presidential system that limits the

---

46 Kruse and Zelizer 2019.

47 Fitts 1996, p. 835.

48 Linz, J. J. (1994). Presidential or Parliamentary Democracy: Does It Make a Difference? In Linz, J. J. and Valenzuela, A. (Eds.), *The Failure of Presidential Democracy: Comparative Perspectives*, Vol. 1. Baltimore, MD: Johns Hopkins University Press, 3-87; Linz, J. J. (1990). The Perils of Presidentialism. *Journal of Democracy*, 1 (1), 51-69.

49 Mainwaring, S. and Shugart, M. S. (1997). Juan Linz, Presidentialism, and Democracy: A Critical Appraisal. *Comparative Politics*, 29 (4), 449-471.

50 This argument is in line with the contention of the recently debated phenomenon of "presidentialization," referring to an increasing concentration of power in the executive in the political process and more direct communication with the citizens in parliamentary systems. Poguntke, T. and Webb, P. (2005). *The*

president's legislative power imposes a reasonable degree of discipline on those holding public office and reduces the degree of party fragmentation or polarization, demonstrating the viability of presidentialism.[51] In this regards, Shugart and Carey developed a catalogue of criteria for gauging the power of presidents, based on a constitutional division of legislative and non-legislative power. The criteria include the degree of the president's authority over package and partial vetoes and the introduction of legislation, budgeting, proposing referenda, and issuing decrees; it also comprises the extent of presidential power regarding cabinet formation, cabinet dismissal, assembly dissolution, and restriction of censure by the assembly.[52] This concerns the limits of presidential government systems per se and the power relationship between the president and parliament, the prime minister, political parties, and the president's office.[53] For the Korean case, four domains have been identified in which presidential powers can vary.[54] The separation of executive powers within the administration includes aspects such as checks and balances in the executive, authority of the presidential office, and presidential appointment powers. Concerning the presidential power vis-à-vis the legislation, legislative and jurisdictive powers of the president, as well as of the political party organization, are central criteria. Presidential power vis-à-vis the judicature is important regarding questions of appointment and amnesty powers. Finally, presidential power is dependent on political culture, which refers to traditions, customs, and habits as well as perceptions, opinions, and attitudes of the citizenry and presidential leadership.

The president's individual *personality* is naturally an important factor for how they realize the presidency, because the structure presidents operate in might restrict their actions but still leave room for interpretation.[55]

Presidentialization of Politics: A Comparative Study of Modern Democracies. Oxford: Oxford University Press.

51 Mainwaring and Shugart 1997, p. 469.
52 Shugart, M. S. and Carey, J. M. (1992). *Presidents and Assemblies: Constitutional Design and Electoral Dynamics*. Cambridge: Cambridge University Press, p. 150.
53 Hong 2002, pp. 155-165.
54 Mosler, H. B. (2020). Characteristics and Challenges of South Korea's Presidential Government System. In Mosler, H. B. (Ed.), *South Korea's Democracy Challenge. Political System, Political Economy, and Political Society*. Berlin: Peter Lang Academic Publishers, 25-66, pp. 32-33.
55 Hong 2002, pp. 153-155; Pak, Y. S. (2016). Han'guk-ŭi chewangjŏk taet'ongnyŏng [The Imperial Presidency by Evasion of the Political Laws in Korea]. *Han'gukchŏngch'i Yŏn'gu*, 25 (2), 27-55, pp. 42-49; Ham, S.-D. (2003). *Taet'ongyŏng-hak [President Research]*. Seoul: Nanamch'ulp'an, pp. 91-98; Ham, S.-D. (2018).

In this vein, Pak rightly argues that one needs to pay more attention to non-institutional conditions such as the expediency in executing the office and adds that these "non-institutional conditions are closely related to the balance of political forces, which is constituted by a combination of the will to make use of institutional gaps and keeping this in check, and this in turn is linked to historical-structural conditions."[56] This agency aspect is also reflected in the discussion of dealing with the US imperial presidency in the 1970s[57] and its partial re-emergence at the beginning of the 21st century, when Kruse and Zelizer purport that "[t]he reformers of the 1970s missed the ways in which reforms simply cannot restrain a president who doesn't care about institutions. The most important source of presidential restraint has been the character of the person in office."[58] In other words, the president's personality, character, psychological state of mind, world-view, and style are important traits that influence how they interpret the office and act out the job. From this perspective, one can simply argue that a more authoritarian person will more likely become an imperial president compared to someone who is lenient in character. Of course, an elected president is not completely free to do what they like to do; the president is dependent to a certain degree on the historical situation, available opportunities, relationship between government and opposition parties, demands or expectations by the people, and circumstances interna-tionally as well as domestically. And, yet, the person in office does make an individual difference.

Besides flawed institutional design and misinterpretation of the office according to the character of the person in office, the general *political culture* is often invoked as yet another factor benefitting imperial presiden-cy.[59] In other words, approving of the abuse or privatization of office and accepting the president's supra-legal and evasional behavior is made possible and potentially even induced by a respective political culture among the political elites as well as in Korean society at large.[60] Whether

---

Chewangjŏk taet'ongyŏng-ŭi chongŏn [The End of the Imperial Presidency]. Koyang: Sŏmaensŏm, pp. 46-50.

56 Pak 2016, p. 51.
57 Weko, T. J. (1995). *The Politicizing Presidency*. Lawrence: University of Kansas Press, pp. 107-126.
58 Kruse and Zelizer 2019.
59 Hong 2002; Mosler 2020.
60 Hong 2002, pp. 165-166.

Korea has an "antidemocratic culture,"[61] and whether this is rooted in its Confucian heritage,[62] is subject to an ongoing debate. A general tendency that has been found for Korea is a political culture even after democratization is said to be characterized by a general preference for strong and centralized government, stiff hierarchical orders in organizations, the rule of bureaucracy, and the obedience of submissive citizens,[63] whereas elites see ordinary citizens as objects for control and mobilization.[64] Meanwhile, more recent accounts contend a continuous change in the civic virtues of the Korean populace, and attest them having become "much more critical of their leaders and raise their voices whenever the government goes against the people's will."[65] At the same time, however, surveys still indicate some pockets of authoritarian attitudes, at least relative to other developed democratic countries.[66] While a final conclusion on this matter is still due, against the backdrop of a recent series of mass demonstrations since 2002, Korean political culture seems to be oscillating between favoring an omnipotent leader-president to whom citizens delegate their power on one hand and the preference to directly execute their sovereignty if the president oversteps a red line on the other.[67] Eventually, this leads to the people giving the president generous leeway in conducting the office that allows him or her to act out his or her personally preferred interpretation of the post.

---

61 Huntington, S. (1991). *The Third Wave: Democratization in the Late Twentieth Century*. Norman and London: University of Oklahoma Press, p. 298.

62 Yi, C.-H. (2008). Han'guktaet'ongyŏngje-ŭi wŏnsukhan unyŏngŭl wihan jeŏn [Suggestions for the Smooth Operation of the Korean Presidential System]. In Yang, K. et al. (Eds.), *Saeroun hŏnbop p'iryohan'ga [Do We Need a New Constitution?]*. Seoul: Taehwamunhwasa, 188-208, pp. 193-194.

63 Kim, U.-T. et al. (Eds.) (1999). *Han'gukchŏngch'iron [Korean Politics]*. Seoul: Pakyŏngsa, p. 262.

64 Kim, H.-J. (1995). *Han'gukchŏngch'ich'ejeron [The Political System of Korea]*. Seoul: Pakyŏngsa, p. 332.

65 Kim, J.-Y. (2020). Political Culture and Behavior. In Moon, C.-I. and Moon, M. J. (Eds.), *Routledge Handbook of Korean Politics and Public Administration*. London: Routledge, 41-58, p. 55.

66 This concerns, for example, the tendency of answers to survey questions regarding the army or experts (technocrats) ruling government, people obeying their rulers, having a strong ruler, and protecting people's liberties from state oppression (see World Values Survey, https://www.worldvaluessurvey.org).

67 See Mosler 2020, pp. 46-49.

Consequences of Falling Into the Imperial President Trap

The above elaborations reveal that too much unchecked presidential pow-er attracts actors such as the president herself or himself, close aides, staff, loyalists, entrepreneurs, friends, relatives, and others to take advantage of this power source for personal gains or political interests. This, in turn, leads to violations of law and infringement of the principle of division of powers that is central to a sound democracy. An imperial president fosters expectations by the people of the president as an omnipotent savior, and it increases disappointment, political apathy, or antipathy in the people when the president cannot deliver what they had imagined. What is more, excessive use of power by the president often prompts equally strong reactions by those who are subjected to it such as the opposition, the legislative branch, prosecutors, and, ultimately, the people. This results in a "paradox of power,"[68] wherein imperial presidents are outmatched in the power game, leading to stalemates in parliament or crises in the political system. Against this backdrop, this section introduces the term *presidential power trap* as an alternative to "imperial president" to better demonstrate the dynamics and complexities involved in the phenomenon at hand. Of course, even the depiction of an imperial president does not exclude a connotation of power challenges or even intrigues against and overthrow of the ruler, and it does not necessarily preclude alluding to situations in which the incumbent unintentionally or unknowingly committed mal-practice with negative effects to them personally, the office, and the polity at large. Nevertheless, too often,

> "[t]he imperial presidency is, in many ways, propped up by media par-tisans who insist that the naked emperor has glorious new clothes."[69]

Many scholarly accounts, too, tend to disregard this crucial dark spot of the matter that has negative repercussions on a given democratic sys-tem. Therefore, using the notion of the presidential power trap provides a critical and more obviously negative connotation from the outset. In this way, "presidential power trap" is less prone to misrepresenting the phenomenon as an always omnipotent president but allows for alluding to situations or times when a president is trapped and thus restricted in conducting the office properly. In addition, the metaphorical device of a "trap" also allows for more easily thinking of different reasons for sliding

---

68 Fitts 1996.
69 Kruse and Zelizer 2019.

into such a situation. For example, presidents can be "lured into a trap" (by other actors), they can "walk right into a trap" with their eyes open, and they can "fall into their own trap." What is more, the metaphorical trap does not have to be limited to capturing the president but can be extended to describing the aftermath of the resulting power dynamics that are harmful to the president's aides, the political system, or society at large. In other words, the presidential power trap can better accommodate the three main causes involved in the too-powerful president: flawed constitutional design (formal), misinterpretation of the office (informal), and people's perceptions and attitudes (cultural).

Operationalizing the Presidential Power Trap

Based on the above discussion of the existing literature on the phenomenon of the imperial president in Korea three analytical categories were established for analyzing the first three years of Moon's presidency (2017-2020). First, the way the incumbent organizes the presidential office allows evaluating the concentration of power in a few hands. Put differently, the more authority and discretion the presidential office and its staff are given, the higher the danger of excessive use of power. This can be operationalized in formal terms of quantities such as number of staff, amount of the office's budget, and organizational structures as well as in informal appointment practices of the president's close aides regarding their professional qualification, their ethic conduct, and popular reputation. Another variable concerns in how far the office's communication with the citizens promotes or impedes proper efficacy of the office. Second, the category of operating government serves as indicator regarding how presidents uses their power within the executive branch. This concerns to what degree they make use of their authority to share power within the administration's center with the prime minister, to appoint members of the cabinet or state council (*kungmuhoeŭi*), that is ministers, how much authority they cede to executive ministries, and to what extend they abstain from the practice of revolving door policy as a way of rewarding political support. Third, the category of 'cooperating with the branches' aims at evaluating the actual practice of the principle of separation of powers among the three branches. Here, the variable of the degree of diffusing power is operationalized based on the extend the president encroaches upon rights of the legislature and judiciary, and the section thus examines government's extent and style of legislative activities as well as the quantity and quality of making use of powerful rights such as the presidential pardoning right.

2. Analysis

2.1 Organizing the Presidential Office (Blue House)

Scale of Resources

Similar to Nixon's White House, the growth of scale of the Korean Blue House (*Ch'ŏngwadae*) started in the 1970s (with President Park Chung-hee) and has been continuing since then.[70] This most visible result of increased power regards an office staff that grew from 209 persons in the 1970s to 395 in the end of the 1990s to 443 under President Park Geun-hye. In other words, personnel in the Blue House more than doubled during the last 24 years between father and daughter. Accordingly, the budget of the president's office skyrocketed from KRW eight billion in the 1970s to KRW 30 billion at the end of the 1990s to KRW 80 billion under Park Geun-hye.[71] The Blue House under President Moon saw a growth in budget to KRW 90 billion and in his personnel to about 450 people.[72] Naturally, part of this remarkable growth can be attributed to a generally more complex society and global developments that simply led to the need for a greater organizational scope to cope with the growing complexity. Other qualitative developments in the Blue House, however, are outcomes closely related to the phenomenon of increased concentration of power. The following paragraphs address two main aspects central to the question of the imperial presidency that are mutually enforcing. One regards the actual power wielded by the exclusive elite of presidential personnel – how powerful they are vis-à-vis the rest of the executive and administration, and vis-à-vis the legislature as well as the judicature. The other aspect regards the power of the president and the Blue House vis-à-vis the people.

Personnel Decisions and Activities

Personnel decisions and activities concern, most crucially, the powerful staff in the president's office, the Blue House – that is, the chief of staff and the senior secretaries. In theory, the Blue House staff has the function of gathering, processing, and evaluating the information coming in from the

---

70 Pak 2018.
71 Ibid., p. 66.
72 Ibid.

various government organs and agencies and other sources to provide the president with the necessary, comprehensive data to make policy decisions. To this end, the various units in the presidential office are organized so that they mirror the most important ministries or sections that have to be monitored and administered. In other words, the presidential office's original function is that of a control tower that organizes the various communications and policy actions. However, due to the concentration of power around the president, the office staff influences the ministries and other organs to a degree that their autonomy is excessively restricted.[73] While formally, the secretaries are on the level of deputy ministers, in fact, they wield power equal to or even higher than the ministers. Likewise, the presidential chief of staff is formally on the ministerial level but has authority exceeding this level. This has the effect of leading to less autonomy of the cabinet members, ministries, and lower echelons of the bureaucracy. An additional problem is that these close and powerful aides to the president are gatekeepers between the ministries and the president. On the one hand, this is an important source of their power in the first place, because they can decide who has access to the president when, how, and why. On the other hand, this means they control the flow of information that reaches the president on the basis of which she or he makes decisions. Due to this kind of firewall of the presidential office, there is a danger of insulating the president from the rest of the executive and administration, not to speak of the legislature and judicature, with the risk of the president's "withdrawal from external reality."[74] Moreover, these powerful staff of the president are not elected and thus are not accountable to the people but are handpicked by the president. At the same time, it is actually them who have the power to influence the government agencies, which are headed by ministers who at least were decided on by parliament as the representative body of the people's will. Also, when things go wrong, it is mostly the ministers who are sacrificed, not the presidential office's staff, who might have led the ministry to make the critical decisions. In addition, when the president promotes a culture within the office where the staff are not allowed to express or at least are discouraged from voicing criticism or differing views, the president's decision power grows respectively.

---

73 Cho, S.-J. and Im, T.-B. (2010). *Han'guk haengjŏngjojiknon [Korean Administration Theory]*. Seoul: Bŏmmunsa, pp. 114-136; Hong 2002, pp. 163-165; Pak 2018, pp. 69-72.

74 Schlesinger 1973, p. 223.

The most controversial staffing decisions at the Blue House under President Moon have concerned former Senior Protocol Administrative Staffer T'ak Hyŏn-min, former Senior Secretary for Civil Affairs Cho Kuk, and former Chief of Staff Im Jeong-seok (*Im Chong-sŏk*). The first controversy around T'ak Hyŏn-min, a former professor of mass communication at Sungkonghoe University (*Sŏnggonghoe taehakkyo*), arose in May 2017 when he was appointed senior protocol administrative staffer at the Blue House and was linked to a series of explicit sexist and misogynic remarks in two books he authored before joining then presidential candidate Moon's campaign team in 2011.[75] A second controversy emerged when, in November 2017, T'ak went on trial for carrying out an unlawful election campaign activity during a ceremony in the run-up to the presidential election half a year earlier. In the first as well as the second instance, the courts acquitted him of accusations regarding violations of the Political Finance Act but found him guilty of having violated the Public Office Election Act and fined him KRW 700,000.[76] During this time, President Moon made repeatedly clear that he would not give up T'ak despite strong demands for his resignation by women's rights groups and the Minister for Gender Equality. T'ak finally resigned in January 2019, but shortly afterwards was assigned as a member of the newly established Advisory Committee for Presidential Event Management.[77] In Spring 2020, T'ak eventually made his comeback to the Blue House's inner power circle, when he was promoted to protocol secretary.[78]

When Cho Kuk, professor of law at Seoul National University (*Sŏul taehakkyo*), was appointed senior secretary for civil affairs at the Blue House

75 Chŏng, W.-S. (2018). T'ak Hyŏn-min-ŭi 1-yŏn, nollan-esŏ sat'oe-ggaji [One year T'ak Hyŏn-min, from controversy to resignation]. *The Hankyoreh*, June 30, 2018. Available at: https://h2.khan.co.kr/201806301601001 [Accessed January 12, 2020].

76 Ko, T.-U. (2018). Pulbŏp sŏn'gŏundong T'ak Hyŏn-min 2-sim pŏlgŭm 70-manwŏn [Fine of KRW 700,000 for T'ak in the Second Instance]. *Yonhapnews*, November 2, 2018. Available at: https://www.yna.co.kr/view/AKR2018110204925 1004?input=1195m [Accessed January 12, 2020].

77 Im, M.-H. (2019). Mun taet'ongnyŏng haengsagihoek chamunwiwŏn sinsŏl, T'ak Hyŏn-min wich'uk [President Moon Established Advisory Committee for Presidential Event Management, Makes T'ak Hyŏn-min Member]. *MBC News*, February 21, 2019. Available at: https://imnews.imbc.com/news/2019/politics/article/51 74599_29092.html [Accessed January 12, 2020].

78 Sŏng, Y.-C. (2020). T'akhyŏnmin ch'ŏngwadae ŭijŏnbisŏgwan-ŭro pokkwi [T'ak Hyŏn-min Returns to the Blue House as Protocol Secretary]. *The Hankyoreh*, May 26, 2020. Available at: http://www.hani.co.kr/arti/politics/bluehouse/946553.html [Accessed May 26, 2020].

in May 2017, the criticism was that he had been involved in left-leaning activism and that he used to criticize academics who went into politics as irresponsible. A serious scandal arose in autumn 2019 when he resigned and then was appointed Minister of Justice, and allegations arose that he had been involved in various cases of malpractice while in office. The prosecution indicted him in January 2020 on twelve different charges including bribery and graft. He is accused of a whole set of allegations including receiving bribes, graft, violating the public servants' ethics code, business obstruction, unlawful interference in public duties, forging documents, and instigation of tampering and hiding evidence.[79] Besides allegations concerning grafting certificates for and taking tests instead of his two children, Cho is accused of malpractice (*chikkwŏnnamyong*) while serving in the Blue House. In its bill of indictment, the prosecution charges Cho with having illegally suspended a probe (*kamch'al*) in the presidential office in late 2017 that was looking into bribery allegations of former Busan Vice Mayor Yoo Jae-soo (*Yu Chae-su*). In addition, Paek Wŏn-u, the president's former Presidential Secretary for Civil Affairs, and Pak Hyŏng-ch'ŏl, former Presidential Secretary for Anticorruption, allegedly had been partaking in the illegal activities.[80] The prosecution charged them with having given in to requests by close aides of President Moon and former Blue House staff to turn a blind eye to the mayor's case, as he had become close to Moon while serving in the Blue House under President Roh Moo-hyun.[81]

In addition, Cho is accused of another case of malpractice regarding an election-meddling scandal with then Chief of Staff Im Jeong-seok at the center.[82] Im was a controversial personnel decision in the first place regarding his student movement background. Conservatives criticized his

79 Kim, E.-B. and Lee, S.-E. (2020). Cho Kuk Indicted on 12 Charges, Blue House Slams 'Narrow' Results. *Korea Joongang Daily*, January 1, 2020. Available at: http://koreajoongangdaily.joins.com/news/article/article.aspx?aid=3072083 [Accessed January 12, 2020].

80 Kim, S.-M., Lee, G.-Y., and Lee, S.-E. (2019). Cho Faces Questions in Ex-Busan Vice Mayor Probe. *Korea Joongang Daily*, December 17, 2019. Available at: http://koreajoongangdaily.joins.com/news/article/article.aspx?aid=3071547 [Accessed January 12, 2020].

81 Kim, H.-C. (2020). Yu Chae-su pwajunŭn kŏn ŏt'ŏk'ennŭnya [How About Turning a Blind Eye on Yu Chae-su?]. *Kyunghyang Sinmun*, January 20, 2020. Available at: http://news.khan.co.kr/kh_news/khan_art_view.html?art_id=202001201329001 [Accessed January 20, 2020].

82 Sŏng, T.-H. (2020). Cho Kuk ch'ŏngwadae-e 21-hoe pogo [Cho Kuk Reported 21 Times to the Blue House]. *Yonhapnews*, February 5, 2020. Available at: https://ww

appointment, arguing that he was a pro-North Korean leftist activist, which they saw confirmed when Im was at the center of organizing the North-South summit in 2018 with discretion apparently exceeding those of the Prime Minister, Minister for Unification, or Minister for Foreign Affairs. Besides criticism of the imbalanced power vis-à-vis the administration, it was pointed out that the chief of staff is supposed to focus on assisting the president.[83] This is related to the problem of transgressing other state organs' discretion, as well as Im going beyond his job description and engaging in political malpractice, which is another issue that was raised. It was deemed inappropriate, for example, when the chief of staff became an increasingly visible actor in the rapprochement process with North Korea, including appearances in the media when visiting North Korea or the demilitarized zone (DMZ), which led some to call him the "royal chief of staff (wangsiljang)."[84] Legally far more concerning is that Im was summoned by the prosecution as a criminal suspect in a case of alleged power abuse in relation to the Ulsan mayoral elections in 2018. The accusation stands that several high-level Blue House staff, including Im, pressured Ulsan police to investigate former Ulsan Mayor Kim Ki-hyŏn shortly before the election on possible corruption allegations to produce negative publicity, thus helping rival candidate Song Ch'ŏl-ho, who is close to President Moon. Other suspects indicted by the prosecution are former Senior Presidential Secretary for Political Affairs Han Pyŏng-do, former Presidential Secretary for Civil Affairs Paek Wŏn-u, and former Presidential Secretary for Anticorruption Pak Hyŏng-ch'ŏl.[85]

Another noteworthy development are the high numbers of former Blue House staff resigning to run for office in the general elections in April 2020. No less than around 40 former presidential office personnel

---

w.yna.co.kr/view/AKR20200205075600004?input=1195m [Accessed February 6, 2020].

83 Kim, T.-H. (2018). Chaggu k'ŭnŭn Im Chong-sŏk [Im Chong-sŏk Is Continually Growing]. *Chugan Chosŏn*, March 25, 2018. Available at: http://news.chosun.com/ site/data/html_dir/2018/03/23/2018032302132.html [Accessed January 12, 2020].

84 Kim, N.-H. (2018). DMZ sich'al, Begun myŏndam ... wangsiljang nollan hipsa'in Im Chong-sŏk [Inspection of the DMZ, Meeting With Begun ... Im Chong-sŏk Is Embroiled in Royal Chief of Staff Controversy]. *JTBC News*, October 30, 2018. Available at: http://news.jtbc.joins.com/article/article.aspx?news_id=NB11719193 [Accessed January 12, 2020].

85 Ser, M.-J. and Bae, J.-S. (2020). Im Jong-seok to Face Questioning on Power Abuse. *Korea Joongang Daily*, January 30, 2020. Available at: http://koreajoongan gdaily.joins.com/news/article/article.aspx?aid=3073151 [Accessed February 12, 2020].

will be applying for a candidacy at the government party, and another roughly 30 persons are using their relationship with President Moon as a central advertisement point on their application.[86] While running for office is a decision by those individuals that was not necessarily initiated by the president, the fact that so many make use of their relationship with the incumbent president demonstrates the excessive symbolic power that emanates from the office. It has been suggested that many even see their employment at the Blue House as only a preparatory step, adding this particular valuable experience for the ultimate aim of running for office. This is particularly true for the competitive selection process in the government party through which candidacies are decided.[87] Out of about 70 original contenders 30 were appointed candidate by the ruling party, while in the end 19 were elected into office.[88] Thus, once more the name of the president alone wielded the desired power, and thus to a certain extent, prove this point.

The Presidential Office's Webpage's Publicity Vortex

As for symbolic power, the Moon administration made efforts to present the president's office in a more accessible and approachable light. A case in point is the Blue House's online petition board (*kungminch'ŏngwŏn*). This online petition board is modelled after the Obama administration's "We the People." Citizens can file petitions directly at the presidential office, and the government is required to respond to every petition that receives more than 200,000 consenting signatures from other citizens within 30 days. According to the president's office, the online petition board was intended to make its webpage into yet another platform for citizens

---

86 Chŏng, Y.-I. (2020). 'Ch'ŏngwadae kyŏngnyŏk' ch'ongsŏn pŭrimiŏm toeilgga? [Will the 'Blue House Experience' Become an Election Premium?]. *Kyunghyang Weekly*, January 10, 2020. Available at: https://weekly.khan.co.kr/khnm.html?mode=view&artid=202001101639211&code=113 [Accessed January 12, 2020].

87 Yun, C.-W. (2020). Ch'ŏngch'ulsin yŏktaegŭp inwŏn-i ch'ongsŏn-e nasonŭn paegyŏng [Background on the Reasons Why So Many Former Blue House Staff Are Running for Public Offices]. *Maeil Kyŏngje*, January 20, 2020. Available at: http://m.raythep.com/AllNew/AllNew/View/21181 [Accessed February 4, 2020].

88 Kim, K.-C. (2020). 4-15 ch'ongsŏn, 'chŏnggwŏn simp'an'-boda 'kukchŏng anjŏng' [April 15 General Elections Rather Reflected 'Government Stability' Than 'Judgment of Government']. *Issue Maker*, April 24, 2020. Available at: http://www.issuemaker.kr/news/articleView.html?idxno=31607 [Accessed May 26, 2020].

communication.[89] Despite the supposed intentions, the online petition has the effect of concentrating even more attention and thus power in the Blue House and the president. At the time of writing, the government has responded to 135 out of almost 700 petitions since the board opened in mid-August 2017. Most of the petitions regard political reforms, human rights and gender equality matters, and issues related to safety and the environment.[90] At the time of writing, the petition with the most consenting signatures requested to dissolve the conservative opposition Liberty Korea Party (*Chayuhan'guktang*) for obstructing the government from enacting policies on behalf of the people (1.8 million), followed by a petition urging a tough punishment for a killer who committed a brutal murder at an Internet café in a western Seoul district in October 2018 (1.2 million), and the demand to appoint Cho Kuk as Justice Minister despite the allegations against him and his wife (760,000). In addition, about 740,000 people asked to reinvestigate the case surrounding celebrity Jang Ja-yeon (*Chang Cha-yŏn*), who committed suicide after having been coerced by her agency to give sexual and other favors; roughly 710,000 users opposed the around 500 Yemenis who landed in 2016 on Cheju Island and applied for refugee status; and amid the coronavirus crisis in early 2020, around 700,000 users demanded to stop Chinese citizens from entering Korea.[91]

Major effects of the petition board have been problematic for two reasons. First, it amplifies the image of the president as an omnipotent king or savior who can solve any problem of their subjects. This leads to even higher expectations in the president and accordingly results in stronger disappointment. The petitions enjoy strong media attention, which in turn induces sensationalist petitions that oversimplify problems. This can then again lead to amplifying conflicts rather than solving them. The petition with the most likes so far, demanding the dissolution of the opposition Liberty Korea Party, received almost two million signatures. The second

---

89 Kwŏn, H.-U. (2017). Sot'ong-ŭi 'mun'-ŭl yŏlda – ch'ŏng: 'kungmin-sot'ongp'ŭlaetŭp'om' pongyŏk kadong [Opening the Door to Communication – Blue House: Full-Scale Operation of the Public Communication Platform]. *CBS Nokŏt'ŭnyusŭ*, August 17, 2017. Available at: http://www.nocutnews.co.kr/news/4 832273 [Accessed July 20, 2018].

90 Yi, C.-Y. (2019). Kungminch'ŏngwŏn haru p'yŏnggyun 851-kŏn [Citizens' Petition Board Receives on Average 851 Petitions Per Day]. *Seoul Sinmun*, November 7, 2019. Available at: https://www.seoul.co.kr/news/newsView.php?id=201911070 09010&wlog_tag3=naver [Accessed January 10, 2020].

91 Ch'ŏngwadae (2020). *Kungminch'ŏngwŏn [Citizens' Petition Board]*. [Online]. Available at: https://www1.president.go.kr/petitions [Accessed February 11, 2020].

aspect is that the more people focus their petitions to the central site of the Blue House, the fewer petitions are filed to those government agencies that are actually in charge of the matters at hand. This means not only less authority of the government agencies vis-à-vis the Blue House, but also less effectiveness of the institution of petitioning the administration as such. Moreover, the effect is that the concentration on the president as a kind of savior who can solve all the problems in the world, if they can only hear what the people say, is increased, thus promoting the weakening of institutions such as political parties and parliament.[92] Put differently, the electronic petition board contributes to this vicious cycle of trust in the president and relative distrust in almost all other political institutions. Another problem identified in this regard is that through the online petition board, citizens tend to cede their sovereignty to the president instead of themselves actively working towards a certain goal, and then demand the president to implement a respective policy.[93] Put differently, it promotes passive behavior of political subjects, who tend to expect to be helped by an omnipotent savior.

Besides the petition board, the presidential office's webpage also includes additional functions allowing citizens to appeal to government and administration agencies (*kungminsinmun'go*), make suggestions for how to allocate the budget (*kungminch'amyŏyesan*), and forward proposals for whom to appoint to public offices (*injaech'uch'ŏn*). While these weblinks refer the user to the webpages of the respective institutions, other functions such as the "discussion room" (*t'oronbang*) and the online petition board belong to the website of the Blue House. To sum up, good intentions and some good effects cannot be denied, but in the end, the online petition at the Blue House contributes to the imperial president phenomenon rather than lessening it by concentrating even more attention, and thus power in the presidency.

92 See Kwŏn, K.-S. (2018). Chikchŏp minjujuŭi vs yŏronmori agyong – 'yangnar-ŭi k'al' doen kungminch'ŏngwŏn [Abuse of Direct Democracy Versus Public Opinion – The National Petition Has Become a Double-Edged Sword]. *Segye Ilbo*, September 9, 2018. Available at: http://www.segye.com/newsView/20180909002 693 [Accessed September 24, 2018].

93 Pak, S.-H. (2017). Ch'ŏngwadae kungminch'ŏngwŏn-ŭn minju-jŏgilgga [Is the Blue House Public Petition Democratic?]. *Dong-A Ilbo*, December 19, 2017. Available at: http://news.donga.com/3/all/20171219/87808886/1 [Accessed May 18, 2018].

2.2 Operating Government

Prime Minister

Regarding power structures within the executive, the imbalanced division of powers between the president and the prime minister as well as between the president and the cabinet are particular sources of power concentration in the president. Despite constitutionally regulated discretion of the prime minister (*kungmuch'ongni*), in practice the prime minister's fate is wholly in the hands of the president, thus leaving the prime minister factually significantly under-empowered. Because of that, the prime minister in Korea has only seldom played a significant role at the top of the executive, usually acting as an assistant to the president, and a merely symbolic or ceremonial figure who can be shed as ballast when the government has to take responsibility.[94] Moon's first prime minister Lee Nak-yon (*Yi Nag-yŏn*) became Korea's longest serving prime minister since democratization and rightly received favorable appraisal across political camps for his service. However, even Lee was not given, and apparently did not claim, the full range of powers that the constitution potentially allows, and which could help check and balance the president adequately.

Members of Cabinet

The power relationship between the president and ministers or cabinet members are similarly lopsided, because appointment and removal of state council (*kungmuhoeŭi*) members – that is, ministers – is fully up to the president.[95] Problems stemming from democratic deficits regarding personnel decisions for ministerial and other higher posts usually manifest in the appointment process. In 2000, the Personnel Hearing Act (*insach'ŏng-munhoebŏp*; PHA) was introduced as a way of empowering parliament concerning this matter, and in 2005, ministers as well as members of the state council – that is, the cabinet – were included as well. Before a candidate can finally be appointed to their post, there has to be a hearing at the Na-

---

94 Hong 2002, pp. 159-161; Mosler 2020; Myŏng, J. J. (2007). Kungmuch'ongnije-ŭi hamni-chŏk unyong-ŭi han'gye-wa kaehŏn p'iryosŏng [The Operational Limits of the Prime Minister's Power and the Necessity of Constitutional Revision]. *Hŏnbŏp Yŏn'gu*, 13 (1), 155-185.
95 Constitution of the Republic of Korea, Articles 86, 87.

tional Assembly and a respective bill agreed upon by a Special Committee on Personnel Hearings and passed in the plenary session. The candidate is approved when the National Assembly adopts a positive report on the candidate in question. However, even if the candidate did not appear before such a hearing, or the hearing report was not adopted, the president can appoint the person, because there is no ultimate means parliament can use for forcing the executive to act according to their position.[96] Since the introduction of the PHA, under every government so far there have been cases, though to differing degrees, whose appointments were enforced by the president despite nonadoption by parliament.

Comparing the last three governments under Presidents Lee Myung-bak (*Yi Myŏng-bak*), Park Geun-hye, and Moon Jae-in shows that the share of cases in which the personnel hearing report of the National Assembly for high officials was not adopted was 15.3%, 11.2%, and 33.8% respectively.[97] The percentage of cases in which neither a hearing nor the adoption of the report took place and the person was appointed regardless were 20.0%, 11.2%, and 34.3% respectively.[98] In other words, regarding the use of the executive's appointment power for high officials, the Moon government is already visibly more disregarding of the principle of equal partnership between the executive and the legislature. To be fair, the stern behavior of the Blue House is also a reaction to the extreme uncooperative, if not sabotaging, attitude displayed by the conservative opposition. However, this, too, has to be understood as an effect of the presidential power trap on the not completely groundless pretext of being overpowered by the administration's authority.

The appointment of former Senior Secretary for Civil Affairs Cho Kuk to Minister of Justice in 2019 is a case in point. The nomination prompted an outcry by the rightist conservatives, which shortly afterwards spread to major portions of the citizenry. The majority of the public and the opposition party rejected Cho to be appointed Minister of Justice for

---

96 Sim, K.-S. (2017). Kwŏllyŏkpullip-kwa taet'ongnyŏng-ŭi immyŏnggwŏn [Separation of Powers and the Appointment Power of President]. *Hŏnbŏp Yŏn'gu*, 23 (3), 295-332, pp. 300-301. For more on the power relation between the president and the legislature see section below.

97 Sŏk, H.-W. (2019). Nŭrŏnanŭn kukhoe p'aesing kwagŏ chŏngbu-nŭn ŏddaenna? [Increasing National Assembly Passing, How Was It under Former Governments?]. *KBS News*, June 17, 2019. Available at: http://news.kbs.co.kr/news/view.d o?ncd=4284401 [Accessed October 25, 2019].

98 Ibid. Regarding the statistics on the Moon administration, the numbers are as of June 2019.

legal reasons, as well as for moral reasons, but President Moon appointed him nonetheless. Only 30 days after his inauguration, Cho had to resign because of the above-mentioned allegations against his family, including his wife, as well as suspicions regarding private equity investment and manipulation of his daughter's college admission. President Moon publicly apologized twice for appointing Cho despite the opposition. The vacancy of the Minister of Justice was shortly afterwards filled with government party deputy Choo Mi-ae (*Ch'u Mi-ae*). One of Choo's first actions was to reassign several public prosecutors of the Supreme Prosecutor's Office in Seoul who had been investigating Blue House allegations to posts in distant provinces, bringing to mind the attempts under the Nixon administration to deploy civil servants to remote locations.[99] While the Blue House denies any allegations, it nevertheless does add to plausible suspicions that this reshuffle was to punish the prosecutors or to hamper investigations.[100]

An additional measure for gauging critical personnel decisions is the ratio of members of the state council who belong either to the president's election camp, have similar political or ideological inclinations, and/or are members of the governing Democratic Party (*Tŏburŏminjudang*, DP). In this respect, the Moon administration, with a ratio of 65%, has so far has been worse than Park (62%) but better off than Lee (84%).[101] These questionable appointments do not only potentially reduce the autonomy of the organization in question but are also manifestations of the still strongly prevailing political clientelism – the president being the super patron.

Executive Ministries and Policy Decisions

Due to their strong dependency on the president, executive ministers are restricted in their ministerial autonomy vis-à-vis the president or the Blue House key staff. In this regard, Korean ministers are famous for their short

99 Waterman 2009, p. 5.
100 The Economist (2020). *Going South: South Korea's President Curbs the Power of Prosecutors*, January 16, 2020. Available at: https://www.economist.com/asia/2020 /01/16/south-koreas-president-curbs-the-power-of-prosecutors [Accessed January 20, 2020].
101 Kim, K.-Y. and Kim, T.-B. (2019). Mun K'aemk'odŏ insa Pak-poda mank'o MB-boda chŏkta [Moon's Questionable Personnel Decisions More Than Park, Less Than Lee]. *Nocutnews*, April 10, 2019. Available at: https://www.nocutnews.co.kr /news/5132380 [Accessed January 12, 2020].

office terms. Since 1987, ministers were in office in average for not more than 15 months, while the average for a minister in the US, for example, is three years.[102] As mentioned above, chief secretaries at the presidential office wield strong influence on the agenda of the ministries designated to them. The following examples will suffice to show the degree to which the Blue House is overly seizing jurisdiction over matters delegated to the ministries.

In 2019, President Moon in his budget speech at the National Assembly stated that admission policies of domestic universities will be changed to have a greater share of regular selection vis-à-vis special selection. In other words, it will become more important for prospective students to do well on the College Scholastic Ability Test (CSAT). The reasoning is that increasing the weight of alternative admission criteria had led to an advantage for students from privileged families. Until now, students could increase their portfolio by collecting certificates or recommendations by doing costly extracurricular activities and out-of-class volunteer work. Also, since these activities cannot be regulated and controlled as tightly as the CSAT, potential malpractice can profit those who misuse the system. Irrespective of whether the one or the other admission policy is more desirable, President Moon's statement caught the Ministry of Education completely unprepared. President Moon began to push education policy reform preparations in early September 2019, and the Minister of Education had made clear several times that a change in the university admission modus was not part of the new policy plans. A month before President Moon announced the about-face during his speech in parliament, Minster of Education Yoo Eun-hae (*Yu Ŭn-hye*) responded to a question of an opposition deputy that there would be no change in this regard.[103] One day before the president's statement, government party deputies in charge of education policy, too, were still advocating against expanding the portion of students universities admit based on standardized testing,

102 Kim, S.-J. (2017). Han'guk changgwan chae'im kigan 1-yŏn 2-gaewŏl vs miguk changgwan 3-nyŏn pan [Korean Ministers' 1 Year and 2 Months Office Term vs US-Ministers' 3 Years]. *YTN*, June 25, 2017. Available at: https://www.ytn.co.kr/_ln/0101_201706250515367569 [Accessed October 23, 2019].

103 Yi, H.-S. (2019). Yu Ŭn-hye, tae'ipkaep'yŏn, chŏng.susi piyul chojŏng anin hakchong kongjŏngsŏng chego [Yu Ŭn-hye, Improving Equity of the Early Admission System Rather Than Adjusting the Standardized Modus]. *Yonhapnews*, September 4, 2019. Available at: https://www.yna.co.kr/view/AKR201909041070 52004?input=1195m [January 10, 2020].

that is CSAT.[104] However, only 24 hours later, the President contradicted his Minister of Education in public and without prior notice.[105] Because of this sudden change in education policy, which contradicts policies hitherto planned by the Moon administration, it is widely suggested that Moon made this change to avert further disadvantage due to the Cho Kuk scandal (see above). In only 2018, the Ministry of Education finalized university admission policy by way of a year-long public deliberation and decided on applying more than 30% of the regular admission modus for the academic year 2022. Against this backdrop, newspaper editorials called the president's move "populist" and an "arbitrary decision" made out of "political interest" based on a "flawed decision process" due to "ignorance of the Blue House secretaries regarding education policy."[106] To summarize, first, the president contradicted his Minister of Education in public without prior notice, let alone any other form of communication. While the president has final authority over policies in the ministries, to expose one of his ministers in public with a 180-degree about-turn is not only embarrassing but signals to the public, as well as to his cabinet, that the president can overturn any policy anytime. Second, this case demonstrates that regardless of the policy's importance or establishing background (ex-

---

104 Chŏng, Ŭ.-H. (2019). Chŏngsi hwaktae ŏptadŏn kyoyukpu [The Ministry of Education That Were Against Expanding the CSAT]. *TV Chosun*, October 22, 2019. Available at: http://news.tvchosun.com/site/data/html_dir/2019/10/22/2019 102290077.html [Accessed January 12, 2020].

105 Song, C.-S. (2019). Sunŭng chŏngsi hwaktae-ro tae'ipchedo kaep'yŏn [Decision to Reform College Entrance System by Extending the CSAT Proportion]. *Kyunghyang Sinmun*, October 22, 2019. Available at: http://news.khan.co.kr/k h_news/khan_art_view.html?artid=201910221706001&code=940401 [Accessed January 10, 2020].

106 Chosun Ilbo (2019). *Cho Kuk ttal t'ase tto ipsi pyŏn'gyŏng, 4-nyŏn-e 4-bŏn pagg-windani [The Entrance Exam Changed Again, Changing Four Times in Four Years, Because of Cho Kuk's Daughter]*, November 11, 2019. Available at: https://www .chosun.com/site/data/html_dir/2019/11/29/2019112903288.html [Accessed November 30, 2019]; Dong-A Ilbo (2019). *Kyoyukpo "chŏngsi 40% hwaktae," kaljija kyoyukchŏngch'aek ŏnje tto paggwilji [Ministry of Education "Expansion of On-Time 40%," When Will the Education Policy Change Again?]*, November 29, 2019. Available at: https://www.donga.com/news/Opinion/article/all/20191128/ 98587080/1 [Accessed November 29, 2019]; Chosun Ilbo (2019). *Mun chŏngwŏn munŭngŭi tto tarŭn p'ihaeja, 'kyoyuk'-kwa 'haksaeng hakpumo' [Additional Other Victims of the Moon Regime's Incompetence, 'Education' and 'Students and Parents']*, October 25, 2019. Available at: https://www.chosun.com/site/data/html_dir/2019 /10/24/2019102403447.html [Accessed November 29, 2019].

pert knowledge and deliberation process), the president can scrap even long-term policies if they please or see the need due to political challenges.

Revolving Door to Para-Public Organization Posts

Another major characteristic of imperial presidency in Korea is the practice of appointing government loyalists and/or high-ranking officials after their retirement to para-public organizations in the manner of a revolving door mechanism. This practice is called parachute personnel reshuffling (*nakhasan insa*) because personnel is specifically dropped from high-ranking posts to organizations lower in the state organ hierarchy based on personal networks established during their time in government. Most of those persons earned their merits helping the president during election campaigning or even before in their political career. This is understood as a kind of gift appointment to reward efforts and loyalty to the leader and to prevent defecting and possibly even changing sides. A central criterion for identifying the parachute appointments is that the person in question lacks sufficient expertise in the field they will be working, and such appointments are also marked by an uncompetitive appointment process. According to a statistic produced by the middle-of-the-road Bareun Party (*Parŭnjŏngdang*), there have been 515 parachute appointments since the inauguration of President Moon.[107] While there is no exact empirical data for a direct comparison with preceding governments, this number is relatively high in light of the fact that the first year of the administrations of Presidents Lee and Park accounted for only 169 and 107 such appointments, respectively.[108]

107 Pak, Y.-H. (2019). Mun chŏngbu nakhasan 500-myŏng nŏmŏ [Parachute Personnel Re-Shuffling Under the Moon Government Exceeds 500 Persons]. *Kyunghyang Sinmun*, October 13, 2019. Available at: http://news.khan.co.kr/kh_news/khan_art_view.html?art_id=201910131052001 [Accessed January 12, 2020].

108 Chungang Ilbo (2018). *Uri-nŭn mujŏk-ŭi nakhasan pudae [We Are the Parachute Unit Without Enemies]*, May 24, 2018. Available at: https://news.joins.com/Digital special/297 [Accessed January 12, 2020].

2.3 Cooperating with the Branches

The Legislature

According to Korea's Constitution, the president has the right to introduce not only normal bills to the National Assembly, but even constitutional reform bills.[109] This particular legislative power of the president was added to the constitution by strongman Park Chung-hee in 1972 and thus is a highly controversial norm in itself. Nevertheless, President Moon used this authority for the first time for a constitutional reform attempt in 2017 along the lines of "if Congress will not do their job, at least we can do ours."[110] However, the bill failed to be passed in parliament because all political parties except the government party refused to take part in the vote. Besides opposition to some of the proposal's contents, the most decisive objection concerned the legislation procedure. Even the floor leader of the leftist-progressive Justice Party *(Chŏngŭidang)* stated that some of the proposal's contents were more progressive than his own party's proposal, but that his party rejected the bill because it was made and introduced to parliament in a one-sided manner.[111] Again, this example shows quite well how the president – well-intended or not – makes use of his excessive powers, how his attempts are met with opposition due to the lack of democratic legitimacy, how powerless he becomes in the end, and how this does not help to solve conflict and stalemate in the political system, but rather increases these problems.[112]

Additionally, the three reform bills that were fast-tracked through parliament by a reform coalition spearheaded by the governing DP over the year 2019 represent the imbalanced relationship between the branches as a result of presidential unilateralism. Election law was changed to allow 18-year-olds to vote, and the share of proportional representative seats was increased somewhat to improve representation, including those of minor parties; the unleveled playing field in favor of prosecutors' over police's discretion was balanced; and a special independent agency *(kongsuch'ŏ)*

---

109 Constitution of the Republic of Korea, Articles 52, 128.

110 Obama, Barak [Barak Obama] (2014). "If Congress will not do their job, at least we can do ours." – President Obama #ActOnReform [Tweet]. *Twitter*, June 30, 2014. Available at: https://twitter.com/barackobama/status/483692659236540416 [Accessed January 12, 2020].

111 Kim, C.-D. (2018). Kukhoebonhoeŭi Hoeŭirok 360(4) [Minutes of the Plenary Session 360(4)], *Office of the National Assembly*, May 24, 2018.

112 Mosler 2020.

was established to investigate corruption among high-ranking officials. Meanwhile, the conservative opposition Liberty Korea Party vehemently objected to the reforms, claiming the revision was aimed at "perpetuating the life of the leftist dictatorship."[113] This exaggerated allegation is obviously part of a smear campaign against the government, while the basic idea behind the reforms is indeed aimed at improving the political system. At the same time, it is likewise true that this aggressive unilateral behavior by the executive claiming to be pursued in the name of the will of the people contributes to perpetuating the presidential power trap.

Another issue with the power relationship between the executive and the legislative branches is that parliament has insufficient rights to effectively veto presidential decrees (*taet'ongnyŏngnyŏng*), which can circumvent representative control. Often, this has led to misappropriating administrative legislation because the parliament lacks control mechanisms sufficient to veto these presidential transgressions. Recent examples include changes in presidential decrees regarding the National Finance Act (*kukkajaejŏngbŏp*) in 2009; the Sewol Ferry Special Act (*sewŏlho t'ŭkpyŏlbŏp*) as well as the Education Act on Primary, Middle, and High Schools; and the Newspaper Act in 2015.[114] According to official records, the National Assembly has filed 152 cases of legal violations through administrational ordinances (*sihaengnyŏng*) between 2008 and 2014; however, there has been no response from the administration.[115] During his first three years in office, President Moon issued on average about 840 presidential decrees,[116]

---

113 Chŏn, H.-G. (2019). Chwap'a tokchae yŏnggujipkwŏn sido seryŏkŭrobut'ŏ chayudaehandmin'gukŭl chik'yŏnaegaessŭmnida [We Will Protect a Free Republic of Korea From the Forces That Attempt to Rule Permanently under the Leftist Dictatorship]. *Naver*, April 27, 2019. Available at: https://news.naver.com /main/read.naver?mode=LSD&mid=sec&sid1=123&oid=156&aid=0000025804 [Accessed April 30, 2019].

114 Pak 2016, pp. 42-44.

115 Mun, T.-Y. (2015). Kukhoe pŏpchesil, mobŏp-e ŏgŭnnan haengjŏng'ippŏp p'yŏngga sarye palgan [The National Assembly's Legislation Office Publishes Administrative Legislation Evaluation Cases That Violate Upper Law]. *Globalnewsagency*, June 1, 2015. Available at: www.globalnewsagency.kr/news/articl eView.html?idxno=37115 [Accessed October 23, 2019]. Recent analysis again found that out of 3391 administrative legislations, 139 cases contain issues regarding their respective upper law. National Assembly Legislation Office (2016). *Che-19-dae kukhoe haengjŏngippŏp punsŏk-p'ŏngga sarye [19th National Assembly Administrative Legislative Analysis and Evaluation Cases].*

116 Ministry of Legislation (2020). *Kongp'ohyŏnhwang [Current State of Promulgations].* Available at: https://www.moleg.go.kr/esusr/mpbStaSts/stastsList.es?mid=a 10110020000&srch_csf_cd=120002 [Accessed February 12, 2020].

which hypothetically can be extrapolated to up to more than 4,200 presidential decrees until the end of his term, an increase of around 20% compared to his predecessor.[117]

The Judiciary

Likewise, the decision by Minister of Justice Choo Mi-ae to part with custom and not to disclose the prosecution's bill of indictments regarding the case of President Moon's allies who were allegedly involved in an election-meddling scandal (see above) is a manifestation of unilateral actions by the executive vis-à-vis the legislature. The ministry rejected the National Assembly's request to publish the indictment documents because during the criminal justice process, this would violate right to a trial and infringe upon various fundamental rights. While it is undeniable that disclosing details of indictments of public interest have hitherto had negative repercussions, let alone being a questionable practice in light of rule of law principles, this sudden break with this bad habit in this particular case of alleged malpractice of Blue House staff casts a bad light on the executive branch. This abrupt covertness resembles practices that have been characterized as "far-reaching claims of exclusive access to information and power"[118] or simply "presidential abuse of the secrecy system,"[119] leading to loss of confidence in the presidency.

Another excessive power of the president based on the Korean Constitution, Article 79, is the authority to pardon, which allows for amnesty (*sa'myŏn*), commutation (*kamhyŏng*), and the restoration of rights (*pokkwŏn*). In addition, the president can reduce or exempt from penalties (*kammyŏn*), grant pardon for disciplinary actions (*chinggye sa'myŏn*), or delete penalty points (*pŏljŏm sakche*). In other words, the president is bestowed with an extraordinary discretion that potentially allows them to challenge and overturn certain decisions by the judiciary. While it is common even in so-called established liberal democracies to make use of special exempting or pardoning as a way of alleviating social hardships and fostering social integration, the practice is justifiably criticized for undermining the rule of law. In particular, if the pardoning right is mo-

---

117 See Im, C.-H. and Yun, S.-M. (2019). T'ukhamyŏn ippŏp pasing [Very Often Legislation Is Bypassed]. *Chungang Ilbo*, November 4, 2019. Available at: https://news.joins.com/article/23623288 [Accessed January 10, 2020].

118 Crouch et al. 2017, p. 566.

119 Schlesinger 1973, p. 366.

nopolized by a single person such as a president, not only might excessive pardoning limit both the rights of public prosecutors (*soch'u'gwŏn*) and the jurisdiction of courts (*chaep'an'gwŏn*), but it might also be used and/or seen as misusage by that person. In Korea, even though in 2012 the Amnesty Act (*sa'myŏnbŏp*) was strengthened to curb presidential abuse by various measures, in the end the president still has room to maneuver and push through arbitrary pardons.[120]

In quantitative terms, Moon complies with the trend of reduced pardoning. The number of pardoning has been continuously decreasing with the presidency of Roh Moo-hyun (2003-2008), who pardoned in total 40,893 persons. During the succeeding presidency of Lee Myung-bak (2008-2013), this number dropped to 27,797, only to decrease once more under President Park Geun-hye (2013-2017) to 17,328 persons.[121] President Moon, in just his third year in office, has already pardoned 15,996 persons, and it remains to be seen whether there will be additional pardoning under his administration, through which the number could exceed those of his predecessor.[122] Meanwhile, when looking at whom he pardoned, in qualitative terms, the picture becomes slightly more critical. This is because Moon has already twice granted amnesty to a series of politicians who belong to his party and/or have worked closely with him in the past. In 2017, Moon ordered to restore the passive electoral rights of the controversial former member of parliament Chong Pong-ju (*Ch'ŏng P'ŏng-ju*), who was found guilty of violating election law by spreading false information and served his term in prison. In 2019, former province governor of Kangwŏn-do Yi Kwang-jae's right to hold public office, as well as his pas-

---

120 Lee, S.-J. (2016). Taet'ongnyŏng-ŭi sa'myŏn'gwŏn-e taehan pip'an-chŏk koch'al [A Critical Appraisal of the Presidential Amnesty Right]. *Pŏphak Yŏn'gu (Yonsei)*, 26 (4), 1-38, pp. 26-28; Shin, G. H. (2016). Taet'ongnyŏng-ŭi sa'myŏn'gwŏn t'ongje-e kwanhan yŏn'gu [A Study on the Control of Presidential Pardoning Power]. *Kach'ŏn Pŏphak*, 9 (3), 124-148, p. 137; Ko, M.-H. (2007). Chewangjŏk taet'ongnyŏngje-ŭi t'ŭkching-ŭrosŏ sa'myŏn'gwŏn haengsa-ŭi t'ongjebangan [A Proposal for Controlling the Presidential Pardoning Power as an Element of the Imperial Presidency]. *Segyehŏnbŏp Yŏn'gu*, 13 (2), 1-36.

121 Regarding this number, it has to be taken into account that Park did not complete her five years in office.

122 Also, the penalties of another 1.7 million citizens for minor violations were reduced. It has been common to reduce penalties for minor violations, and the number per presidential term has often exceeded several million beneficiaries. Pak, C.-J. (2015). Yŏktae chŏngbu taet'ongnyŏng sa'myŏn taehaebu [Analysis of Presidential Pardoning Under Previous Governments]. *Hankook Weekly*, May 9, 2015. Available at: http://daily.hankooki.com/lpage/politics/201505/dh20150509 094918137430.htm [Accessed January 12, 2020].

sive electoral rights, were restored. Yi, who is a long-term member of the DP and its predecessor parties, had been convicted several times since 2005 for having been involved in corruption cases and receiving illegal political funds. Of course, Moon also pardoned politicians from the opposition, but the very fact of reducing penalties for politicians who violate election law is seen problematic in itself, especially against the background that Moon himself specifically pledged not to pardon these violations of election law. The pardoning of former President Park Geun-hye in December 2021 only months before the end of Moon's term was not only highly controversial in itself but also an illustrative example of abusing this overly powerful right as a president. In this way, the pardoning right and especially excessive utilization do not only pose a potential threat for the division of powers but also contribute to the image of the president as an "almighty savior" who can decide on individuals' fates comparable to an emperor who, by showing a thumb up or down, decides on the life and death of a human.[123]

Conclusion

This chapter investigated manifestations of the *presidential power trap* phenomenon in Korea after the impeachment and removal of President Park Geun-hye in 2017. The assumption was that a shock to the system such as a political crisis in the form of an impeachment motion might have the effect of destabilizing the equilibrium of the existing institution of the imperial president trap, thus opening the way for deviating from the beaten path. The role of the institution of impeachment can be compared to the reset function of a computer, allowing the system to be shut down in case of a grave error that seriously obstructs normal operation. This was the case when the deteriorating quality of democracy in Korea over the course of a decade[124] accumulated to the point of a political crisis that climaxed in the impeachment of Park. According to most observers and indices, such as the Varieties of Democracy Index, this downward trend appeared to be reversing since President Moon Jae-in's election in 2017.

---

123 Chŏng 2004, p. 191.
124 Mosler, H. B. (2015). The Deterioration of South Korean Democracy. In Howe, B. (Ed.), *Democratic Governance in Northeast Asia: A Human-Centred Approach to Evaluating Democracy*. London: Palgrave Macmillan, 25-50; Mosler, H. B. et al. (Eds.) (2018). *The Quality of Democracy in Korea: Three Decades after Democratization*. Basingstoke: Palgrave Macmillan.

However, three years into his presidency this positive trend turns out to be not as straightforward as it seemed in the beginning as was demonstrated above for selected issues in relation to the presidential power trap. The analysis found that despite the Moon's pledge and actual attempts, his endeavor to root out the bad habits of wielding imperial power has, in several respects, not been successful.

First, the examination of the way the presidential office has operated under Moon revealed that besides an ever-bigger Blue House, the behavior of key aides at the office, as well as the popular attention drawn through the office's website, contributed to maintaining imperial president features. Second, the investigation discussed not only that Moon appointed more high-level officials without consent of parliament than his predecessors, but that the revolving door custom has been continuing, if not increasing, under his administration. Moreover, President Moon has been conducting state affairs in a fashion that often led the Blue House and the president to encroach upon the executive ministries' discretion. Third, studying the relationships between the executive branch and the legislature and the judiciary showed that the good intentions by the government to lessen institutional incentives for overly concentrating power in the presidential office through legal reforms have backfired because basic principles of procedural democracy were often disregarded in the course of unilateral action with even the government party reduced to a mere subordinate partner.

Based on these results, it can be argued that the political system might not work even after restarting it through impeachment (of President Park Geun-hye), as long as serious errors remain. It is one thing to remove a corrupt president, but if the system's hardware (institutional design) or society's software (political culture) are incompatible, removing some rotten apples might not do the job. This does not mean the institution of impeachment is ineffective. On the contrary, even though, for example, Trump was eventually acquitted, and even if, after successfully unseating Park, Moon maneuvered himself into the presidential power trap again, the two democracies would have been much worse off without this crucial safety device. In other words, the importance of the institution of impeachment for the consolidation of democracy becomes obvious even when it is not or cannot be invoked, eventually. Impeachment is, thus, a necessary condition for consolidating democracy; sufficient conditions must be provided by other means. Regarding the case of Korea, the presidential power trap is one of the largest hindrances for further democratic consolidation by making even reformist presidents such as Moon Jae-in to repeat the mistake of trying to change politics by taking too much power. To remedy these deficiencies in the way presidents organize the presidential office, operate government, and cooperate with the branches, it is

"important to remember that the 'imperial presidency' will outlive any one president unless more is done to institute real checks and balances on the office itself."[125]

References

Ch'ŏngwadae (2020). *Kungminch'ŏngwŏn [Citizens' Petition Board].* [Online]. Available at: https://www1.president.go.kr/petitions [Accessed February 11, 2020].

Cho, S.-J. and Im, T.-B. (2010). *Han'guk haengjŏngjojiknon [Korean Administration Theory].* Seoul: Bŏmmunsa.

Choi, J.-J. (2004). *Minjuhwa ihu-ŭi minjujuŭi [Democracy after Democratization].* Seoul: Humanitas.

Chŏn, H.-G. (2019). Chwap'a tokchae yŏnggujipkwŏn sido seryŏkŭrobut'ŏ chayudaehandmin'gukŭl chik'yŏnaegaessŭmnida [We Will Protect a Free Republic of Korea From the Forces That Attempt to Rule Permanently under the Leftist Dictatorship]. *Naver*, April 27, 2019. Available at: https://news.naver.com/main/read.naver?mode=LSD&mid=sec&sid1=123&oid=156&aid=0000025804 [Accessed April 30, 2019].

Chŏng, C.-S. (2004). *Hŏnbŏp Yŏn'gu [Constitutional Theory].* Seoul: Pakyŏngsa.

Chŏng, Ŭ.-H. (2019). Chŏngsi hwaktae ŏptadŏn kyoyukpu [The Ministry of Education That Were Against Expanding the CSAT]. *TV Chosun*, October 22, 2019. Available at: http://news.tvchosun.com/site/data/html_dir/2019/10/22/2019102290077.html [Accessed January 12, 2020].

Chŏng, W.-S. (2018). T'ak Hyŏn-min-ŭi 1-yŏn, nollan-esŏ sat'oe-ggaji [One Year T'ak Hyŏn-min, From Controversy to Resignation]. *The Hankyoreh*, June 30, 2018. Available at: https://h2.khan.co.kr/201806301601001 [Accessed January 12, 2020].

Chŏng, Y.-I. (2020). 'Ch'ŏngwadae kyŏngnyŏk' ch'ongsŏn pŭrimiŏm toeilgga? [Will the 'Blue House Experience' Become an Election Premium?]. *Kyunghyang Weekly*, January 10, 2020. Available at: https://weekly.khan.co.kr/khnm.html?mode=view&artid=202001101639211&code=113 [Accessed January 12, 2020].

Chosun Ilbo (2019). *Cho Kuk ttal t'ase tto ipsi pyŏn'gyŏng, 4-nyŏn-e 4-bŏn paggwindani [The Entrance Exam Changed Again, Changing Four Times in Four Years, Because of Cho Kuk's Daughter],* November 11, 2019. Available at: https://www.chosun.com/site/data/html_dir/2019/11/29/2019112903288.html [Accessed November 30, 2019].

---

125 Kruse and Zelizer 2019.

Chosun Ilbo (2019). *Mun chŏnggwŏn munŭngŭi tto tarŭn p'ihaeja, 'kyoyuk'-kwa 'haksaeng hakpumo' [Additional Other Victims of the Moon Regime's Incompetence, 'Education' and 'Students and Parents'],* October 25, 2019. Available at: https://w ww.chosun.com/site/data/html_dir/2019/10/24/2019102403447.html [Accessed November 29, 2019].

Chungang Ilbo (2018). *Uri-nŭn mujŏk-ŭi nakhasan pudae [We Are the Parachute Unit Without Enemies],* May 24, 2018. Available at: https://news.joins.com/Digitalspec ial/297 [Accessed January 12, 2020].

Constitution of the Republic of Korea. Available in English at: https://korea.asse mbly.go.kr:447/res/low_01_read.jsp?boardid=1000000035 [Accessed April 15, 2021].

Constitution of the United States. Available at: https://www.senate.gov/civics/const itution_item/constitution.htm [Accessed April 15, 2021].

Crouch, J., Rozell, M. J., and Sollenberger, M. A. (2017). The Law: The Unitary Executive Theory and President Donald J. Trump. *Presidential Studies Quarterly,* 47 (3), 561-573.

Democratic Party (2017). *Nara-rŭl naradapke. 19-tae taet'ognyŏngsŏn'gŏ tŏburŏminjudang chŏngch'aekkungyakchip [Making the Country Country-Like. The Democratic Party's 19ᵗʰ Presidential Election Manifesto].* Seoul: Democratic Party.

Dong-A Ilbo (1974). *Chumokpannŭn miguk-ŭi tu chŏsŏ [Two US-American Books That Receive Attention],* January 21, 1974, p. 5.

Dong-A Ilbo (2019). *Kyoyukpo "chŏngsi 40% hwaktae," kaljija kyoyukchŏngch'aek ŏnje tto paggwilji [Ministry of Education "Expansion of On-Time 40%," When Will the Education Policy Change Again?],* November 29, 2019. Available at: https://www. donga.com/news/Opinion/article/all/20191128/98587080/1 [Accessed November 29, 2019].

Fitts, M. A. (1996). The Paradox of Power in the Modern State: Why a Unitary, Centralized Presidency May Not Exhibit Effective or Legitimate Leadership. *University of Pennsylvania Law Review,* 144 (3), 827-902.

Ham, S.-D. (1999). *Taet'ongnyŏnghak [The Korean Presidency].* Seoul: Nanam.

Ham, S.-D. (2002). The Institutional Development of the Blue House in the Park Chung Hee Presidency. *Asian Perspective,* 26 (2), 101-130.

Ham, S.-D. (2003). *Taet'ongyŏnghak [President Research].* Seoul: Nanamch'ulp'an.

Ham, S.-D. (2018). *Chewangjŏk taet'ongyŏng-ŭi chongŏn [The End of the Imperial Presidency].* Koyang: Sŏmaensŏm.

Holloway, J. (2002). *Change The World Without Taking Power.* London: Pluto Press.

Hong, T.-P. (2002). Chewangjŏk taet'ongnyŏngnon: Kŭ t'ŭkching-kwa wŏnin-ŭl chungsim-ŭro [The Concept, Characteristics, and Causes of the Imperial President]. *Kungminyulli Yŏn'gu,* 50, 145-171.

Huntington, S. (1991). *The Third Wave: Democratization in the Late Twentieth Century.* Norman and London: University of Oklahoma Press.

Im, C.-H. and Yun, S.-M. (2019). T'ukhamyŏn ippŏp pasing [Very Often Legislation Is Bypassed]. *Chungang Ilbo,* November 4, 2019. Available at: https://news.jo ins.com/article/23623288 [Accessed January 10, 2020].

Im, M.-H. (2019). Mun taet'ongnyŏng haengsagihoek chamunwiwŏn sinsŏl, T'ak Hyŏn-min wich'uk [President Moon Established Advisory Committee for Presidential Event Management, Makes T'ak Hyŏn-min Member]. *MBC News*, February 21, 2019. Available at: https://imnews.imbc.com/news/2019/politics/article/5 174599_29092.html [Accessed January 12, 2020].

Kelley, C. (2008). The Unitary, or Unilateral Executive? Presidential Power in the Bush Administration. *The American Review of Politics*, 29, 181-196.

Kim, C.-D. (2018). Kukhoebonhoeŭi Hoeŭirok 360(4) [Minutes of the Plenary Session 360(4)], *Office of the National Assembly*, May 24, 2018.

Kim, E.-B. and Lee, S.-E. (2020). Cho Kuk Indicted on 12 Charges, Blue House Slams 'Narrow' Results. *Korea Joongang Daily*, January 1, 2020. Available at: http://koreajoongangdaily.joins.com/news/article/article.aspx?aid=3072083 [Accessed January 12, 2020].

Kim, H.-J. (1995). *Han'gukchŏngch'ich'ejeron [The Political System of Korea]*. Seoul: Pakyŏngsa.

Kim, H.-C. (2020). Yu Chae-su pwajunŭn kŏn ŏt'ŏk'ennŭnya [How About Turning a Blind Eye on Yu Chae-su?]. *Kyunghyang Sinmun*, January 20, 2020. Available at: http://news.khan.co.kr/kh_news/khan_art_view.html?art_id=202001201329 001 [Accessed January 20, 2020].

Kim, J.-Y. (2020). Political Culture and Behavior. In Moon, C.-I. and Moon, M. J. (Eds.), *Routledge Handbook of Korean Politics and Public Administration*. London: Routledge, 41-58.

Kim, K.-C. (2020). 4-15 ch'ongsŏn, 'chŏnggwŏn simp'an'-boda 'kukchŏng anjŏng' [April 15 General Elections Rather Reflected 'Government Stability' Than 'Judgment of Government']. *Issue Maker*, April 24, 2020. Available at: http://www.issu emaker.kr/news/articleView.html?idxno=31607 [Accessed May 26, 2020].

Kim, K.-Y. and Kim, T.-B. (2019). Mun K'aemk'odŏ insa Pak-poda mank'o MB-boda chŏkta [Moon's Questionable Personnel Decisions More Than Park, Less Than Lee]. *Nocutnews,* April 10, 2019. Available at: https://www.nocutnews.co.k r/news/5132380 [Accessed January 12, 2020].

Kim, N.-H. (2018). DMZ sich'al, Begun myŏndam … wangsiljang nollan hipsa'in Im Chong-sŏk [Inspection of the DMZ, Meeting With Begun … Im Chong-sŏk Is Embroiled in Royal Chief of Staff Controversy]. *JTBC News*, October 30, 2018. Available at: http://news.jtbc.joins.com/article/article.aspx?news_id=NB11 719193 [Accessed January 12, 2020].

Kim, S.-J. (2017). Han'guk changgwan chae'im kigan 1-yŏn 2-gaewŏl vs miguk changgwan 3-nyŏn pan [Korean Ministers' 1 Year and 2 Months Office Term vs US-Ministers' 3 Years]. *YTN*, June 25, 2017. Available at: https://www.ytn.co.kr/ _ln/0101_201706250515367569 [Accessed October 23, 2019].

Kim, S.-M., Lee, G.-Y., and Lee, S.-E. (2019). Cho Faces Questions in Ex-Busan Vice Mayor Probe. *Korea Joongang Daily*, December 17, 2019. Available at: http://ko reajoongangdaily.joins.com/news/article/article.aspx?aid=3071547 [Accessed January 12, 2020].

Kim, T.-H. (2018). Chaggu k'ŭnŭn Im Chong-sŏk [Im Chong-sŏk Is Continually Growing]. *Chugan Chosŏn*, March 25, 2018. Available at: http://news.chosun.c om/site/data/html_dir/2018/03/23/2018032302132.html [Accessed January 12, 2020].

Kim, U.-T. et al. (Eds.) (1999). *Han'gukchŏngch'iron [Korean Politics]*. Seoul: Pakyŏngsa.

Ko, M.-H. (2007). Chewangjŏk taet'ongnyŏngje-ŭi t'ŭkching-ŭrosŏ samyŏn'gwŏn haengsa-ŭi t'ongjebangan [A Proposal for Controlling the Presidential Pardoning Power as an Element of the Imperial Presidency]. *Segyehŏnbŏp Yŏn'gu*, 13 (2), 1-36.

Ko, T.-U. (2018). Pulbŏp sŏn'gŏ'undong T'ak Hyŏn-min 2-sim pŏlgŭm 70-manwŏn [Fine of KRW 700,000 for T'ak in the Second Instance]. *Yonhapnews*, November 2, 2018. Available at: https://www.yna.co.kr/view/AKR20181102049251004?inpu t=1195m [Accessed January 12, 2020].

Kruse, K. M. and Zelizer, J. E. (2019). Have We Had Enough of the Imperial Presidency Yet? *The New York Times*, January 9, 2019. Available at: https://ww w.nytimes.com/2019/01/09/opinion/president-trump-border-wall-weak.html [Accessed January 12, 2020].

Kwŏn, H.-U. (2017). Sot'ong-ŭi 'mun'-ŭl yŏlda – ch'ŏng: 'kungmin-sot'ongp'ŭlaetŭp'om' pongyŏk kadong [Opening the Door to Communication – Blue House: Full-Scale Operation of the Public Communication Platform]. *CBS Nokŏt'ŭnyusŭ*, August 17, 2017. Available at: http://www.nocutnews.co.kr/news/ 4832273 [Accessed July 20, 2018].

Kwŏn, K.-S. (2018). Chikchŏp minjujuŭi vs yŏronmori agyong – 'yangnar-ŭi k'al' doen kungminch'ŏngwŏn [Abuse of Direct Democracy Versus Public Opinion – The National Petition Has Become a Double-Edged Sword]. *Segye Ilbo*, September 9, 2018. Available at: http://www.segye.com/newsView/20180909002693 [Accessed September 24, 2018].

Lee, S.-J. (2016). Taet'ongnyŏng-ŭi sa'myŏn'gwŏn-e taehan pip'an-chŏk koch'al [A Critical Appraisal of the Presidential Amnesty Right]. *Pŏphak Yŏn'gu (Yonsei)*, 26 (4), 1-38.

Lim, S. H. (1998). A Paradox of Korean Democracy: 50 Years' of Experience of the Imperial Presidency and the Peripheral Legislature. *Korea and World Affairs*, 22 (4), 522-538.

Linz, J. J. (1994). Presidential or Parliamentary Democracy: Does It Make a Difference? In Linz, J. J. and Valenzuela, A. (Eds.), *The Failure of Presidential Democracy: Comparative Perspectives*, Vol. 1. Baltimore, MD: Johns Hopkins University Press, 3-87.

Linz, J. J. (1990). The Perils of Presidentialism. *Journal of Democracy*, 1 (1), 51-69.

MacKenzie, J. P. (2008). *Absolute Power: How the Unitary Executive Theory Is Undermining the Constitution*. New York: The Century Foundation Press.

Mainwaring, S. and Shugart, M. S. (1997). Juan Linz, Presidentialism, and Democracy: A Critical Appraisal. *Comparative Politics*, 29 (4), 449-471.

Ministry of Legislation (2020). *Kongp'ohyŏnhwang [Current State of Promulgations]*. Available at: https://www.moleg.go.kr/esusr/mpbStaSts/stastsList.es?mid=a10110 020000&srch_csf_cd=120002 [Accessed February 12, 2020].

Moon, J.-I. (2017). *Mun Chae-in taet'ongnyŏng yŏnsŏlmunjip 2017-nyŏn 5-7-wŏl [Selected Speeches of President Moon Jae-in of the Republic of Korea, May-July 2017]*. Seoul: Korean Culture and Information Service.

Mosler, H. B. (2015). The Deterioration of South Korean Democracy. In Howe, B. (Ed.), *Democratic Governance in Northeast Asia: A Human-Centred Approach to Evaluating Democracy*. London: Palgrave Macmillan, 25-50.

Mosler, H. B. (2017). The Institution of Presidential Impeachment in South Korea, 1992-2017. *Verfassung und Recht in Übersee*, 2, 111-134.

Mosler, H. B. et al. (Eds.) (2018). *The Quality of Democracy in Korea. Three Decades after Democratization*. Basingstoke: Palgrave Macmillan.

Mosler, H. B. (2020). Characteristics and Challenges of South Korea's Presidential Government System. In Mosler, H. B. (Ed.), *South Korea's Democracy Challenge: Political System, Political Economy, and Political Society*. Berlin: Peter Lang Academic Publishers, 25-66.

Mun, T.-Y. (2015). Kukhoe pŏpchesil, mobŏp-e ŏgŭnnan haengjŏng'ippŏp p'yŏngga sarye palgan [The National Assembly's Legislation Office Publishes Administrative Legislation Evaluation Cases That Violate Upper Law]. *Globalnewsagency*, June 1, 2015. Available at: www.globalnewsagency.kr/news/articleView.html?idx no=37115 [Accessed October 23, 2019].

Myŏng, J. J. (2007). Kungmuch'ongnije-ŭi hamni-chŏk unyong-ŭi han'gye-wa kaehŏn p'iryosŏng [The Operational Limits of the Prime Minister's Power and the Necessity of Constitutional Revision]. *Hŏnbŏp Yŏn'gu*, 13 (1), 155-185.

National Assembly Legislation Office (2016). *Che-19-dae kukhoe haengjŏngippŏp punsŏk-p'ŏngga sarye [19th National Assembly Administrative Legislative Analysis and Evaluation Cases]*.

Obama, Barak [Barak Obama] (2014). "If Congress will not do their job, at least we can do ours." – President Obama #ActOnReform [Tweet]. *Twitter*, June 30, 2014. Available at: https://twitter.com/barackobama/status/483692659236540416 [Accessed January 12, 2020].

Pak, C.-J. (2015). Yŏktae chŏngbu taet'ongnyŏng sa'myŏn taehaebu [Analysis of Presidential Pardoning Under Previous Governments]. *Hankook Weekly*, May 9, 2015. Available at: http://daily.hankooki.com/lpage/politics/201505/dh20150509 094918137430.htm [Accessed January 12, 2020].

Pak, S.-H. (2017). Ch'ŏngwadae kungminch'ŏngwŏn-ŭn minju-jŏgilgga [Is the Blue House Public Petition Democratic?]. *Dong-A Ilbo*, December 19, 2017. Available at: http://news.donga.com/3/all/20171219/87808886/1 [Accessed May 18, 2018].

Pak, S.-H. (2018). *Ch'ŏngwadae chŏngbu [Blue House Government]*. Seoul: Humanitas.

Pak, Y.-H. (2019). Mun chŏngbu nakhasan 500-myŏng nŏmŏ [Parachute Personnel Re-Shuffling Under the Moon Government Exceeds 500 Persons]. *Kyunghyang Sinmun*, October 13, 2019. Available at: http://news.khan.co.kr/kh_news/khan_a rt_view.html?art_id=201910131052001 [Accessed January 12, 2020].

Pak, Y. S. (2016). Han'guk-ŭi chewangjŏk taet'ongnyŏng [The Imperial Presidency by Evasion of the Political Laws in Korea]. *Han'gukchŏngch'i Yŏn'gu*, 25 (2), 27-55.

Poguntke, T. and Webb, P. (2005). *The Presidentialization of Politics: A Comparative Study of Modern Democracies*. Oxford: Oxford University Press.

Rudalevige, A. (2005). *The New Imperial Presidency. Renewing Presidential Power after Watergate*. Ann Abor: University of Michigan Press.

Schlesinger, A. (1973). *The Imperial Presidency*. Boston: Houghton Mifflin.

Ser, M.-J. and Bae, J.-S. (2020). Im Jong-seok to Face Questioning on Power Abuse. *Korea Joongang Daily*, January 30, 2020. Available at: http://koreajoongangdaily.j oins.com/news/article/article.aspx?aid=3073151 [Accessed February 12, 2020].

Shin, G. H. (2016). Taet'ongnyŏng-ŭi sa'myŏn-gwŏn t'ongje-e kwanhan yŏn'gu [A Study on the Control of Presidential Pardoning Power]. *Kach'ŏn Pŏphak*, 9 (3), 124-148.

Shugart, M. S. and Carey, J. M. (1992). *Presidents and Assemblies: Constitutional Design and Electoral Dynamics*. Cambridge: Cambridge University Press.

Sim, K.-S. (2017). Kwŏllyŏkpullip-kwa taet'ongnyŏng-ŭi immyŏnggwŏn [Separation of Powers and the Appointment Power of President]. *Hŏnbŏp Yŏn'gu*, 23 (3), 295-332.

Song, C.-S. (2019). Sunŭng chŏngsi hwaktae-ro tae'ipchedo kaep'yŏn [Decision to Reform College Entrance System by Extending the CSAT Proportion]. *Kyunghyang Sinmun*, October 22, 2019. Available at: http://news.khan.co.kr/k h_news/khan_art_view.html?artid=201910221706001&code=940401 [Accessed January 10, 2020].

Sŏk, H.-W. (2019). Nŭrŏnanŭn kukhoe p'aesing kwagŏ chŏngbu-nŭn ŏddaenna? [Increasing National Assembly Passing, How Was It under Former Governments?]. *KBS News*, June 17, 2019. Available at: http://news.kbs.co.kr/news/view. do?ncd=4284401 [Accessed October 25, 2019].

Sŏng, T.-H. (2020). Cho Kuk ch'ŏngwadae-e 21-hoe pogo [Cho Kuk Reported 21 Times to the Blue House]. *Yonhapnews*, February 5, 2020. Available at: https://w ww.yna.co.kr/view/AKR20200205075600004?input=1195m [Accessed February 6, 2020].

Sŏng, Y.-C. (2020). T'akhyŏnmin ch'ŏngwadae ŭijŏnbisŏgwan-ŭro pokkwi [T'ak Hyŏn-min Returns to the Blue House as Protocol Secretary]. *The Hankyoreh*, May 26, 2020. Available at: http://www.hani.co.kr/arti/politics/bluehouse/94655 3.html [Accessed May 26, 2020].

The Economist (2020). *Going South: South Korea's President Curbs the Power of Prosecutors*, January 16, 2020. Available at: https://www.economist.com/asia/2020 /01/16/south-koreas-president-curbs-the-power-of-prosecutors [Accessed January 20, 2020].

Waterman, R. W. (2009). The Administrative Presidency, Unilateral Power, and the Unitary Executive Theory. *Presidential Studies Quarterly*, 39 (1), 5-9.

Weko, T. J. (1995). *The Politicizing Presidency*. Lawrence: University of Kansas Press.

Yang, K. (2003). Irŭnba chewangjŏk taet'ongnyŏng nonŭi-e kwanhan sogo [A Study of the Debate on the Imperial Presidency]. *Segyehŏnbŏp Yŏn'gu*, 8, 113-124.

Yi, C.-H. (2008). Han'guktaet'ongyŏngje-ŭi wŏnsukhan unyŏngŭl wihan jeŏn [Suggestions for the Smooth Operation of the Korean Presidential System]. In Yang, K. et al. (Eds.), *Saeroun hŏnbop p'iryohan'ga [Do We Need a New Constitution?]*. Seoul: Taehwamunhwasa, 188-208.

Yi, C.-Y. (2019). Kungminch'ŏngwŏn haru p'yŏnggyun 851-kŏn [Citizens' Petition Board Receives on Average 851 Petitions Per Day]. *Seoul Sinmun*, November 7, 2019. Available at: https://www.seoul.co.kr/news/newsView.php?id=2019110700 9010&wlog_tag3=naver [Accessed January 10, 2020].

Yi, H.-S. (2019). Yu Ŭn-hye, tae'ipkaep'yŏn, chŏng.susi piyul chojŏng anin hakchong kongjŏngsŏng chego [Yu Ŭn-hye, Improving Equity of the Early Admission System Rather Than Adjusting the Standardized Modus]. *Yonhapnews*, September 4, 2019. Available at: https://www.yna.co.kr/view/AKR201909041 07052004?input=1195m [January 10, 2020].

Yi, K.-I. (2008). Chewangjŏk taet'ongyŏng-ŭi kiwŏn [The Origin of the Imperial Presidency]. *Hwanghaemunhwa*, 60, 117-138.

Yun, C.-W. (2020). Ch'ŏngch'ulsin yŏktaegŭp inwŏn-i ch'ongsŏn-e nasonŭn paegyŏng [Background on the Reasons Why So Many Former Blue House Staff Are Running for Public Offices]. *Maeil Kyŏngje*, January 20, 2020. Available at: http://m.raythep.com/AllNew/AllNew/View/21181 [Accessed February 4, 2020].

The Political Role of Courts in the Trials of South Korea's 2016-2017 Impeachment Scandal

Justine Guichard

Introduction

"The respondent is removed from the office of President."[1] So did the Constitutional Court of Korea conclude the ruling that its judges rendered on March 10, 2017, terminating the term of Park Geun-hye (*Pak Kŭn-hye*) a year before its supposed ending.[2] The following day, the last of twenty mass protest rallies held every Saturday since October 2016 to demand Park's ousting took place to celebrate the so-called candlelight movement's (*ch'otpuljiphoe*) victory. To the members and observers of this movement symbolized by its crowds of light-holding participants, the Constitutional Court's verdict meant the institutional consecration of the popular struggle to defend South Korea's democratic order against the president's abusive and corrupt use of her power.[3]

---

1 Constitutional Court of Korea, 2016Hun-Na1, March 10, 2017, p. 63 (English translation), available at http://search.ccourt.go.kr/xmlFile/0/010400/2017/pdf/e 2016n1_1.pdf [last consulted on July 10, 2020]. The original Korean decision is accessible through the court's case search engine (hyphens in the case numbers need to be omitted), available at http://search.ccourt.go.kr/ths/pt/selectThsPt010 1List.do (last consulted on July 10, 2020). This chapter's analysis is based on the original Korean text, abbreviated as CCK 2016Hŏn-Na1 in future references, but it occasionally relies on the English translation. When that is the case, the source is abbreviated as CCK 2016Hun-Na1 (English translation). See also references for information on how to access this and the following rulings online.

2 South Korean presidents serve for a five-year, non-renewable term (Constitution of the Republic of Korea. Available in English at: https://korea.assembly.go.kr:447/re s/low_01_read.jsp?boardid=1000000035 [Accessed April 15, 2021], Article 70). As Park Geun-hye was elected on December 19, 2012, and took office on February 25, 2013, her term was supposed to last until February 2018.

3 As recounted by Sungmoon Kim, "[f]or Koreans, Park's abuse of power in extorting millions of dollars from big corporations (also known as chaebol) to fund foundations created by Choi Soon-sil, her private confidante, Choi's improper and illegal meddling in governmental affairs, and Choi's daughter's shady admission into one of the most prestigious universities in Korea using the connection to the president all signaled the culmination of [various] accumulated evils, which ought

A close reading of the impeachment ruling, however, reveals a number of gaps between the upholders of democracy in the streets – a large and diverse coalition of citizens – and the guardians of its order on the bench – usually nine but in this case eight magistrates. While having obtained from the Constitutional Court what it fought for, the candlelight movement was indeed obliterated from the ruling. This obliteration operated not only lexically – the candlelight demonstrations being never mentioned or acknowledged in the judgment – but also substantially – several of the anti-Park movement's grievances and demands appearing excluded from the text's scope and content. To put it differently, the court "blew out the candle" of citizens' mobilization in a double direction, realizing their main wish – removing Park Geun-hye from office – while denying having fulfilled what they wanted.

This negation of civil society's influence on the process and probably outcome of impeachment may not come as a surprise if interpreted as necessary to make the trial impartial.[4] But, as this chapter contends, the Constitutional Court's dissociation of its juridical decision from popular contestation does not simply reflect the institution's commitment to act legally rather than politically. Judges expectedly claimed and strived to rule in such a way, thus erasing the candlelight movement from their considerations as part 1 of this chapter elaborates. Yet, the court's effort to avoid partiality and partisanship did not imply that it was able to fully evade politics.

On the contrary, this chapter argues that the Constitutional Court acted politically not in the sense of taking a side but of shaping a certain vision of the polity. Its members can indeed be said to have articulated a specific understanding of what democracy is as part 2 of this chapter examines. This invites us to question whether the courts of the ordinary judicial system have done the same when judging not only Park Geun-hye but also the business actors involved in the 2016-2017 impeachment scandal, starting with the de facto head of South Korea's largest conglomerate, Lee

---

to have been overcome in order for Korea to live up to its normative ideal or its true name as a democratic republic—hence the slogan '*ige naranya* 이게 나라냐? (Is this a country?)' throughout the protest." Kim, S. (2018). Candlelight for Our Country's Right Name: A Confucian Interpretation of South Korea's Candlelight Revolution. *Religions*, 9 (11), 330, p. 1.

4 In this light, the ruling can be read as having blown out the candle by which it was penned to ensure that no shadow would be cast on the court's stature as an impartial adjudicator. My thanks to Chaihark Hahm for this thoughtful suggestion.

Jae-yong (*Yi Chae-yong*) from Samsung. As part 3 of this chapter analyzes, Park's and Lee's criminal trials appear to confirm the political role that courts can play as shapers of the democratic order.

1. The Constitutional Court's Claim and Care to Act Apolitically: Ruling in Favor of Impeachment but Not of the Candlelight Movement

The impeachment of Park Geun-hye was voted on December 9, 2016, by South Korea's unicameral parliament, the National Assembly. It was upheld three months later by the Constitutional Court's eight sitting members.[5] The judges did not rule with one voice only as two separate but concurring opinions were written by Justices Kim Yi-su (*Kim I-su*) and Lee Jin-sung (*Yi Chin-sŏng*) on the one hand, as well as Justice Ahn Chang-ho (*An Ch'ang-ho*) on the other hand in addition to the majority decision.[6] This chapter's first part focuses on the majority decision and uncovers how the court claimed and strived in it to act apolitically, ruling in favor of impeachment but not of the candlelight movement.

1.1 Constructing the Case's Background and Removing the Candlelight Movement's Influence

The majority decision opened with a review of the case's background.[7] The storytelling in which judges engaged can be described as institution-centric, leaving out of frame the mass protests without which the trial to impeach Park Geun-hye would not have taken place. Setting it in motion actually required more than two votes in parliament: a first one by over half

---

5 The vacancy left by the non-replacement of a ninth member did not affect the court's competence to adjudicate this matter or the procedure according to which the vote of at least six justices is statutorily required for impeachment to be confirmed. In addition to impeachment, the Constitutional Court's functions include reviewing the constitutionality of laws upon the request of ordinary courts, dissolving political parties, arbitrating competence disputes between different state agencies and/or government levels, as well as adjudicating the constitutional complaints that any individual alleging a violation of constitutional rights can directly file. Constitution of the Republic of Korea, Article 111.

6 The other members were Justices Cho Yong-ho (*Cho Yong-ho*), Kang Il-won (*Kang Il-wŏn*), Kim Chang-jong (*Kim Ch'ang-jong*), Seo Ki-seok (*Sŏ Ki-sŏk*), and Lee Jung-mi (*Yi Chŏng-mi*), the court's then president.

7 CCK 2016Hŏn-Na1, pp. 9-10.

of the National Assembly's 300 members to introduce the impeachment motion and a second one by at least two thirds of representatives to adopt it, thus triggering the impeachment trial that the Constitutional Court adjudicated.[8] Needless to say, the nationwide rallies held every Saturday since October 29, 2016, were instrumental in prompting the National Assembly to act. Yet, no mention of civil society's mobilization in general, or of the candlelight movement in particular, was made when justices examined the roots of the crisis that led the parliament to intervene.

Both lexical and narrative, this twin absence of the candlelight movement was all the more salient since the "people" or "citizens (*kungmin*)" featured in the court's account of the case's background.[9] But they were envisioned as a passive rather than as an active collective body, the audience of press reports and presidential apology statements. Portraying South Koreans as having received a "shock (*ch'unggyŏk*)" following the media revelations surrounding Park Geun-hye and the intervention in state affairs of her longtime friend and unofficial aide, Choi Soon-sil (*Ch'oe Sun-sil*), the court treated citizens' reactions as a matter of public opinion but not as a source of political mobilization.[10] The crux of the story behind the contestation and eventual demise of Park Geun-hye's presidency was thus expunged from the ruling, a gap that the separate but concurring opinions did not fill.

The chronology of events was reconstituted by the court as follows. News reports about the Blue House's (*Ch'ŏngwadae*) role in establishing two nonprofit foundations under the control of Choi Soon-sil began to surface in July 2016. By September, the two organizations called Mir and K-Sports had attracted the attention of a parliamentary audit due to the KRW 50 billion (close to EUR 40 million) they had collected from South Korean business conglomerates known as *chaebŏl*. The next month, on October 24, revelations broke out in the press about confidential documents found in the possession of Choi Soon-sil and her secret involvement in

---

8 Constitution of the Republic of Korea, Article 65, Section 2.
9 CCK 2016Hŏn-Na1, p. 9.
10 Ibid. South Korean cable television network JTBC was the one to unleash the scandal on October 24, 2016, "by uncovering a tablet computer belonging to Choi Soon-sil, a friend of Ms Park who held no official position in the government. Documents found on the computer suggest[ed] Ms Choi ha[d] received confidential presidential documents and edited key speeches." The first candlelight demonstration took place five days later, on October 29. Harris, B. (2017). Timeline: Downfall of Park Geun-hye. *The Financial Times*, March 10, 2017. Available at: https://www.ft.com/content/9e5b361e-bde8-11e6-8b45-b8b81dd5d080 [Accessed April 8, 2021].

state affairs. Owing to the above-cited shock received by many citizens and the rise of discontented public opinion, Park Geun-hye delivered on October 25 the first of three apology statements. The second came on November 4 amidst reports about the continuing role played by Choi Soon-sil in state affairs, contradicting presidential allegations that Choi's involvement had only been temporary. That same month, Choi Soon-sil and two top presidential aides, Ahn Jong-beom (*An Chong-bŏm*) and Jeong Ho-seong (*Chŏng Ho-sŏng*), were arrested while discussions about impeaching the president started in the National Assembly.

The majority decision closed its review of the case's beginning with Park Geun-hye's November 29 third apology statement. It then moved on examining the process behind the National Assembly's impeachment trial request. Out of the various paragraphs that compose these two sections, none included a reference to the cumulative mobilization of millions of South Korean citizens peacefully taking to the streets once a week since the end of October 2016, a movement that was instrumental in pressuring the National Assembly into voting for the impeachment of Park Geun-hye despite the initial reluctance of political parties. The judges' account of the developments that led to such an outcome was procedural only. In other words, they contented themselves with retracing the institutional trajectory of the impeachment trial request, from its introduction in the parliament to its transmission to the Constitutional Court.[11]

The court's ruling is consequently characterized by its deletion of the candlelight movement from the events that led to Park Geun-hye's downfall. The account not only articulated by the majority but also subscribed to by other justices relied on a complete omission of mass politics, obliterating the role of civil society's 2016-2017 demonstrations in demanding and obtaining Park's removal from office. Instead, the review of the context constructed by the court rested on selective facts while centering on institutional steps. In so doing, constitutional judges not only erased the direct influence of the candlelight rallies on the impeachment process but also negated the political background of the case and, as a result, of the court's intervention itself.

---

11 More specifically, a proposal to impeach the president was submitted by 171 members of the National Assembly on December 8, 2016, and adopted by 234 representatives the following day, triggering per the Korean Constitution's Article 49, Section 2, the intervention of the Constitutional Court as the institution in charge of adjudicating impeachment trials.

1.2 Constructing the Impeachment Grounds and Ignoring the Candlelight Movement's Demands

The Constitutional Court further erased the candlelight movement from its ruling when constructing the acts on the basis of which Park Geun-hye was removed from office. First of all, it must be stressed that out of the four grounds examined in the impeachment ruling, the court only retained one as justifying Park's ousting: the abuse of her authority (*kwŏnhan namyong*), a category under which she was found guilty to have violated her obligation to serve the public interest, the freedom and property rights of private enterprises, as well as her duty of confidentiality. By contrast, the president was not found to have abused her power to appoint public officials (*kongmuwŏn immyŏn kwŏn*), to have infringed on the freedom of the press (*ŏllon-ŭi chayu*), or to have violated her obligation to protect the right to life (*saengmyŏng kwŏn poho ŭimu*). Additionally, Park's obligation to faithfully execute her duties (*pulsŏngsilhan chikch'aek suhaeng ŭimu*) was not considered as a proper matter of review.

Particularly the rejection of the last two grounds contributed to leaving the April 16, 2014 sinking of the Sewol ferry (*Sewŏlho*) and the ensuing scandal caused by the death of 304 passengers (most of whom were high school students on a class trip) beyond the scope of the majority decision. Political anthropologist Nan Kim has highlighted how, in so ruling, the Constitutional Court

> "excluded from the grounds for impeachment the issue that figured highly into the Candlelight protests: the former president's handling of the Sewol Ferry disaster. The National Assembly bill in December recognized the issue among the reasons for impeachment, stating that Park was derelict in her duty and failed to protect the lives of the disaster's victims. The families of the Sewol victims and their advocates had been at the forefront of the movement that first brought widespread attention to the issue of Park's incompetence. It was therefore surprising that the Constitutional Court excluded their claims from the ruling, which stated that political incompetence did not constitute sufficient grounds for a presidential impeachment."[12]

Yet, the responsibility of Park Geun-hye in unresponsively handling the sinking of the Sewol ferry may not be the only candlelight movement's

---

12 Kim, N. (2017). Candlelight and the Yellow Ribbon: Catalyzing Re-Democratization in South Korea. *Asia-Pacific Journal: Japan Focus*, 15 (14), no. 5, 1-17, p. 7.

claim excluded from the ruling as a close reading of the majority decision reveals. As a matter of fact, even the violations recognized as justifying the president's removal from office can be seen as having been constructed by the judges in ways that departed from public perceptions and demands. This divergence especially manifested itself in the court's treatment of *chaebŏl* as victims of corruption rather than as actors of government-business collusion. Conglomerates were indeed exculpated as the justices held that Park Geun-hye had forced their executives to provide donations and favors to her entourage, thus not only violating her obligation to serve the public interest (*kongik silhyŏn ŭimu*) but also infringing upon the freedom and property rights of enterprises (*kiŏp-ŭi chayu-wa chaesan kwŏn*).

Both offenses factually had to do with Park's direct role in establishing at the end of the year 2015 the Mir and K-Sports foundations, coercing financial contributions from various conglomerates to fund them. As in the National Assembly's impeachment motion, concerned firms and their chairs were uniformly described as having been forced to comply with the president's scheme, primarily out of "fear (*turyŏum*)" of being negatively impacted rather than in exchange for benefits. In so reasoning, legislators and judges articulated a vision of corruption that was unilateral as opposed to reciprocal (i.e., as only emanating from the political side) and individual as opposed to systemic (i.e., as only emanating from the immorality of Park Geun-hye and Choi Soon-sil).[13] By contrast, the candlelight movement had identified state-business collusion as one of South Korea's "deep-seated vices (*chŏkp'ye*)," which led protesters to eventually ask for "a new world with the imprisonment of Park Geun-hye and *chaebol* owners."[14]

---

13 CCK 2016Hŏn-Na1, p. 29. In addition to the establishment of the Mir and K-Sport foundations, a number of other ventures were examined and found to further demonstrate Park Geun-hye's use of her position to serve the private interests of Choi Soon-sil and her suite.

14 Lee, Y. (2019). Articulating Inequality in the Candlelight Protests of 2016-2017. *Korea Journal*, 59 (1), 16-45, p. 36. According to the author, the "vices" denounced during the candlelight demonstrations "included democracy without equality, as in the unbridled power of the *chaebol*, state-business collusion, and the implementation of anti-labor laws, state failures at public safety and accountability, as in the Sewol ferry disaster, the haunting persistence of authoritarian politics, as in government-sponsored history textbooks, blacklisting of dissidents, muzzling of the press, and the occasions of subservient diplomatic relations, as with the agreement with Japan over the 'comfort women' issue and the questionable installation of the American THAAD project." Ibid., p. 35. See also the chapter by Juliette Schwak in this volume.

As for the three rejected grounds, the majority found it difficult based on available evidence to conclude that Park had abused her power to appoint civil servants by taking disciplinary measures against employees from the Ministry of Culture; that she had violated the freedom of the press by exerting pressure on newspapers such as the *Segye Ilbo*; or that she had deserted her duty to protect the right to life by taking inappropriate or insufficient measures in response to the sinking of the Sewol ferry. Furthermore, the charge that the president unfaithfully performed her functions during this emergency was deemed beyond the possible scope of an impeachment trial because the determination of such an issue would be political rather than legal. As explored in the next section, this distinction was at the heart of how the court framed its role in this decision.

1.3 Constructing Impeachment as an Apolitical Trial

The obliteration of the candlelight movement appears consistent with the Constitutional Court's effort to characterize impeachment as a "normative (*kyubŏmjŏk*)" rather than "political (*chŏngch'ijŏk*)" trial, a procedure for preserving the constitution by ensuring that no one can be placed above.[15] Adjudicating this trial falls within the duties of the court as the institution in charge of safeguarding South Korea's constitutional order (*hŏnpŏp chilsŏ*), an expression mentioned fifteen times in the ruling. Accordingly, impeachment is understood as a defense mechanism against acts that seriously endanger this order, also once referred to in the majority decision as the "basic order of liberal democracy (*chayu minjujŏk kibon chilsŏ*)."[16]

The above-mentioned gravity requirement is not explicitly prescribed in the Constitution of the Republic of Korea, enacted in 1948 but last amended in 1987, or in the Constitutional Court Act, passed in 1988.[17] Both texts

---

15 CCK 2016Hŏn-Na1, p. 20.

16 Ibid. On this notion also translatable as the "free" or "liberal democratic basic order," see Mosler, H. B. (2017). Decoding the 'Free Democratic Basic Order' for the Unification of Korea. *Korea Journal*, 57 (2), 5-34. For a discussion of the political meaning of the expression's different translations, see Kim, S. (2019). From Remonstrance to Impeachment: A Curious Case of Confucian Constitutionalism in South Korea. *Law & Social Inquiry*, 44 (3), 586-616, note 3, p. 587.

17 The creation of the Constitutional Court was introduced by the 1987 revision of the constitution. On the process and outcome of this amendment, the ninth since the founding of the Republic of Korea in 1948, see Cho, J. (2004). The Politics of Constitution-Making During the 1987 Democratic Transition in South Korea. *Korea Observer*, 35 (2), 171-206.

limit themselves to specify that impeachment can be activated against the president and a number of high-ranking public officials when they have violated the constitution or other laws in the course of performing their functions.[18] The court has come to define this provision more narrowly in the two presidential impeachment verdicts it has rendered so far: in favor of Roh Moo-hyun (*No Mu-hyŏn*) on March 14, 2004, and against Park Geun-hye on March 10, 2017.

As stipulated in both rulings, the head of state faces the possibility of being removed from office not merely if he or she has committed violations of existing norms but provided that these violations are "unpardonable from the perspective of protecting the Constitution."[19] Not any kind of behavior that contravenes the law may present this degree of seriousness as exemplified by the 2004 constitutional decision against the impeachment of Roh Moo-hyun.[20] In it, the court confirmed that the then president had not respected his obligation to remain neutral in electoral times but still did not pronounce his removal from office.[21] Whereas the violations committed by Roh were not deemed grave enough to endanger the constitutional order and justify his ousting, Park's were on the contrary seen as posing a deep threat and thus requiring an extreme remedy, despite its own consequences.

In the court's words, "the considerable political chaos that may occur by removing a President elected by the public from office should be deemed an inevitable cost of democracy paid by the nation in order to protect the

---

18 Constitution of the Republic of Korea, Article 65, Section 1; Constitutional Court Act [of the Republic of Korea]. Downloadable in English from the website of the Constitutional Court: https://english.ccourt.go.kr/site/eng/main.do [Accessed April 15, 2021], Article 48.

19 CCK 2016Hun-Na1 (English translation), p. 63.

20 Constitutional Court of Korea, 2004Hun-Na1, March 14, 2004. English translation available at http://search.ccourt.go.kr/xmlFile/0/010400/1/pdf/e2004n1_1.pdf [Accessed July 11, 2020].

21 The political formation that Roh openly supported ahead of the April 2004 legislative elections was the Uri Party *(Uridang)*, founded by his closest followers in November 2003 after they seceded from the ruling Millennium Democratic Party *(Saech'ŏnnyŏnminjudang)*. Representatives from both the ruling camp and conservative opposition therefore joined forces to pass the motion that impeached Roh Moo-hyun on March 12, 2004, for having violated his obligation to remain neutral in electoral times. On South Korean electoral laws and their political restrictions, see Mobrand, E. (2015). The Politics of Regulating Elections in South Korea: The Persistence of Restrictive Campaign Laws. *Pacific Affairs*, 88 (4), 791-811.

basic order of liberal democracy."[22] As articulated here, ruling in favor of impeachment did not amount for judges to a political intervention but a constitutional responsibility imposing itself out of necessity: protecting "the basic order of liberal democracy," an expression borrowed from the preamble of the constitution. The meaning of this basic order was not explained in the case at hand but can be clearly distinguished from that of democracy as popular sovereignty, with which it was put in balance: removing the president from office was indeed said to unavoidably hurt the latter for the sake of safeguarding the former.

Impeachment was therefore found to pass the proportionality test employed by many constitutional courts around the world.[23] To South Korean judges, the "benefits of protecting the Constitution" were indeed considered to "overwhelmingly outweigh" the costs of removing a democratically elected president from office given how grave the violations committed were – to the point that they resulted in "a betrayal of the people's confidence."[24] Yet, while it is generally admitted that "in criminal adjudication proportionality provides a politically neutral principle for normative balancing," as pointed out by political theorist Sungmoon Kim, the same is not true in the context of constitutional adjudication where "it is highly controversial whether the principle of proportionality can assume a similar neutralist posture," leaving courts room to make determinations involving political rather than legal judgment.[25]

I would add that political judgment intervenes not only in the act of weighing competing interests but also in that of defining the very aim towards which they are balanced: protecting the "basic order of liberal democracy." In its name, the Constitutional Court of Korea has accomplished a lot since it began to operate in 1988, including validating restrictions of citizens' fundamental rights such as in the frame of the National Security Act.[26] Among its recent and notorious decisions, the institution has appealed to the necessity of safeguarding the "basic democratic order" to dissolve the minority left-wing Unified Progressive Party (*T'onghapchin-*

---

22 CCK 2016Hun-Na1 (English translation), p. 20.
23 Jackson, V. and Tushnet, M. (Eds.) (2017). *Proportionality: New Frontiers, New Challenges*. Cambridge: Cambridge University Press.
24 CCK 2016Hun-Na1 (English translation), p. 63.
25 Kim 2019, pp. 593–594.
26 Guichard, J. (2016). *Regime Transition and the Judicial Politics of Enmity: Democratic Inclusion and Exclusion in South Korean Constitutional Justice*. New York: Palgrave Macmillan.

bodang) on December 19, 2014, a decision that was pronounced by the same justices who voted in favor of removing Park Geun-hye from office.[27]

Through its commitment to defend this order, the Constitutional Court has shaped the contours of South Korea as a democratic polity in ways that importantly invite to relativize the apparent victory of the candlelight movement in the impeachment ruling. For the court, confirming the president's ousting did not mean acknowledging, let alone upholding, the existence and demands of the anti-Park movement. On the contrary, the vision of democracy that transpired through the 2014 and 2017 judgments appears premised on a model of politics fearful of ideological pluralism in the first case and of popular mobilization in the second, as this chapter's next part unveils.[28]

The court's depoliticization of impeachment as a procedure therefore ought not to make us blind to the political dynamics at work and at stake in the task and claim of protecting the constitutional order. Defending and defining this order imply no less than determining what is compatible or incompatible with democracy, which actors respect or endanger it and can consequently be included in or excluded from the polity. While this chapter concedes that adjudicating an impeachment trial may not be a political matter in the partisan sense of choosing a side – and the Constitutional Court was very careful in its ruling not to side with the anti-Park camp – the court can still be said to have acted politically in the deeper sense of embracing a certain model of politics from which the claims and practices of the candlelight movement were largely excluded.

---

27 Appointed for a six-year renewable term, the Constitutional Court's members are selected by the different branches of government: the executive (who nominates all justices but only chooses three), the legislative, and the judiciary. Among the eight justices who sat over the impeachment trial, Cho Yong-ho and Seo Ki-seok had been picked by Park Geun-hye herself while Ahn Chang-ho had been recommended by the then ruling conservative Saenuri Party (*Saenuridang*). Therefore, it should be noted that all the judges designated by Park or her camp voted in favor of her impeachment contrary to expectations.

28 Constitutional Court of Korea, 2013Hun-Da1, December 19, 2014. English translation available at http://search.ccourt.go.kr/xmlFile/0/010400/2014//pdf/e2013d1_2.pdf [Accessed July 11, 2020].

2. The Constitutional Court's Covert Understanding of Democracy: (De)mobilizing Civil Society

Various limitations of the majority ruling were addressed in the two concurring but separate opinions filed by Justices Kim Yi-su and Lee Jin-sung
on the one hand, and Justice Ahn Chang-ho on the other hand. These
two texts consequently appear more critical of Park Geun-hye's presidency.
Relatedly, they dedicated more attention to civil society, either identifying
its members with the victims of the Sewol ferry sinking or apprehending
citizens as the actors of needed constitutional reforms. Yet, these forms of
inclusion hardly translated into a celebration of contentious mass politics
as embodied in the candlelight movement. As argued in this chapter's
second part, the people in whose name the three judges wrote were only
mobilized along certain lines – those of collective suffering and political
deliberation – while alternative modalities of their presence and participation in the public space – namely, street protests – were clearly discounted.
Ultimately, Park Geun-hye was not found to have infringed upon the
fundamental rights of citizens but only those of enterprises.

2.1 Accounting for Collective Suffering: Citizens as Victims of the Sewol Ferry Sinking but Not of the President's Violation of Her Duties

The first concurring but separate opinion focused on revisiting the sinking of the Sewol ferry and the response by Park Geun-hye to what was
construed as a national crisis in which the saving of 476 persons was at
stake. The orders given by the crew that all passengers remain onboard
indeed prevented an evacuation of the ship that could have lessened the
eventual toll of 304 dead. Even so, Justices Kim Yi-su and Lee Jin-sung
declared themselves in agreement with the majority over refusing to rule
that the president had contravened her duty to protect the right to life, not
holding her directly responsible for the event and its tragic outcome. In
opposition to their colleagues, however, they considered that the violation
of the president's obligation to faithfully perform her duties could be a
basis for impeachment, leading them to reexamine in detail Park's actions
on the day of the incident.

To begin with, both justices held that the obligation in question was
legal (*pŏpchŏk*) rather than just moral (*toŭijŏk*) or political (*chŏngch'ijŏk*),

making it a legitimate matter of review.[29] They further reasoned that two criteria could be identified to assess whether a violation had been committed: first, the occurrence of a national crisis; and second, the failure of the president to faithfully carry his or her duty to react to such an emergency. This obligation on the part of the country's leader was interpreted as being less one of result than one of conduct, which Park Geun-hye was not found to have honored.

For Justices Kim and Lee, Park was principally derelict in her duty as a result of not having gone to her office while the sinking and rescue operations of the Sewol ferry were unfolding. Instead, she stayed at her residence on a regular workday and during a crisis whose monitoring and management required her presence in the Blue House Situation Room. In addition, the two judges strongly rejected the president's claims that she was misled in her understanding of the situation by erroneous news reports and only came to realize its gravity in the late afternoon. According to their opinion, she could and should have been aware of the existence of an emergency earlier than she did, which would have enabled the taking of swift and appropriate measures.

As stressed by Kim Yi-su and Lee Jin-sung, the demonstration of leadership necessary during a national crisis entails a concrete and symbolic dimension. Presidential actions are not only directed to the relevant agencies in charge of handling the situation on the ground, but they are also addressed to citizens. In this respect, Justices Kim and Lee designated victims and their families as the ones to whom the president's treatment of the situation as a top priority can bring not only "hope (*hŭimang*)" but also, after the facts, "strength (*him*)."[30] Their opinion's careful review of the Sewol ferry incident and Park Geun-hye's (lack of) response therefore extended to taking into account the collective suffering of directly affected citizens, not only aggrieved in this case by the loss of dear ones but also by the non-ineluctability of this tragedy had more been done to prevent it.

In so reasoning, Kim Yi-su and Lee Jin-sung can be said to have acknowledged better than the majority decision an issue at the heart of the 2016-2017 anti-Park protests. Their text thus included within its scope citizens excluded from the rest of the impeachment ruling. Yet, this acknowledgment rested on an empathetic mode that entirely evaded the candlelight movement's politicization of the Sewol ferry scandal, a point to which our analysis will return later. To this reservation must be added

---

29 CCK 2016Hŏn-Na1, p. 49.
30 Ibid., p. 58.

the conclusion reached by the two judges at the end of their opinion: that the violation Park Geun-hye committed of her obligation to faithfully react to a national crisis such as the Sewol ferry sinking did not suffice, in and of itself, to justify her removal from office.

In Justices Kim and Lee's words,

> "although the respondent violated the obligation to faithfully execute the President's duties prescribed under the Constitution and the duty of fidelity under the State Public Officials Act, this alone cannot serve as a ground for removal from office for it is not, in and of itself, a cause for losing public trust to the extent that the democratic legitimacy vested in the President by the people should be forfeited before the presidential term ends."[31]

This last sentence may be read as a particularly strong dismissal of the candlelight rallies, in which millions of citizens voiced having lost confidence in Park Geun-hye's moral ability to act as president and traced this betrayal to the Sewol ferry sinking. Justices Kim Yi-su and Lee Jin-sung's position to blame Park for her handling of the crisis without finding that her legitimacy was harmed to the point of justifying her removal from office rang particularly dissonant with the popular mobilization in favor of impeachment.

2.2 Calling for Constitutional Reform: Citizens as Public Deliberators but Not Protesters

In light of the limitations displayed both by the majority decision and the first concurring but separate opinion examined so far, the one filed by Justice Ahn Chang-ho appears to carry a radical critique of Park Geun-hye's presidency. While agreeing with the rest of the court that the violations Park committed were unforgivable from the perspective of protecting the constitution and thus made necessary her removal from office, Justice Ahn also searched deeper than his colleagues for the structural causes in which such abuses could be rooted.

His opinion offered as an answer the notion of "imperial presidency (*chewangjŏk taet'ongnyŏngje*),"[32] mentioned both in Korean and English in the text as Ahn Chang-ho acknowledged having borrowed it from debates

---

31   CCK 2016Hun-Na1 (English translation), p. 82.
32   See also the chapter by Hannes B. Mosler in this volume.

about the nature of the US presidency following the Watergate scandal.[33] Blaming the hyper-concentration of power characteristic of this system on "our constitution's power structure" (*uri hŏnpŏp-ŭi kwŏllyŏk kujo*), Justice Ahn denounced South Korea's imperial presidency as an emanation of institutional rather than circumstantial factors.[34] His text therefore incriminated what the rest of the court sought to preserve, condemning the flaws of current constitutional arrangements and calling for their reform. This position stood in sharp contrast with the court's hegemonic discourse. Contrary to it, Justice Ahn construed the constitution not solely as being in danger and deserving protection but also as posing a threat. This happened to be the case because its provisions failed to diffuse power in a democratic way.

According to Ahn Chang-ho, although the revision that the constitution underwent with South Korea's 1987 regime change enhanced the democratic legitimacy of the presidency and introduced some checks on it (in particular through the direct election of the head of state and the non-renewability of their five-year term), these new norms confirmed rather than altered the excessive concentration of power vested in South Korea's highest office. Ahn Chang-ho went on identifying three harmful effects arising from existing structures: the intervention in state affairs of unofficial aides (*pisŏn chojik-ŭi kukjŏng kaeip*), the presidency's ingrained tendency to abuse its vast authority (*taet'ongnyŏng-ŭi kwŏnhan namyong*), and the collusion between government and big businesses (*chaebŏl kiŏp-kwa-ŭi chŏnggyŏng yuch'ak*).[35]

These three phenomena overlap with the grounds justifying Park Geun-hye' s ousting in the Constitutional Court's majority ruling while also departing from them in important ways. Whereas the majority constructed the violations committed by Park as instances of personal misbehavior on her part, Justice Ahn's opinion brought to light how the abuses in question were not only a matter of individual responsibility but also of institutional entrenchment. This led him to diagnose that removing Park Geun-hye from office would not suffice to remedy the pathologies of South Korean politics. To that end, constitutional revisions imposed themselves. The ones advocated in Ahn Chang-ho's opinion did not prescribe specific power arrangements as much as a general direction for change: diffusing power at a multiplicity of levels, including through finding an

---

33 CCK 2016Hŏn-Na1, p. 60.
34 Ibid.
35 Ibid., p. 62.

alternative to the presidential system, privileging local autonomy over administrative centralization, and making political parties more representative of society.

At the center of these reforms' process and outcome, Ahn Chang-ho placed citizens' participation, insisting on the necessity to incorporate their views and opinions. This concern can be particularly contrasted with the institution-centric approach of the majority decision, in which citizens were hardly envisioned as political actors even in the context of contesting Park Geun-hye's power. Yet, the definition proposed by Justice Ahn of the modalities of public participation primarily revolved around deliberation through "reasonable dialogue (*isŏngjŏk taehwa*)."[36] This makes it difficult to read his text as a tribute to the candlelight movement, whose demands for change were formulated through contentious mobilization. Therefore, not only is Ahn Chang-ho's opinion devoid of any reference to the 2016-2017 candlelight demonstrations, like the rest of the impeachment ruling, but the kind of citizens' involvement he celebrated also appears far from the occupation of the public space by protests.

Ultimately, Justice Ahn's critique can be read as having articulated a vision of democracy fearful of political conflict. Under his pen, the "basic order of liberal democracy" was defined as being premised on "autonomy and harmony (*chayul-kwa chohwa*)," two values also attached to it in the preamble of the constitution.[37] It is also through "harmony" that economic democratization should be achieved as the judge highlighted, this time quoting the constitution's Article 119.[38] Although Ahn Chang-ho, contrary to the majority, did not treat conglomerates as victims but as accomplices of the Park Geun-hye administration, his call for undoing the collusion between government and big businesses nonetheless expressed deep confidence in the market economy system. Justice Ahn's concluding words thus praised the ability of this system and, by extension, of its actors to contribute to "the freedom, equality, safety and happiness of the Korean people and future generations,"[39] a belief that does not appear fully aligned with the pronounced anti-*chaebŏl* stance of the candlelight movement.

---

36 CCK 2016Hŏn-Na1, p. 66.
37 Ibid., p. 70.
38 Ibid., p. 64.
39 CCK 2016Hun-Na1 (English translation), p. 98.

2.3 A Hidden Discursive Commonality: Extinguishing Contentious Mass Politics

Citizens feature differentially in the Constitutional Court's impeachment ruling when paying close attention to the three texts that compose it. If the candlelight movement's existence and demands were substantially excluded from the majority decision even as it ruled in favor of removing Park Geun-hye from office, the two concurring but separate opinions seem to have offered anti-Park activists some form of inclusion. This was accomplished, on the one hand, through Justices Kim Yi-su and Lee Jin-sung's scrutiny of the presidential failure to respond adequately to the Sewol ferry crisis and, on the other hand, through Justice Ahn Chang-ho's call for citizens to play a central role in needed constitutional reforms – two positions that resonated with the 2016-2017 mobilization of civil society.

Yet, stopping the analysis at this conclusion risks obscuring a discursive commonality shared by all justices: their deployment of arguments to contain, and even extinguish, the flame of contentious mass politics. If a place was recognized for citizens in the impeachment ruling, it did not coincide with the streets where the candlelight rallies momentously unfolded for twenty consecutive weeks. The implications of this sidelining go beyond the necessity for the court to write in the name of all the people rather than some if impeachment is to be defended as an apolitical, nonpartisan form of trial. As contended in this chapter, the arguments articulated in the constitutional ruling may express justices' preference not for a given side but for a certain model of politics: one in which democratic contention should keep within limits both in terms of claims and practices.

Let us recall that the majority decision constructed Park Geun-hye's abuses as a source of public shock but never as a trigger of political mobilization. In addition, the issue of her wrongdoings' structural causes was evacuated as justices succumbed to the "occult of personality," blaming Park for her immorality while exonerating economic actors from any responsibility.[40] Finally, how Park reacted to the Sewol ferry sinking was found to be outside the scope of the impeachment trial. This point was firmly contested in the first concurring but separate opinion although, in the end, the fact that the president violated her duty to faithfully respond

---

40 Doucette J. (2017). The Occult of Personality: Korea's Candlelight Protests and the Impeachment of Park Geun-hye. *Journal of Asian Studies*, 76 (4), 851-860.

to a national crisis was not deemed to have harmed her legitimacy to the degree of justifying her removal from office.

Justices Kim Yi-su and Lee Jin-sung's interpretation of the Sewol ferry scandal thus deeply conflicted with the one articulated through the candlelight protests. As analyzed by Nan Kim, the 2016-2017 demonstrations contributed to recasting this tragedy's significance. In contrast to the apolitical emphasis on mourning and remembrance that prevailed in the wake of the event, invoking it had become two years later a matter of open challenge against the Park Geun-hye administration. This displacement was particularly exemplified in the public space by the shifting meaning of the yellow ribbons meant to commemorate the victims of the sinking. According to Nan Kim, "[o]ne of the historical ironies about the yellow ribbon in South Korea [...] is that the symbol was initially circulated in 2014 not as a political symbol but as an apolitical gesture of hope after the Sewol disaster," a hope for the safe return of the missing passengers that soon turned into an expression of national grief and support for the bereaved families before being eventually displayed as "an emblem of dissent" during the candlelight movement.[41]

The language of hope was precisely the one that Justices Kim and Lee mobilized in their opinion, which invested the president with the symbolic role of inspiring such a feeling during a national emergency. Their construction of the Sewol ferry crisis thus remained inscribed in a frame of understanding that prevailed in 2014 but no longer did in 2016-2017. Their account accordingly demonstrated compassion for a specific portion of citizens, namely victims and their families, while disregarding the larger and political significance taken by this event for a vast segment of the population.

Justice Ahn Chang-ho's concurring but separate opinion appears as the only contribution that endowed citizens with an active role, which they were called to play in the context of needed constitutional reforms. What Justice Ahn envisioned was no less than a transformation of South Korean politics through the design of new mechanisms to diffuse power. Yet, his conception of this transformation as having to unfold through "reasonable dialogue" suggests an implicit critique of another form of democratic participation: protest mobilization in the streets as characteristic of the candlelight rallies. Although Justice Ahn saw citizens as agents of political change, his opinion clearly favored a model of democracy premised on harmony and fearful of conflict. His position can thus be interpreted as a

---

41 Kim 2017, pp. 12-13.

form of distantiation vis-à-vis the candlelight movement distinct from, but converging with, other modes of dissociation resorted to in the rest of the constitutional decision.

In conclusion, the Constitutional Court justified Park Geun-hye's impeachment by invoking that her "acts of violating the Constitution and law [were] a betrayal of the people's confidence, and should be deemed grave violations of the law unpardonable from the perspective of protecting the Constitution."[42] As this chapter has demonstrated, this rare reference to the people was ridden with limitations. In addition to civil society's voicing of said betrayal being silenced in the ruling, the concession that citizens' confidence in the president had been damaged did not entail the recognition that Park's acts had infringed upon their rights. As a matter of fact, the only fundamental rights found to have been violated were not those of citizens but of private enterprises. In this sense, too, the Constitutional Court can be said to have acted politically, by treating *chaebŏl* as victims in the name of protecting the "basic order of free democracy." The next and final part of our analysis turns to the question of whether the ordinary justice system has done the same in deciding the criminal trials brought about by the impeachment scandal.

3. Ordinary Courts as Shapers of the Democratic Order: Judging Government-Business Relations

More than three years after its outbreak, South Korea's 2016-2017 scandal is still on trial. The impeachment of Park Geun-hye was only the start. Since then, not only the Constitutional Court but also the various levels of the judicial system have come to examine and determine the wrongdoings committed by the scandal's protagonists: Park Geun-hye herself; her entourage at the center of which was Park's longtime friend and unofficial aide, Choi Soon-sil; and the heads of family-run conglomerates known as *chaebŏl* including, first and foremost, Lee Jae-yong, Samsung's de facto leader as well as heir.

Taking into consideration the rulings rendered by the Seoul Central District Court, the Seoul High Court, and the Supreme Court against Park Geun-hye and Lee Jae-yong, this chapter's last part highlights how these institutions have responded to the popular demand for holding accountable not only the former president but also economic actors for the close and

---

42 CCK 2016Hun-Na1 (English translation), p. 63.

mutual ties both sides have nurtured. While conglomerates were absolved from any responsibility in the impeachment ruling, the criminal justice system has not fully exculpated them. Yet, the extent to which *chaebŏl* have been found guilty appears limited, revealing the polity-shaping role that ordinary courts played in ruling heavily against Park Geun-hye but leniently against business magnates.

3.1 The Criminal Trial of Park Geun-hye: *Chaebŏl* as Both Victims of Corruption and Accomplices of Collusion

Following her removal from office, Park Geun-hye was arrested on March 31, 2017, and has been detained since. Her trial in two separate criminal cases has gone through several levels of jurisdiction so far. Most recently, it resulted in a combined sentence of twenty years in prison against the ex-president: fifteen for bribery and five for abuse of power and other charges.[43] Without entering in the details of all the rulings, this section focuses on the first and main case involving power abuse and corruption charges, reviewing how the different courts have constructed the government-business relations under examination.[44]

On April 6, 2018, the Seoul Central District Court handed down a sentence of 24 years in prison against the former president. The court advanced several reasons to justify the length and amount, which did not meet those requested by the prosecution (namely, a jail term of 30 years).[45] The first such reason actually rested on two contentions: that the accused had abused the position and power vested in her by the people while she gravely infringed upon the property rights and freedom of occupation of enterprises. The list of specific offenses Park Geun-hye was found to have committed comprised having requested donations from various companies in order to fund the Mir and K-Sports foundations under the control of Choi Soon-sil as well as having made some of the same *chaebŏl* provide a wide range of benefits to Choi and her suite. Like the Constitutional Court before it, the Seoul Central District Court held the coercion of conglomerates as a key element of Park's guilt in this respect.

43　Yonhap News Agency (2020). *Appellate Court Slashes Prison Term of Ex-President Park to 20 Years in Retrial*, July 10, 2020. Available at: https://en.yna.co.kr/view/AE N20200710009300315 [Accessed April 8, 2021].

44　The second and minor case related to the off-the-books funds transferred to Park Geun-hye by the National Intelligence Service, South Korea's intelligence agency.

45　Seoul Central District Court, 2017Kohap364-1, April 6, 2018.

Yet, the court's panel of three judges did not stop there. The second reason put forth to condemn Park Geun-hye encompassed the bribes she solicited and/or received from conglomerates such as Samsung, Lotte, and SK. This money was distinguished from the donations previously examined in so far as it was not given out of coercion but in exchange for benefits, leading the court to recognize the full agency of *chaebŏl* in their dealings with the presidency. Finally, Park was found guilty of a crime that had not been taken into account in the impeachment trial: politically motivated discrimination, which she enforced by ordering that financial support be refused to or withdrawn from individuals and organizations active in the artistic and cultural world but critical of her administration.[46]

On August 24, 2018, the Seoul High Court increased the ex-president's original sentence to 25 years in prison. In laying out the grounds for its decision, the appellate court went further than its lower counterpart in determining the crimes committed by Park.[47] The first of these crimes remained that of having abused her power and position while seriously infringing upon the property rights and freedom of occupation of enterprises. In accordance with the findings of the Seoul Central District Court, the Seoul High Court defined Park's offenses as comprising the request of financial contributions and other favors from conglomerates that were coerced into providing them.

The language of both institutions, however, diverged over the next item considered: the bribes that the former president received from Samsung and Lotte as well as those she solicited from SK. As recalled by the appellate court, the bribes in question had been discussed in one-on-one meetings between Park Geun-hye herself and *chaebŏl* heads. They consisted of vast sums of money that the latter had promised or provided not as a result of undue pressures but in exchange for self-serving demands. Insisting on the reciprocal dimension of government-business collusion, the Seoul High Court concluded that this kind of "immoral dealings (*pudodŏkhan kŏrae*)" between political and economic forces contributed to damaging the "essence of democracy (*minjujuŭi-ŭi ponjil*)" and to distorting the "or-

---

46 It has since been ascertained that more than 9,000 personalities had been blacklisted and denied funding under this policy. Korea Herald (2018). *Truth Committee: More than 9,000 Politically Active Artists Blacklisted under Ex-President Park*, April 10, 2018. Available at: http://www.koreaherald.com/view.php?ud=20180410 000663 [Accessed April 8, 2021].

47 Seoul High Court, 2018No1087, August 24, 2018.

der of market economy (*sijang kyŏngje chilsŏ*)," thus instilling a deep sense of loss and distrust in citizens.[48]

The appellate court additionally characterized the politically motivated discrimination implemented by Park Geun-hye in the cultural and artistic realm as antidemocratic. In the words of Judges Kim Mun-sŏk, Chin Kwang-ch'ŏl, and Pae Yong-jun, Park's policy had amounted to negating the "basic order of liberal democracy," which the ruling described as being premised upon the freedoms of thought, expression, and art. Repeating the formula twice, the three judges went on emphasizing how the ideological and cultural diversity normally supporting this order had suffered a regression under the Park Geun-hye administration.[49]

The Seoul High Court's decision was in turn reversed by the Supreme Court on August 29, 2019, due to a procedural mistake.[50] The case was consequently sent back to the level of jurisdiction below, which was asked to consolidate the two ongoing trials against the ex-president while ruling separately on bribery charges and the rest of alleged offenses. On July 10, 2020, Park's combined sentence of 30 years in prison was reduced to 20 as the Seoul High Court argued that "she seems to have received little personal benefits" regarding bribery.[51] Interestingly, this extenuating circumstance has often had a strong mitigating impact when the heads of conglomerates were tried, accounting for much of the pro-*chaebŏl* bias that South Korean courts are proven to show.[52]

3.2 The Criminal Trial of Lee Jae-yong: A Lesser Condemnation of Government-Business Relations

Paradoxically, Lee Jae-yong's trial has involved the same institutions and facts as those in the case against Park, but it has resulted in a lesser con-

---

48 Seoul High Court, 2018No1087, August 24, 2018.
49 Ibid.
50 Supreme Court, 2018To14303, August 29, 2019.
51 Yonhap News Agency 2020.
52 As shown by existing research, "the judiciary widely accepts 'no private gain' defenses, that a criminal acquires no direct private gain from crimes in question, especially in *chaebol* cases. The judiciary often accepts the claim that the crimes involving in-group transactions are designed to facilitate the interests of a whole business group (e.g. propping troubled affiliates in the group)." Choi, H., Kang, H., and Lee, C. (2018). What Constitutes 'Too Big to Jail?' Evidence from South Korea's Family Business Groups. *Asia-Pacific Journal of Financial Studies*, 47 (6), 881-919, p. 883.

demnation of government-business relations both in terms of reasoning and punishment. On August 25, 2017, the Seoul Central District Court handed down a five-year prison sentence to Lee Jae-yong on the basis of three grounds.[53] The first was Lee's illegal appropriation of Samsung's funds. The embezzled money was used toward the commission of the second offense for which the company's de facto leader was sanctioned, namely, bribery. Finally, the *chaebŏl*'s heir was found guilty of perjury for having falsely testified before the National Assembly during a parliamentary hearing held on December 6, 2016, before Park Geun-hye's impeachment motion was voted. According to Lee's declarations on that occasion, then president Park had "neither mentioned nor asked him to contribute" to the Mir and K-Sports foundations "when the two had a private meeting on July 25, 2015."[54]

As it turned out, Samsung had been asked to contribute to both supposedly nonprofit organizations. The company even sent them eight donations, amounting to KRW 20 billion in total, between November 20, 2015, and February 26, 2016. But this vast sum of money was not the only kind of transfer examined by the criminal justice system. A major point of contention between this system's various levels of jurisdiction and the conflicting rulings they have rendered has concerned the status of three dressage horses bought by Samsung for the use of equestrian Chung Yoo-ra (*Chŏng Yu-ra*), Choi Soon-sil's daughter. The Seoul Central District Court determined that this purchase constituted one of several forms of bribery offered by Lee Jae-yong to Park Geun-hye, who had enjoined him "to buy good horses" back in September 2014.[55] As argued by the prosecution, the purpose and benefit of paying such bribes had been to ensure that the government would support Samsung's leadership transition.[56]

---

53 Seoul Central District Court, 2017Kohap194, August 25, 2017.

54 Park, S. (2016). Samsung Scion to Be Accused of Perjury. *The Korea Times*, January 12, 2016. https://www.koreatimes.co.kr/www/nation/2020/03/113_221978.html [Accessed April 8, 2021].

55 Seoul Central District Court, 2017Kohap194.

56 This transition does not consist in a simple handing over of power from father to son. It has to be understood in the larger context of South Korean conglomerates' ecosystem. Although they are family-run, *chaebŏl* tend to have a complex ownership structure. As in the case of Samsung, the founding and ruling clan is able to exert control over the whole business group not through majority shareholding but, instead, through cross-shareholding. Notwithstanding "his less-than-1 percent stake in Samsung Electronics," Lee Jae-yong has succeeded in consolidating power over his family's empire through the 2015 merger of two of Samsung's parent companies, Samsung C&T and Cheil Industries. The Park

The five years in jail that Lee Jae-yong received from the Seoul Central District Court on August 25, 2017, fell short of the twelve years the prosecution had requested. Less than six months after this verdict, Lee's sentence was momentously shortened on appeal as the Seoul High Court not only reduced his punishment by half but also suspended it. At the heart of this reversal lay the status of the three horses Park Geun-hye had urged Lee Jae-yong to invest in for the benefit of Choi Soon-sil's progeny. Holding that Samsung's scion was not at liberty to ignore or dismiss the former president's demand, the appellate court did not consider that the said horses constituted a form of bribery.[57] To put it differently, Samsung's heir was treated as a victim of Park's corruption but not as an actor of government-business collusion, the occurrence of which was explicitly dismissed. The same court that had characterized the mutually benefitting deals made by political and economic forces as antidemocratic when ruling against the former head of state did not see reciprocity in the case concerning Lee. According to Judges Chŏng Hyŏng-sik, Kang Mun-gyŏng, and Kang Wan-su, no evidence showed that the latter had sought advantages from the presidency.

The Seoul High Court's February 5, 2018, verdict resulted in the freeing of Lee Jae-yong from prison. His early liberation conformed to a larger pattern according to which chairs of conglomerates have evaded punishment as examined in this chapter's next and final section. Not surprisingly, the ruling was appealed to the Supreme Court. On August 29, 2019, this last institution rendered its decision to send back Lee Jae-yong's case to the Seoul High Court after having reviewed several grounds of appeal formulated both by the defendant and the prosecution. While upholding some the grounds raised by Lee and his attorneys, the high court momentously sided with prosecutors on the issue of whether the horses bought for Chung Yoo-ra constituted graft.[58] A majority of justices found the lower court to have erred in determining that neither the animals nor the money used for their purchase represented bribes. The Supreme Court instead

---

Geun-hye administration proved instrumental in facilitating this controversial operation to which some of Samsung C&T's shareholders were strongly opposed. As "the biggest investor in Samsung C&T," the National Pension Service indeed "helped Samsung narrowly win" the approval needed for the merger to proceed. Lee, Y. (2017). Key Issues in Trial of Samsung Heir Charged with Bribery. *AP News*, March 8, 2017. Available at: https://apnews.com/article/30d54176c03f461bb 814a594759cbd74 [Accessed at April 8, 2021].

57 Seoul High Court, 2017No2556, February 5, 2018.
58 Supreme Court, 2018To2738, August 29, 2019.

considered that both could be considered as such even though the horses' property rights had not been transferred to Choi Soon-sil or her daughter.

The institution went on ruling that Lee Jae-yong was guilty not only of bribery but also of embezzlement, having misappropriated funds from Samsung Electronics to finance the acquisition. While recognizing that the buying of the three horses and other acts amounted to favors offered by Lee Jae-yong to Park Geun-hye in exchange for benefits, the Supreme Court did not venture into broad considerations about government-business relations in its decision. Keeping its reasoning centered on the specific details of the case, the high court incriminated Lee more heavily than he had previously been but on a narrow basis. In other words, justices did not use the case against Samsung's heir to articulate a general condemnation of state-*chaebŏl* collusion.

Lee Jae-yong's ongoing retrial raises speculations as to whether or not it will result in a more serious conviction. The public apology he delivered on May 6, 2020, may play in his favor.[59] If not, it remains to be seen how Moon Jae-in (*Mun Chae-in*), South Korea's post-impeachment president who was elected on May 9, 2017, will react. Although Moon has pledged not to grant any presidential pardon in connection with the trials of the 2016-2017 scandal, promising upon his coming into office that "the cozy relationship between political and business circles will completely disappear," he has since become increasingly active in cultivating close ties with Samsung as part of his effort to boost economic growth.[60] This rapprochement points to the structural interdependence existing between the state and business conglomerates, a symbiosis upon which South Korea's development has been historically based and continues to rely to this day. This interdependence helps explain the pattern following which *chaebŏl* heads have evaded punishment from the criminal justice system.

59 Choe, S.-H. (2020). Samsung Heir Apologizes for Corruption and Union-Busting Scandals. *The New York Times*, May 6, 2020. Available at: https://www.nytimes.co m/2020/05/06/business/samsung-lee-apology.html [Accessed April 8, 2021].

60 The Economist (2019). *South Korea's Left-Wing President Loses His Zeal to Humble Big Business*, June 22, 2019. Available at: https://www.economist.com/asia/201 9/06/22/south-koreas-left-wing-president-loses-his-zeal-to-humble-big-business [Accessed April 8, 2021].

3.3 The Polity-Shaping Role of Courts: Comparing Ordinary and Constitutional Justice

So far, several chairs of conglomerates have escaped serving full time behind bars, including Lee Jae-yong's own father, Lee Kun-hee (*Yi Kŏn-hŭi*), demonstrating South Korean judiciary's understanding that *chaebŏl* heads are "too big to jail."[61] Lee Kun-hee most recently succeeded to avoid prison in 2008, when he was found guilty of charges such as tax evasion and received a suspended sentence of three years in prison from the Seoul High Court. He was subsequently pardoned by then president Lee Myung-bak (*Yi Myŏng-bak*), whose own trial for corruption has revealed that the pardon in question was among the favors the former head of state granted to Samsung in exchange for hefty financial compensations.[62] Lee Kun-hee had previously been pardoned after being convicted alongside other *chaebŏl* executives in the frame of the vast corruption scandal for which ex-presidents Chun Doo-hwan (*Chŏn Tu-hwan*) and Roh Tae-woo (*No T'ae-u*) were tried, convicted, and eventually amnestied.[63]

---

61 "Light criminal penalties are connected to the size of *chaebols* (too big to jail) just as a large bailout is connected to the size of systematically important financial institutions (too big to fail, Mishkin et al., 2006). [...] The total sales of the top four family business groups (Samsung, Hyundai Motor Group, LG, and SK) contribute 49.2% of Korea's GDP; the total assets of their affiliates amounted to 43.5% of GDP in 2005 (Solidarity for Economic Reform, 2009). Since a few wealthy families manage *chaebols*, judges worry that harsh sentences against the tycoons may engender economy-wide system risk." Choi et al. 2018, p. 902.

62 Kwaak, J. S. (2017). Samsung Is Under Scrutiny Again as South Korean Police Raid Offices. *The New York Times*, October 18, 2017. Available at: https://www.ny times.com/2017/10/18/business/samsung-investigation-police-raid.html [Accessed April 8, 2021]; Choe, S.-H. (2018). Former South Korean President Gets 15 Years in Prison for Corruption. *The New York Times*, October 5, 2018. Available at: https://www.nytimes.com/2018/10/05/world/asia/lee-myung-bak-south-korea-conv icted.html [Accessed April 8, 2021].

63 Chun Doo-hwan and Roh Tae-woo were tried not only for the colossal amount of money they had amassed in two slush funds but also for their role in the December 1979 military coup d'état and the ensuing suppression of the May 1980 Kwangju uprising. They were respectively sentenced to death and 22 and a half years in prison in August 1996. Their sentences were commuted on appeal to life imprisonment and 17 years in prison, which the Supreme Court of Korea confirmed in April 1997. On December 22 of that same year, however, Chun and Roh were both released after Kim Young-sam (*Kim Yŏng-sam*) granted them a presidential pardon before retreating from office, a gesture that was agreed to by Kim Dae-jung (*Kim Tae-jung*) upon his election.

This time around, it seems unlikely that Park Geun-hye will receive the same clemency, raising the question of whether the ex-president alone will take the fall for the crimes in which economic actors also participated. While the fate of Lee Jae-yong is still pending, another *chaebŏl* executive has already seen his case resolved favorably: Shin Dong-Bin (*Sin Tong-bin*), the CEO of Lotte Corporation. The sentence of 30 months in prison that the Seoul Central District Court handed him on February 13, 2018, was upheld but suspended by the Seoul High Court on October 5 of the same year, freeing Shin after seven months in jail. The Supreme Court confirmed this last ruling on October 17, 2019. Like its lower counterpart, the highest organ of the judiciary recognized Shin as guilty of bribery but did not use his case to forcefully condemn government-business collusion either in terms of argument or punishment.

The only court that has been willing to do so in the trials of the 2016-2017 scandal appears to be the Seoul High Court, but only as part of its ruling against Park Geun-hye and not against Lee Jae-yong or Shin Dong-bin whose sentences the institution suspended. Let us recall that the appellate court found Park guilty of having endangered two features envisioned at the heart of South Korea's "basic order of liberal democracy": on the one hand, the market economy system, which political and economic forces were said to have distorted; on the other hand, ideological diversity, which was deemed to have been hurt by the former president's policy of punishing individuals and organizations from the artistic and cultural world critical of her.

The Seoul High Court's reference to the "basic order of liberal democracy" appears derived from the definition that the Constitutional Court articulated as early as 1990, recognizing both "private property and market economy" as two core components of this order that the institution is committed to defending.[64] The trials of the 2016-2017 scandal acutely raise the question of what is protected behind this notion. To the Constitutional Court, safeguarding South Korea's constitutional order against Park Geun-hye's attacks has meant discursively taking the side of private enterprises against the ex-president's corruption scheme. The opinion of Justice Ahn Chang-ho stands out in the impeachment ruling as the only part where government-business relations were considered as mutually benefiting. In the realm of ordinary justice, the Seoul High Court has not shied away

---

64 Constitutional Court of Korea, 89Hun-Ka113, April 2, 1990. For an analysis of this ruling rendered in connection to the constitutionality of the National Security Act, see Guichard 2016, pp. 73-77.

from judging state-*chaebŏl* collusion as antidemocratic but only in the case against Park. By contrast, the court has proved clement with business executives both in terms of reasoning and sentencing.

Conclusion

This chapter has first offered to analyze the Constitutional Court of Korea's March 10, 2017, decision to remove president Park Geun-hye as having been pronounced in favor of impeachment but not of the candlelight movement. The latter was indeed obliterated from the ruling, not only lexically but also substantially. While the Constitutional Court apparently negated the existence and demands of the candlelight rallies as a result of its claim and commitment to impartiality, this chapter has argued that the institution avoided partisanship without evading politics. Indeed, the court acted politically not in the sense of choosing a side but of promoting a certain vision of the polity, one in which civil society's mobilization was discounted rather than celebrated while conglomerates were treated as victims. Ordinary courts can also be said to have participated in this polity-shaping role as they have judged government-business relations and condemned one side more heavily than the other, letting Park Geun-hye take the fall for antidemocratic threats much larger than her.

References

Cho, J. (2004). The Politics of Constitution-Making During the 1987 Democratic Transition in South Korea. *Korea Observer*, 35 (2), 171-206.

Choe, S.-H. (2018). Former South Korean President Gets 15 Years in Prison for Corruption. *The New York Times*, October 5, 2018. Available at: https://www.nytimes.com/2018/10/05/world/asia/lee-myung-bak-south-korea-convicted.html [Accessed April 8, 2021].

Choe, S.-H. (2020). Samsung Heir Apologizes for Corruption and Union-Busting Scandals. *The New York Times*, May 6, 2020. Available at: https://www.nytimes.com/2020/05/06/business/samsung-lee-apology.html [Accessed April 8, 2021].

Choi, H., Kang, H., and Lee, C. (2018). What Constitutes 'Too Big to Jail?' Evidence from South Korea's Family Business Groups. *Asia-Pacific Journal of Financial Studies*, 47 (6), 881-919.

Constitution of the Republic of Korea. Available in English at: https://korea.assembly.go.kr:447/res/low_01_read.jsp?boardid=1000000035 [Accessed April 15, 2021].

Constitutional Court Act [of the Republic of Korea]. Downloadable in English from the website of the Constitutional Court: https://english.ccourt.go.kr/site/eng/main.do [Accessed April 15, 2021].

Doucette, J. (2017). The Occult of Personality: Korea's Candlelight Protests and the Impeachment of Park Geun-hye. *Journal of Asian Studies*, 76 (4), 851-860.

Guichard, J. (2016). *Regime Transition and the Judicial Politics of Enmity: Democratic Inclusion and Exclusion in South Korean Constitutional Justice*. New York: Palgrave Macmillan.

Harris, B. (2017). Timeline: Downfall of Park Geun-hye. *The Financial Times*, March 10, 2017. Available at: https://www.ft.com/content/9e5b361e-bde8-11e6-8b45-b8b81dd5d080 [Accessed April 8, 2021].

Jackson, V. and Tushnet, M. (Eds.) (2017). *Proportionality: New Frontiers, New Challenges*. Cambridge: Cambridge University Press.

Kim, N. (2017). Candlelight and the Yellow Ribbon: Catalyzing Re-Democratization in South Korea. *Asia-Pacific Journal: Japan Focus*, 15 (14), no. 5, 1-17.

Kim, S. (2018). Candlelight for Our Country's Right Name: A Confucian Interpretation of South Korea's Candlelight Revolution. *Religions*, 9 (11), 330.

Kim, S. (2019). From Remonstrance to Impeachment: A Curious Case of Confucian Constitutionalism in South Korea. *Law & Social Inquiry*, 44 (3), 586-616.

Korea Herald (2018). *Truth Committee: More than 9,000 Politically Active Artists Blacklisted under Ex-President Park*, April 10, 2018. Available at: http://www.koreaherald.com/view.php?ud=20180410000663 [Accessed April 8, 2021].

Kwaak, J. S. (2017). Samsung Is Under Scrutiny Again as South Korean Police Raid Offices. *The New York Times*, October 18, 2017. Available at: https://www.nytimes.com/2017/10/18/business/samsung-investigation-police-raid.html [Accessed April 8, 2021].

Lee, Y. (2017). Key Issues in Trial of Samsung Heir Charged with Bribery. *AP News*, March 8, 2017. Available at: https://apnews.com/article/30d54176c03f461bb814a594759cbd74 [Accessed at April 8, 2021].

Lee, Y. (2019). Articulating Inequality in the Candlelight Protests of 2016-2017. *Korea Journal*, 59 (1), 16-45.

Mobrand, E. (2015). The Politics of Regulating Elections in South Korea: The Persistence of Restrictive Campaign Laws. *Pacific Affairs*, 88 (4), 791-811.

Mosler, H. B. (2017). Decoding the 'Free Democratic Basic Order' for the Unification of Korea. *Korea Journal*, 57 (2), 5-34.

Park, S. (2016). Samsung Scion to Be Accused of Perjury. *The Korea Times*, January 12, 2016. https://www.koreatimes.co.kr/www/nation/2020/03/113_221978.html [Accessed April 8, 2021].

The Economist (2019). *South Korea's Left-Wing President Loses His Zeal to Humble Big Business*, June 22, 2019. Available at: https://www.economist.com/asia/2019/06/22/south-koreas-left-wing-president-loses-his-zeal-to-humble-big-business [Accessed April 8, 2021].

Yonhap News Agency (2020). *Appellate Court Slashes Prison Term of Ex-President Park to 20 Years in Retrial*, July 10, 2020. Available at: https://en.yna.co.kr/view/A EN20200710009300315 [Accessed April 8, 2021].

List of referenced cases

The following rulings are accessible in Korean language through the Constitutional Court of Korea's case search engine under http://search.ccourt.go.kr/ths/pt/selectThsPt0101List.do [Last accessed July 10, 2020]; hyphens in the case numbers need to be omitted.

Constitutional Court of Korea, 89Hun-Ka113, April 2, 1990. English summary available at http://search.ccourt.go.kr/xmlFile/0/010400/88/pdf/e89k113_1.pdf [Accessed July 11, 2020].

Constitutional Court of Korea, 2004Hun-Na1, March 14, 2004. English translation available at http://search.ccourt.go.kr/xmlFile/0/010400/1/pdf/e2004n1_1.pdf [Accessed July 11, 2020].

Constitutional Court of Korea, 2013Hun-Da1, December 19, 2014. English translation available at http://search.ccourt.go.kr/xmlFile/0/010400/2014//pdf/e2013d1_2.pdf [Accessed July 11, 2020].

Constitutional Court of Korea, 2016Hun-Na1, March 10, 2017. English translation available at http://search.ccourt.go.kr/xmlFile/0/010400/2017/pdf/e2016n1_1.pdf [Accessed July 10, 2020].

The following rulings are accessible in Korean language through the legal database https://casenote.kr [Last accessed April 16, 2021].

Seoul Central District Court, 2017Kohap364-1, April 6, 2018.
Seoul Central District Court, 2017Kohap194, August 25, 2017.
Seoul High Court, 2017No2556, February 5, 2018.
Seoul High Court, 2018No1087, August 24, 2018.
Supreme Court of Korea, 2018To14303, August 29, 2019.
Supreme Court of Korea, 2018To2738, August 29, 2019.

Park Geun-hye's Impeachment:
Theorizing a Political Economic Revolt

Juliette Schwak

Introduction

On March 10, 2017, Korea's Constitutional Court ruled in favor of the National Assembly's impeachment vote towards the incumbent President, Park Geun-hye (*Pak Kŭn-hye*), after months of protests that saw large numbers of Korean citizens, across generations, gender, occupational background and socio-economic status, peacefully fill the streets to ask for Park's resignation. The so-called candlelight protests (*ch'otpuljiphoe*) that accompanied Park's impeachment process were sparked by a series of corruption scandals at the Blue House (*Ch'ŏngwadae*). The scandals revolved around the close involvement in state affairs of Park's friend and confident Choi Soon-sil (*Ch'oe Sun-sil*), as well as a series of bribing and corruption cases involving Park, Choi, and major *chaebŏl*, the large family-run conglomerates that have been the backbone of Korea's industrial development and still dominate its economic system. The narratives contemporary to the protests centered around the "occult" nature of Park's rule[1] and of Choi's shamanic involvement in state affairs,[2] overemphasizing the individual personalities of both women and thereby somewhat obscuring the larger political implications of Park's downfall and of the structural elements that could have motivated the candlelight protesters.[3] Indeed, despite popular (and undeniably accurate) sentiment that Park has used her position to pursue private interests,[4] the corruption practices revealed through the Choi gate are not limited to Park's presidency.

---

1 Doucette, J. (2017). The Occult of Personality: Korea's Candlelight Protests and the Impeachment of Park Geun-hye. *The Journal of Asian Studies*, 76 (4), 851-860.
2 Kelly, R. (2016). South Korea's Most Bizarre Corruption Scandal Yet. *The Diplomat*, November 4, 2016. Available at: https://thediplomat.com/2016/11/south-korea s-most-bizarre-corruption-scandal-yet/ [Accessed January 19, 2020].
3 Doucette 2017, p. 853.
4 Bedeski, R. (2017). The Korean State and Candlelight Democracy: Paradigms and Evolution. *Journal of Contemporary Eastern Asia*, 16 (2), 82-92, p. 86.

This chapter moves beyond the intrigues of the Park presidency and asks: What is the nature of Park's impeachment process? It analyzes this process in the broader political economic context of contemporary Korea. By moving away from what Doucette calls "the occult of personality,"[5] my hypothesis here is that the candlelight protests were not only a movement directed towards Park as an individual and a leader, but rather a movement directed at the configuration of Korea's political economy in the race towards global competitiveness, and its material and immaterial consequences on Korean citizens' lives. If this is the case, the impeachment process is also a revolt against the *chaebŏl*, and the state-*chaebŏl* configuration that has emerged in the post-developmental era, rather than exclusively against Park herself.

The article develops this hypothesis through micro-sociological data on Korean citizens' perceptions of the country's political economic situation, characterized by growing inequalities of income but also of opportunities, and increasing social polarization. The data presented in this study was gathered through a mixed-methods approach that combined in-depth semi-structured interviews with a nation-wide survey undertaken in September 2016, a few months before the start of the candlelight protests. It builds upon and complements the existing literature on impeachment, by theorizing impeachment as a form of political economic protest. It also adds to the studies already available on Park's impeachment process and Korea's democratic consolidation by introducing class as an explanatory factor. Indeed, much of the available literature focuses on the path-dependency of anti-authoritarian protests, cultural and institutional factors that explain Park's impeachment process. However, while these studies are certainly helpful to understand Korean democracy, the discussion must also account for political economic factors and explore the very nature of contemporary democracy in the context of changing state-*chaebŏl* relations.

The chapter first provides a discussion of the theoretical and comparative literature on impeachment and situates Park's impeachment within a larger theoretical framework. Connecting Park's impeachment with recent global protests, it shows that impeachment in practice can serve as a medium of political economic protest, along with less institutional forms of protest such as strikes and highly confrontational demonstrations. This is followed by an assessment of the hypothesis that Park's impeachment process was a protest against the state-business nexus in contemporary Korea. The chapter therefore provides an empirical discussion of the shift

---

5 Doucette 2017.

in state-business relations in Korea, the popular perceptions of such shift and its role in shaping Korea's contemporary political economy. It then briefly introduces methodological choices before analyzing the data. The data shows that the impeachment process reveals the economic anxieties of Korean middle-classes in a post-developmental economy dominated by the *chaebŏl*. It is less of a middle-class revolt for the consolidation of Korea's formal democracy against authoritarianism, and more of a class-based protest for the consolidation of Korea's socio-economic democracy against the monopolization of opportunities by its business elite. The article concludes by analyzing the continuities of the protests under Moon Jae-in's (*Mun Chae-in*) presidency, and the limits of Park's impeachment as a mechanism to resolve the socio-economic tensions expressed during the 2016-2017 protests.

1. Theorizing Impeachment in a Global Context

Park's impeachment reveals specific features of Korea's contemporary political economy, but it can also enrich theoretical discussions of the nature of impeachment processes. In other words, the Park case offers a new answer to the broader theoretical question 'What is impeachment?'. Formally, impeachment is a constitutional provision that allows for the removal of a president who is found guilty of crimes that threaten national interests. It allows presidential democracies to limit abuses of power by otherwise powerful chief executives. Impeachment is an exceptional measure aimed at protecting democratic systems and it is therefore a relatively rare occurrence. Impeachment procedures have been initiated against presidents in the United States, in the Philippines, in Korea, in Lithuania, or in Nigeria.[6] Recent cases include Dilma Roussef's impeachment in 2016 and an impeachment process that started in December 2019 against incumbent US president Donald Trump, who was acquitted in February 2020. A series of Latin American presidents also faced impeachment procedures in the

---

6 Pérez-Liñán, A. (2007). *Presidential Impeachment and the New Political Instability in Latin America*. Cambridge: Cambridge University Press.

1990s.[7] The literature on impeachment is largely situated in the field of constitutional theory and tends to be US-centric[8] with some exceptions.[9]

As Pérez-Liñán notes, a "comparative theory of impeachment" is surprisingly lacking although empirical cases reveal that "impeachment is not just a legal recourse to remove presidents who are proven guilty of high crimes."[10] It has been interpreted as a challenge to presidential imperialism and as evidence of democratic stability since it can replace military coups as a procedure to change the chief executive.[11] It has also been interpreted as a legislative weapon to resolve a fierce executive-legislative conflict,[12] as a partisan weapon in the context of strong partisan conflict,[13] and as a class instrument used by business elites to remove leftist presidents.[14]

Scholars have rightly noted that public opinion and popular mobilization, particularly with regards to a president's perceived economic performance, can greatly impact the likelihood of an impeachment.[15] But the Park case suggests that impeachment can also become a form of political economic protest, channeling not only revolt against a misbehaving president but wider frustrations about economic and social inequalities. Various analyses of the Park case have been published and draw initial conclusions from the 2016-2017 impeachment process,[16] notably looking at its

---

7 Pérez-Liñán 2007.
8 See for instance: Sullivan, T. (1998). Impeachment Practice in the Era of Lethal Conflict. *Congress & the Presidency*, 25 (2), 117-128; Labovitz J. R. and Labovitz, M. (1978). *Presidential Impeachment*. New Haven: Yale University Press; Black, C. L. Jr. (1998). *Impeachment: A Handbook*. New Haven: Yale University Press; Gerhardt, M. J. (2019). *The Federal Impeachment Process: A Constitutional and Historical Analysis*. Chicago/London: University of Chicago Press.
9 Kakakhel, M. N. (1978). The Theory of Impeachment in Islamic Polity. *Islamic Studies*, 17 (2), 93-103; Kada, N. (2003). The Role of Investigative Committees in the Presidential Impeachment Processes in Brazil and Colombia. *Legislative Studies Quarterly*, 28 (1), 29-54; Pérez-Liñán 2007.
10 Pérez-Liñán 2007, pp. 2, 9.
11 Ibid., p. 5.
12 Ibid., p. 7.
13 Sullivan 1998.
14 Van Dijk, T. A. (2017). How Global Media Manipulated the Impeachment of Brazilian President Dilma Rousseff. *Discourse and Communication*, 11(2), 199-229.
15 Mosler, H. B. (2017). The Institution of Presidential Impeachment in South Korea, 1992-2017. *Verfassung und Recht in Übersee*, 50 (2), 111-134, p. 118; Pérez-Liñán 2007, p. 3; Whitehead, L. (2002). *Democratization: Theory and Experience*. Oxford: Oxford University Press, p. 104.
16 I refer to the 2016-2017 impeachment process to emphasize the nature of the impeachment decision as the outcome of a social process that started with the

implications for Korea's democratic consolidation.[17] Overall, this literature focuses on the impeachment process as a revolt against undemocratic leadership under Park, heightened by her personal authoritarian heritage as Park Chung-hee's (*Pak Chŏng-hŭi*) daughter; as a revolt against corruption as an individual crime committed by Park; as an embodiment of certain cultural values that persist in contemporary Korea; as evidence of institutional limits of Korea's democratic system. More specifically, scholars highlight the historical continuities and path-dependencies of the 2016-2017 events: Chang sees the protests and the impeachment in continuity with "the authoritarian and democratization legacies" [18] of modern Korea; similarly Shin and Moon show how the events are inscribed in a series of protest-based democratic reforms in modern Korea[19] and argue that the protests expressed revolt against Park's corrupted political practices and undemocratic leadership.[20] Some discuss the role of social media in the polarization of public opinion with regards to Park's impeachment.[21] Other scholars also analyze the events from a culturalist perspective, emphasizing Korea's political culture,[22] the Confucian character of the protests (articulating discourses of shame[23]) the Confucian rationale of the Constitutional Court in its decision to confirm Park's impeachment,[24] and even Korea's shamanic traditions.[25] Mosler notes that while presidential impeachment, in Park's case, has been an effective means to protect Korean democracy, it

---

candlelight protests and is not limited to institutional mechanisms and court rulings.

17 For classical literature on democratic consolidation, see: Diamond, L. (1999). *Developing Democracy: Toward Consolidation*. Baltimore: Johns Hopkins University Press; Diamond, L., and Kim, B. K. (2000). *Consolidating Democracy in South Korea*. Boulder: Lynne Rienner.

18 Chang, P. Y. (2018). Candlelight Protests in South Korea: The Legacies of Authoritarianism and Democratization. *Ehwa Journal of Social Sciences*, 34 (1), 5-18, p. 5.

19 Shin, G. and Moon, R. J. (2017). South Korea After Impeachment. *Journal of Democracy*, 28 (4), 117-131. p. 118.

20 Ibid., p. 120.

21 Hee, M. and Yun, S. (2018). Selective Exposure and Political Polarization of Public Opinion on the Presidential Impeachment in South Korea: Facebook vs KakaoTalk. *Korea Observer*, 49 (1), 137-159.

22 Dostal, J. M. (2017). South Korean Presidential Politics Turns Liberal: Transformative Change or Business as Usual? *The Political Quarterly*, 88 (3), 480-491.

23 Shin and Moon 2017, p. 121.

24 Kim, S. (2019). From Remonstrance to Impeachment: A Curious Case of "Confucian Constitutionalism" in South Korea. *Law and Social Inquiry*, 44 (3), 586-616.

25 Park, S. (2018). The Politics of Impeaching Shamanism: Regulating Religions in the Korean Public Sphere. *Journal of Church and State*, 60 (4), 636-660.

runs the risk of being institutionalized as an ad hoc procedure to resolve weaknesses in Korean democracy; he therefore recommends institutional reforms to protect the quality of Korea's democracy.[26] Shin considers that Park's impeachment can be explained by the weakness of Korea's party system.[27] Liberal-oriented scholars approach Park's impeachment from the perspective of Korea's "imperial presidency,"[28] considering that the significant constitutional power of Korean presidents contains the seeds of such personal abuses of power[29] and that such presidential power should be limited.[30]

While all these analyses have undeniable merit, they ignore one major element that also explains the impeachment process: class. The political economic context, characterized by growing macro-economic inequalities, produces perceptions across large segments of Korean society that meritocracy is breaking down, and that the *chaebŏl*, with state support and protection, are capturing opportunities at the detriment of middle-classes' economic resources but also socio-economic prospects. This chapter therefore assesses the hypothesis that Park's impeachment was also a revolt against the structural power of the state-*chaebŏl* nexus.

If that is the case, as I demonstrate here after, this should not limit the analysis of the impeachment as a specifically Korean event. Korean state-business interdependence should be connected to a global state-capital alliance in the context of the national pursuit of global competitiveness. Park's impeachment may then be interpreted as one localized form of the wider movement of revolt (or at least the worldwide outburst of frustration) against socio-economic sclerosis, middle-class insecurities, and a perceived return to class conflict in a classical Marxist sense.[31] This movement connects a multiplicity of local events. Some scholars have notably interpreted the 2014 Umbrella Movement in Hong Kong as an initial revolt against inequality.[32] A connection can also be made between Park's

---

26 Mosler 2017, p. 134.

27 Shin, S. (2020). The Rise and Fall of Park Geun-hye: The Perils of South Korea's Weak Party System. *The Pacific Review*, 33 (1), 153-183.

28 See also the chapter by Hannes B. Mosler in this volume.

29 Dostal 2017, p. 483.

30 Bedeski 2017, p. 86.

31 Nugent, C. (2020). From Chile to Hong Kong, the World Saw a Lot of Protests in 2019. Here's Why That Trend Is Going to Continue. *Time*, January 16, 2020, [online]. Available at: https://time.com/5766422/protests-unrest-2019-2020/ [Accessed February 6, 2020].

32 Nugent 2020; Ortmann S. (2015). The Umbrella Movement in Hong Kong: From Economic Concerns to the Rejection of Materialism. *Kyoto Review of Southeast*

impeachment process and the Chilean protests[33] but also with the French *gilets jaunes* [yellow vests] movement. This movement started in 2018 on social media platforms as a protest against the Macron government's announced plan to create an environmental tax that would have increased the price of fuel. A great number of protesters have met weekly around roundabouts throughout the country, creating blockades and demonstrating in diverse cities, including the capital city of Paris. Early studies have shown that the yellow vests were mostly factory workers, employees, and retirees. Participants in the movement did not belong to the poorest segments of the French population, but rather to lower-middle classes whose socio-economic status was more and more precarious.[34] As Jellab reports, the yellow vests were supported by "middle classes that experience [social, economic and cultural] downgrading and feel threatened by globalization."[35] The movement has indeed been interpreted as a breakpoint in the post-materialist movement that had seemingly dominated domestic politics in late capitalist societies following the collapse of the USSR.[36] The

---

Asia, 17; Carroll, T. (2014). Hong Kong's Pro-Democracy Movement is about Inequality: The Elite Knows It. *The Guardian*, July 28, 2014, [online]. Available at: https://www.theguardian.com/commentisfree/2014/jul/28/hong-kongs-pro-democracy-movement-is-about-inequality-the-elite-knows-it [Accessed February 6, 2020].

33 Kornbluh, P. (2019). Why Chileans Are Protesting for a New Socioeconomic Order. *The Nation*, December 10, 2019, [online]. Available at: https://www.thenation.com/article/archive/chile-protests-inequality-pinochet/ [Accessed February 6, 2020]; Langman, J. (2019). From Model to Muddle: Chile's Sad Slide Into Upheaval. *Foreign Policy*, November 23, 2019, [online]. Available at: https://foreignpolicy.com/2019/11/23/chile-upheaval-protests-model-muddle-free-market/ [Accessed February 6, 2020]; Shifter, M. (2020). The Rebellion Against the Elites in Latin America. *The New York Times*, January 21, 2020, [online]. Available at: https://www.nytimes.com/2020/01/21/opinion/international-world/latin-america-elites-protests.html [Accessed February 6, 2020].

34 Papuchon, A. and Duvoux, N. (2019). How to Measure Subjective Poverty in France – And What This Tells Us About the Anger of the Yellow Vests. *EUROPP LSE Blog*. Available at: https://ssrn.com/abstract=3312298 or http://dx.doi.org/10.2139/ssrn.3312298 [Accessed January 28, 2020].

35 Jellab, A. (2019). Gilet jaunes: les enjeux d'une mobilization. Les 'gilets jaunes' à l'épreuve de la démocratie et des injustices sociales [Gilets jaunes: Issues around a Mobilization. The 'Gilets jaunes' up against Social Injustice and the Democratic System]. *Futuribles*, 6 (433), 81-94.

36 Bréchon P. (2019). Le mouvement des 'gilets jaunes' ou le retour des valeurs matérialistes ? [The Yellow Vests Movement: Return of Materialist Values?] *Revue Politique et Parlementaire*, 1090, 113-120. Available at: https://www.revuepolitique.fr/le-mouvement-des-gilets-jaunes-ou-le-retour-des-valeurs-materialistes/ [Accessed January 28, 2020].

yellow vests' anger is directed not so much at wealth accumulation and income inequality, but towards an economic and cultural elite perceived as both self-contained and hampering meritocracy by capturing opportunities.[37] In Korea, likewise, protests did not target wealth and inequality of economic outcomes; they targeted inequalities of opportunity. The forms taken by the yellow vests protest reveal "a new form of public expression beyond the classical repertory of collective action."[38] The yellow vests also expressed a feeling of geographical entrapment (which the fuel tax symbolically came to represent) in opposition to a highly mobile French elite evolving in a radically different physical and political space.

Although the candlelight protests and the yellow vests movement took place in different political contexts and in two distant regions of the world, they share a common thread: frustration of materially and ontologically insecure middle-classes against the capture of economic and social opportunities by an elite that is perceived as self-contained and exclusive. In this perspective, impeachment now belongs to a new repertory of protest forms that goes beyond the traditional forms of collective action. In democratic systems, it functions as a demand for the political economic consolidation of democracy, beyond institutional or cultural consolidation.

2. Methods

In order to test the hypothesis that Park's impeachment was a protest against Korea's growing socio-economic inequalities and *chaebŏl*'s structural power, I have gathered micro-sociological data on Korean citizens' perceptions of the country's political economic situation. The data was gathered in 2015-2016 through a mixed-methods approach. I conducted qualitative semi-structured interviews with Korean citizens of different generations, genders, and socio-economic status. In addition, I conducted a nation-wide online anonymous survey in Korean in September 2016, a few months before the candlelight protests started. 400 respondents (200 men, 200 women, aged 14-65, with slightly over half of respondents residing

---

37 Guilluy, C. (2016). *Le Crépuscule de la France d'en Haut [Twilight of the Elites: Prosperity, the Periphery, and the Future of France]*. Paris: Flammarion.

38 Algan, Y., Beasley, E., Cohen, D., Foucault, M. and Peron, M. (2019). Qui sont les Gilets jaunes et leurs soutiens? [Who are the Yellow Vests and Their Supporters?] *Observatoire du Bien-etre du CEPREMAP et CEVIPOF*. Available at: https://www.sci encespo.fr/cevipof/sites/sciencespo.fr.cevipof/files/-Qui-sont-les-Gilets-jaunes-et-leu rs-soutiens-1.pdf [Accessed January 28, 2020].

in regions of the country beyond Seoul and neighboring Kyŏnggi-do) participated in the survey (which corresponded to a 10% response rate).

The data on perceptions was complemented by macro-economic data available in existing studies. One limit of the method I used is that the data is not representative of the entire Korean population, but rather of those who accepted to answer my questions during interviews and those who volunteered to take the survey. The data thus represents segments of the Korean public who were largely unsatisfied with the political economic situation of the country. Since this is an explorative study into an under-researched field, such data groups nonetheless provide empirical ground for the arguments developed in this chapter, which might be further complemented in future studies.

3. State-Business Relationships in Contemporary Korea

The candlelight protests took place in a specific political economic context. While Park's management of the 2014 Sewol ferry (*Sewŏlho*) disaster, in which hundreds of school children died on a sinking ferry off the coast of Chindo island, had been largely criticized by the Korean public, the candlelight protests also result from a series of scandals involving state-business collusion. Indeed, while much media focus has centered on the almost literary figure of Choi and her personal involvement in state affairs, the Park presidency was also marked by corruption practices and a series of irregular relationships, including the exchange of economic favors, between Park, Choi, and major *chaebŏl*. These include the favored admission to Ehwa Women's University (*Ihwayŏja taehakkyo*) of Choi's daughter, bribes received from Samsung by Park and Choi, and a series of scandals related to Korea's development assistance provision, in which appointments to key posts and selection of projects were made to economically favor Choi and Park.[39] However, Park is not the first Korean president to be tried and sentenced for corruption and collusive practices with big business. In 2018, her predecessor Lee Myung-bak (*Yi Myŏng-bak*) was sentenced to fifteen years in jail for bribery. Presidents Roh Moo-hyun (*No Mu-hyŏn*), Roh Tae-woo (*No T'ae-u*), and Chun Doo-hwan (*Chŏn Tu-hwan*) were all under investigation for corruption; Roh Moo-hyun committed

---

39 Schwak, J. (2019a). Dangerous Liaisons? State-Chaebol Cooperation and the Global Privatisation of Development. *Journal of Contemporary Asia*, 49 (1), 104-126, p. 115.

suicide while he was under investigation, while Roh Tae-woo and Chun Doo-hwan received presidential pardons after being convicted.

The recurrence of state-business collusion in Korean politics has created popular narratives about the *chaebŏl*'s greed and thirst for power. Recent Korean cinema illustrates this popular narrative. Many Korean films have recently depicted cases of corruption, including Woo Min-ho's (*U Min-ho*) 'Inside Men' (2015), Cho Ui-sok's (*Cho Ŭi-sŏk*) 'Master' (2016), or Im Sang-soo's (*Im Sang-su*) 'The Housemaid' (2010) and 'The Taste of Money' (2012). These films[40] reveal an economic imaginary of a corrupted and immoral ruling class of politicians and *chaebŏl*.[41] While the state-directed *chaebŏl* are largely identified by political economists as the backbone of Korea's economic miracle, a moral discourse has emerged in Korean society about the greediness of national capital in the context of a post-developmental, stagnating economy. Choe[42] characterizes the *chaebŏl* narratives in Korean popular culture[43] as "chaebol affect" – "an internationalized sense of insurmountable socioeconomic injustice and intolerable self-contempt located in those who observe chaebol privilege from the outside."[44] The dominant elite narrative is that a tight ruling class operating in both formal and informal ways,[45] notably through social circles in which its actors evolve and communicate.[46] Perhaps more importantly than their wealth accumulation, it is the self-contained and exclusive nature of the *chaebŏl* that popular narratives target. The immoral character of the *chaebŏl* as represented in recent Korean cinema sets them aside; immorality provides a distinctively elitist cultural code of conduct. The spaces in which elite characters evolve are enclosed and exclusive. Elite spaces are particularly exclusive in Bong Joon-ho's (*Pong Chun-ho*)

---

40 'Inside Men' and 'Master' are two box office successes with respectively USD 63 million and USD 48 million of revenues generated.

41 An interesting parallel to the recent films depicting resistance to the Japanese during the colonial era (Ryoo Seung-wan's (*Ryu Sŭng-wan*) 'Battleship Island' with USD 47 million, Choi Dong-hoon's (*Ch'oe Tong-hun*) 'Assassination' with USD 85 million, Kim Jee-woon's (*Kim Chi-un*) 'The Age of Shadows' with USD 55 million of revenues) in which selfless national heroes offer a stark contrast with the selfish and greedy *chaebŏl* winners of Korea's catch-up development.

42 Choe, Y. (2018). Chaebol Affect: Emotional Capital and the Interiority of Wealth in Im Sang-soo's 'The Housemaid' and 'The Taste of Money'. *Cinema Journal, 57* (4), 25-46.

43 For an evolution of these narratives: Choe 2018, pp. 27-30.

44 Choe 2018, p. 26.

45 Ibid., p. 28.

46 Schwak 2019a, p. 100.

acclaimed 'Parasite' (2019), where an inside-out narrative and visual mechanism distinguishes the two worlds that interact in the film. In 'Parasite,' the wealthy often communicate in English for purposes of distinction but also, perhaps more importantly, to indicate an inability of the two represented social classes to communicate in a common language.

Such narratives are in large part a reflection of a new political economic reality: the national imperative to achieve competitiveness in the global market, which has rendered state and *chaebŏl* organically interdependent and amplified "the inequality that many Koreans had begun to feel,"[47] notably through a lax legal system which tolerates *chaebŏl*'s illegal practices to maintain their economic competitiveness. If Koreans now call their country 'the Samsung Republic,' it is because the *chaebŏl* are perceived as dominating the state, thereby limiting popular sovereignty and weakening Korea's democracy.

The existing literature on the state-*chaebŏl* relation suggests a general shift from subordination to domination. The developmental state literature presents the *chaebŏl* from the Park Chung-hee government as dependent upon the Korean state's economic directions and credit allocation.[48] Regardless of the present character of the Korean state,[49] the *chaebŏl* have undoubtedly achieved greater independence from the Korean state from the 1980s. Thanks to the Kim Young-sam (*Kim Yŏng-sam*) government's *segyehwa* [globalization] policy, they began investing in foreign capital markets and integrating Global Value Chains. This lessened their financial dependence on the state and allowed them to effectively operate as Transnational Corporations (TNCs)[50] with both political authority and

---

47 Choe 2018, p. 27.
48 For such classical arguments: Chang, H.-J. (2006). *The East Asian Development Experience: The Miracle, the Crisis and the Future*. Penang: Third World Network; Amsden, A. (1989). *Asia's Next Giant: South Korea and Late Industrialisation*. New York: Oxford University Press; Woo-Cumings, J.E. M. (1999). *The Developmental State*. Ithaca, NY: Cornell University Press.
49 Kim, Y.-T. (1999). Neoliberalism and the Decline of the Developmental State. *Journal of Contemporary Asia*, 29 (4), 441-460; Pirie, I. (2018). Korea and Taiwan: The Crisis of Investment-Led Growth and the End of the Developmental State. *Journal of Contemporary Asia*, 48 (1), 133-158; Pirie, I. (2007). *The Korean Developmental State: From Dirigisme to Neoliberalism*. London: Routledge; Thurbon, E. (2016). *Developmental Mindset: Revival of Financial Activism in South Korea*. Ithaca, NY: Cornell University Press; Kalinowski, T. and Park, M. (2016). South Korean Development Co-operation in Africa: The Legacy of a Developmental State. *Africa Spectrum*, 51 (3), 61-75.
50 Yeung, H. (2014). Governing the Market in a Globalising Era: Developmental states, Global Production Networks and Intra-Firm Dynamics in East Asia. *Review*

channels of discussion and negotiation with the Korean state.[51] While the Kim Dae-jung (*Kim Tae-jung*) government attempted to limit the power of the *chaebŏl* in the aftermath of the 1997 crisis,[52] they have only grown even more powerful, particularly under the Lee Myung-bak government.[53] Lee's pledge to restore economic growth made the state heavily dependent upon the *chaebŏl* since, despite their status of TNCs, they are the core pillars of Korea's competitiveness in the global economy. State-business collusion in contemporary Korea should not come as a surprise.

The hyper globalist thesis[54] suggested that with globalization, states were becoming increasingly powerless in their ability to shape the global economy and regulate transnational flows of capital.[55] It follows that firms are largely operating in autonomy from governments and can assert authority over these through various forms of political pressure, including financial contributions and lobbying. In response, some have suggested that states retain their ability to direct national economies,[56] act to regulate national economies but also function as "agencies" in new architectures of global governance,[57] and are transforming into a new form of state (a "global state").[58]

Beyond the state and globalization debate, the pressures exercised by capital onto the state to shape policies are widely considered as corrup-

---

of International Political Economy, 21 (1), 70-101; Kim, Y. (2008). *Bureaucrats and Entrepreneurs: The State and the Chaebol in Korea*. Seoul: Jimoondang.

51 See the Federation of Korean Industries, for instance, in Schwak 2019a, pp. 113-114.

52 Hundt, D. (2005). A Legitimate Paradox: Neo-Liberal Reform and the Return of the State in Korea. *Journal of Development Studies*, 41 (2), 242-260; Dent, C. M. (2018). East Asia's New Developmentalism: State Capacity, Climate Change and Low-Carbon Development. *Third World Quarterly*, 39 (6), 1191-1210.

53 Kalinowski, T. (2009). The Politics of Market Reforms: Korea's Path from Chaebol Republic to Market Democracy and Back. *Contemporary Politics*, 15 (3), 287-304, p. 288.

54 Hirst, P. and Thompson, G. (1995). Globalization and the Future of the Nation State. *Economy and Society*, 24, 409-442.

55 Ohmae, K. (1995). *The End of the Nation State: The Rise of Regional Economies*. New York: Simon and Schuster.

56 Weiss, L. (1997). Globalization and the Myth of Powerless State. *New Left Review*, 225, 3-27.

57 Hirst and Thompson 1995.

58 Shaw, M. (1997). The State of Globalization: Towards a Theory of State Transformation. *Review of International Political Economy*, 4 (3), 497-513, p. 504.

tion.[59] The concept of corruption fails to integrate the structural changes in the form and function of the state, and its relationship with capital, in an era of global competitiveness. Firms do not always actively attempt to shape policies because they do not need to. In an era of "competition states,"[60] numerous governments are strongly committed to liberal economic policies to pursue national competitiveness. In order to achieve national competitiveness, they rely on national companies (even when those operate as TNCs[61]). Governments are hence fully aware of firms' interests (and can even shape those interests[62]) and they organically integrate those corporate interests into policymaking. The power of capital is not instrumental and the result of lobbying efforts;[63] it is structural. It shapes states' policy preferences and political economic strategies and visions. State and capital are connected by a relationship of structural interdependence.

In Korea, three factors explain this structural interdependence between the state and the *chaebŏl*. On the one hand, path-dependent developmentalism characterizes policymaking, creating a "continuous informal and structural inclusion of business actors in both domestic and foreign policymaking,"[64] through both personal connections developed in shared social circles, and the maintenance of "institutional frameworks and interactions with state elites."[65] On the other hand, from the authoritarian Park Chung-hee to the liberal government of Kim Young-sam, the *raison d'etre* of the Korean state has been the pursuit of competitiveness in the global econ-

---

59 See discussions in: Theobald, R. (2002). Containing Corruption. *New Political Economy*, 7 (3), 435-449; Hopkin, J. (2002). States, Markets and Corruption: A Review of Some Recent Literature. *Review of International Political Economy*, 9 (3), 574-590; Harriss-White, B. and White G. (1996). Introduction: Liberalization and the New Corruption. *IDS Bulletin*, 27 (2), 1-5.

60 Cerny, P. G. (1997). Paradoxes of the Competition State: The Dynamics of Political Globalisation. *Government and Opposition*, 32 (2), 251-274.

61 Starrs, S. (2013). American Economic Power Hasn't Declined – It Globalized! Summoning the Data and Taking Globalization Seriously. *International Studies Quarterly*, 57 (4), 817-830.

62 Woll, C. (2008). *Firm Interests*. Ithaca, NY: Cornell University Press.

63 I am of course not arguing here that lobbying does not take place to achieve specific policies. But the structural framework that benefits capital is also achieved and reproduced without the need for such pressures from business interest groups.

64 Schwak 2019a, p. 110.

65 Kim 2008, p. 236.

omy.[66] Under Park's regime of developmentalism, this meant industrial catch-up with Organization of Economic Cooperation and Development (OECD) member states and competitiveness of Korean products on the world market. Under Kim Young-sam and his successors' "developmental liberalism,"[67] the political obsession shifted to the achievement of state competitiveness itself – making Korea a (financially, legally, culturally) attractive location for different forms of global capital. The *chaebŏl* are key partners of the government in both configurations. While they needed state support and protection to grow in the catch-up era, Korea's economy is now dependent upon them, both to generate growth but also to create a dynamic and innovative business environment in the country. Therefore "national economic interest is more often than not assumed to align with the chaebol interests."[68]

Additionally, the power to make political economic decisions and enact regulations still lies in the hands of governments. Capital cannot operate as it wishes without states' (tacit or explicit) support. In Korea, while the *chaebŏl* are able to operate autonomously by integrating Global Value Chains, this renewed dependence of the *chaebŏl* upon the state is particularly clear in foreign aid policymaking, a sector in which the state eases market access for the *chaebŏl* in developing countries.[69]

This changing relationship explains the instances of state-business collusion against which the candlelight protesters revolted.[70] Scholars[71] and the Korean public regularly analyze these forms of collusion as corruption. This is problematic. Corruption is imagined as a distortion of a well-functioning liberal economic system. In this system, the state and the market are construed as two distinct entities that can cooperate through competitive mechanisms (e.g. a call for tender for a Public Private Partnership[72]), but that must be independent of one another. However, this purely transparent and competitive market economy in which corruption is

66 Schwak, J. (2016a). Branding South Korea in a Competitive World Order: Discourses and Dispositives in Neoliberal Governmentality. *Asian Studies Review*, 40 (3), 426-443.
67 Chang, K.-S. (2019). *Developmental Liberalism in South Korea: Formation, Degeneration, and Transnationalization*. Basingstoke: Palgrave Macmillan.
68 Schwak 2019a, p. 110.
69 Schwak 2019a; Schwak, J. (2019b). Nothing under the Sun: Korea's Developmental Promises and Neoliberal Illusions. *Third World Quarterly*, 41 (2), 302-320.
70 Dostal 2017, p. 488.
71 Kalinowski, T. (2016). Trends and Mechanism of Corruption in South Korea. *The Pacific Review*, 49 (4), 625-645, p. 633.
72 Kalinowski 2016, p. 629.

but a distortion that can be removed with liberal measures[73] is an economic myth. This very economic myth is reproduced by some articles of Korea's constitution, which motivated the Constitutional Court's decision to impeach Park.[74] Park is found guilty of having "pressured private companies to extort funds and intervene in internal decisions, such as with personnel, which violates the constitutional guarantee of property rights (Art. 23, Sec. 1), market economy order (Art. 119, Sec.1), and the freedom to choose one's occupation (Art. 15)."[75] Park is found guilty of having distorted Korea's competitive market economy, while it is precisely the need to maintain a nationally competitive economy that creates the structural conditions of state-business collusion. The *chaebŏl*'s structural power over the Korean economy and society is the outcome of both local specificities (the developmental experience) and global realities (the pursuit of states' economic competitiveness as the only horizon of policymaking since the 1980s).

4. Park's Impeachment: Class Conflict and Middle-Class Anxieties

The candlelight protesters wanted to oust Park from the Blue House, Korea's presidential palace, but they also protested the more persistent state-*chaebŏl* collusion, whose mechanisms I have now highlighted. The whole process of Park's impeachment can therefore be read through a class lens. Rather than an exclusive middle-class revolt against authoritarianism, the impeachment process reveals the economic anxieties of the Korean middle-class in a post-developmental, stagnating economy dominated by the *chaebŏl* and characterized by high youth unemployment, dramatic elderly poverty,[76] growing labor precarity,[77] and lack of opportunities. It is therefore a demand for political economic democracy, rather than merely electoral democracy.

---

73 Kalinowski 2016, pp. 626, 633.
74 Guichard, J. (2022). The Political Role of Courts in the Trials of South Korea's 2016-2017 Impeachment Scandal. In Dumin, J. (Ed.), *South Korea after the 2017 Impeachment: Implications for Politics, Society, and Democracy*. Baden-Baden: Nomos, 67-96.
75 Cited in Mosler 2017, p. 130.
76 Kim, Y.-Y., Baek, S.-H. and Lee, S. S.-Y. (2018). Precarious Elderly Workers in Post-Industrial South Korea. *Journal of Contemporary Asia*, 48 (3), 465-484.
77 Lee, Y. (2015). The Birth of the Insecure Class in South Korea. *Globalizations*, 12 (2), 184-202.

The animosity against the state-*chaebŏl* conundrum, as staged in popular culture and narratives evoked above, represents a new expression of class conflict as a growing portion of the Korean middle-class increasingly finds itself unsure of its socio-economic status in an increasingly unequal society.[78] This argument is in line with Kim's study on "spoon theory,"[79] which looks at popular discourses in contemporary Korea on a hereditary elite that can afford to eat with golden or silver spoons while the rest of Koreans must do with clay spoons. This study is a welcome re-contextualization of Park's impeachment in circumstances of "popular discontent over the loss of opportunities for social mobility based on family ties" and inherited inequality.[80] Dostal also rightly notes that the candlelight protests revealed a "tangible lack of fit between the self-image of a middle-class society and concrete social realities."[81]

Recent studies have demonstrated that Korea is an increasingly polarized society, suffering from economic polarization[82] and income inequality.[83] According to Statistics Korea, Korea's GINI index was 0.304 in 2016 (latest available data).[84] Overall, this index has increased since the 1997 crisis.[85] Korea's labor market has greatly suffered from the shock of the 1997 Asian financial crisis and its aftermath, particularly the flexibilization of labor reforms implemented by the Kim Dae-jung government. This has led to the emergence of a divide between regular and irregular workers,[86] with

---

78 You, J.-S. (2019). The Political Economy of Inequality and Capture in South Korea. In Park, C.-M. and Uslaner, E. M. (Eds.), *Inequality and Democratic Politics in East Asia*. Abingdon/New York, NY: Routledge; Kim, Y. (2018). Hell Joseon: Polarization and Social Contention in a Neo-liberal Age. In Kim, Y. (Ed.), *Korea's Quest for Economic Democratization*. Basingstoke: Palgrave Macmillan, 1-20.

79 Kim, H. (2017). "Spoon Theory" and the Fall of a Populist Princess in Seoul. *The Journal of Asian Studies*, 76 (4), 839-849.

80 Kim 2017, pp. 840, 843.

81 Dostal 2017, p. 486.

82 Koo, H. (2019). Rising Inequality and Shifting Class Boundaries in South Korea in the Neo-Liberal Era. *Journal of Contemporary Asia*, September 16, 2019, [online]. Available at: https://www.tandfonline.com/doi/abs/10.1080/00472336.2019. 1663242 [Accessed January 20, 2020].

83 Kwon, O. Y. (2019). *Social Trust and Economic Development: The Case of South Korea*. Cheltenham: Edward Elgar Publishing.

84 Data available at: http://kostat.go.kr/portal/eng/pressReleases/6/4/index.board?b mode=read&aSeq=361894&pageNo=&rowNum=10&amSeq=&sTarget=&sTxt= [Accessed February 6, 2020].

85 Kang, S. (2001). *Globalization and Income Inequality in Korea: An Overview*. Available at: https://www.oecd.org/dev/2698445.pdf [Accessed February 6, 2020].

86 Lee 2015.

irregular workers suffering the double burden of economic precariousness and social precariousness.[87] As of January 2018, 46% of employees in Korea were irregular workers,[88] excluded from a stability that has become a privilege of regular workers, or what Kim calls "labor aristocracy."[89]

Most authors recognize that Korea's middle-class has been shrinking since 1997.[90] Perceptions also matter: fewer and fewer Korean citizens consider themselves to belong to the middle-class.[91] This decline of the middle-class is connected to the elite-based nature of capital accumulation in Korea[92] and the increasing concentration of income in the hands of the *chaeböl*,[93] notably income acquired through non-labor revenues.[94] Polarization is not limited to income: it extends to access to real estate, education, and employment.[95]

The result of these different forms of socio-economic polarization is the emergence (or resurgence) of a class-based society, where class divisions deepen long-standing divisions in modern Korean society (regional, ideological, and generational divisions).[96] Although Kim and Park find no conclusive data that connect electoral class and electoral behavior in con-

---

87 Kim, Y. and Park, S. (2018). Emerging Cleavages in Korean Society: Region, Generation, Ideology and Class. In Kim, Y. (Ed.), *Korea's Quest for Economic Democratization*. Basingstoke: Palgrave Macmillan, 63-88, p. 63.

88 This excludes unpaid family workers, see Schwak 2019b, p. 12.

89 Kim, H.-A. (2018). Labor Polarization: Labor Aristocracy versus Irregular Workers in Post-developmental Korea. In Kim, Y. (Ed.), *Korea's Quest for Economic Democratization*. Basingstoke: Palgrave Macmillan, 119-140.

90 Yang, M. (2018). *From Miracle to Mirage: The Making and Unmaking of the Korean Middle Class, 1960-2015*. Ithaca, NY: Cornell University Press; Na, E.Y. (2009). Oehwanwigi ihu kyech'ŭng-ŭi yanggŭkhwa: pyŏnhwadoen ilsang-gwa sobisaenghwal [The Gap between Social Stratification in the Aftermath of the 1997 Crisis: The Change of Living Conditions and Daily Life as a Consumer]. *Chosa Yŏn'gu [Research Study]*, 10 (1), 1-32, p. 9; Im, H.-B. (2018). Globalization, Democracy and Social Polarization in South Korea. In Kim, Y. (Ed.), *Korea's Quest for Economic Democratization*. Basingstoke: Palgrave Macmillan, 89-118; Kim and Park 2018.

91 Na 2009, p. 9.

92 Im, H.B. (2006). Korean Democracy in an Era of Polarization. In *Co-sponsored conference of the Korean Political Science Association and Korean Sociological Association*.

93 Kim, Y. 2018, p. 3.

94 Shin G.-H. and Shin D.-G (2007). Sodŭkpunp'o yanggŭkhwa-ŭi t'ŭksŏng-gwa kyŏngje, sahoejŏk yŏnghyang [Income Polarization and Its Social and Economic Impact]. *Han'gukkyŏngje-ŭi Punsŏk [Korean Economy Analysis]*, 13 (2), 63-123.

95 Im 2018, pp. 29-30.

96 Kim and Park 2018; Suh D. (2018). Democracy Disenchanted and Autocracy Glamorized in Korea. In Kim, Y. (Ed.), *Korea's Quest for Economic Democratization*. Basingstoke: Palgrave Macmillan, 41-62.

temporary Korea, they point to the emergence of a "class consciousness"[97] among Korean citizens who share a similar experience of social downgrading.[98] This is worsened by the lack of opportunities for Korean youth, combined, in parallel, with a rise in the number of suicides among the elderly induced by a weak welfare system.[99]

While income inequality and redistribution of economic resources are surely factors of concern, it is particularly the unequal access to socio-economic opportunities that has angered Korean citizens. Growing anxieties about inequalities of opportunity have been highlighted by the recent *Annyŏngdŭl hasimnikka* [How are we *all* doing?[100]] online protest movement, which denounced the dissolution of the social contract in an increasingly individualistic society, and by online discussions of *Hell Chosŏn*.[101] With the catchphrase *Hell Chosŏn*, predominantly young Koreans expressed their anguish and anger with a society reminiscent of the rigid class structure of Chosŏn society,[102] and above all which is *both* highly competitive and highly exclusive.

My empirical research also revealed a notable perception of the breakdown of Korean meritocracy. Fear of the future and uncertainty were recurrent themes in my discussions with young Koreans, some of them mentioning their desire to escape the country. Among a variety of questions, survey respondents (who belonged to different generations) were asked which qualities they considered to be necessary to success in Korean society. They were provided with a list of nine answers (seven attributes, and 'Other' and 'Prefer not to answer'): Beauty; Good education; Family networks; Self-discipline/diligence; Ambition; Talent/creativity; Money. Most respondents considered that (in order) money, academic training and family networks were key to succeed in Korean society. In contrast, when respondents were provided with the same list of qualities and asked to choose those they considered necessary to succeed in foreign countries,

---

97 Kim and Park 2018, p. 84.

98 Im 2018, p. 29.

99 Schwak, J. (2016b). L'inquiétant taux de suicide des personnes âgées en Corée du Sud [The Worrying Suicide Rate of the Elderly in South Korea]. *Korea Analysis*, 9, 24-28.

100 'dŭl' is a suffix that indicates a plural form. It is facultative, and in this sentence, it is used to emphasize the collective subject that is threatened by growing social polarization.

101 Kim, Y. 2018, p. 1.

102 Chosŏn was the last dynasty that ruled over the Korean peninsula. It had a highly hierarchical and institutionalized social structure in which birth largely determined one's life opportunities.

their answers were significantly different. Outside of Korea, success was perceived as meritocratic, and determined by individual abilities and willingness to work: indeed, respondents gave priority to (in order) creativity, ambition, and discipline. For respondents, meritocracy in Korea had broken down: Korean society was perceived as structurally unequal, and one's socio-economic status determined by factors beyond one's individual will (such as family networks or beauty, a highly deterministic factor one can only seek to overcome through expensive plastic surgery operations). In Korea, class structure was perceived as a major determinant in one's life opportunities, while foreign societies were imagined as unconstrained by class determinants and rewarding of individual qualities.

This perception was corroborated by a set of interviews I conducted. The first interviewee was a young entrepreneur I met in the prosperous district of Sŏch'o-gu in Seoul. He was introduced to me through personal connections. The interview was conducted in English, as the interviewee was a fluent English speaker. He had graduated from a prestigious Seoul university and had grown up in Sŏch'o-gu in a well-off business family. Although his economic situation was unstable when we met, and despite some fierce criticism he held against Korea's competitive education system and labor market, he believed in Korean meritocracy. When I asked him to choose among the attributes needed to succeed in Korean society, he chose "ambition" and "self-discipline."[103]

The second interview was conducted with a group of undergraduate students from Masan. Masan is a predominantly industrial area and is much less cosmopolitan and well-off than the Seoul area. The group interview was organized by one of my colleagues and conducted in Korean (with some translation support from my colleague, who was present during the interview). I asked these students the question I had asked the young entrepreneur and the survey respondents. Consensus quickly emerged among them: to succeed in Korean society, one needs "social networks from school, blood, and local community" (in other words, educational, family, and regional networks). They added that one's experience and appearance also mattered.[104]

In my interviews and during the months I spent conducting fieldwork in Korea in 2015-2016, few grievances were voiced regarding income inequality. The accumulation of wealth itself was not a question that was often discussed. Popular resentment was directed towards the accumula-

---

103 Author's interview, Seoul, April 2016.
104 Author's interview, Masan, April 2016.

tion of social capital and the structural conditions that shaped and limited one's life opportunities. Koreans had imagined themselves as a meritocratic society through the developmental era, which promised fair economic rewards for those who worked hard and invested in their education.[105] However, several interviewees considered that Korea's competitive educational system and labor market were not open to all. A social worker and mother of two I interviewed in Korean at her home in Mapo-gu, in a lower middle-class area of the district, Seoul explained: "To go to SKY[106] universities, there is competition nationally and within Seoul in high schools. But some people cannot participate, it's restrictive."[107]

In this context, Park Geun-hye came to embody the anxieties and frustrations of middle and lower-middle classes, particularly of the post-developmental generation, for whom the meritocratic *'chal sarabose'* [Let's get rich] slogan promoted by Park Geun-hye's father, authoritarian president Park Chung-hee, during the developmental era, is clearly at odds with everyday material realities. Park was particularly resented because she used her *inherited* privileges, thereby embodying the hereditary nature of socio-economic opportunities in contemporary Korea.[108] The collusion she engaged in with the *chaebŏl* was the cherry on an already bitter cake: Park became the visible symptom of a deeper political economic pathology in which the state-*chaebŏl* relationship is resented as a corrupted relationship that limits opportunities for the majority of Korean citizens. The Korean 2016-2017 impeachment was a popular outburst against Park, but it expressed deeper frustrations about the state-*chaebŏl* relationship and inherited opportunities. Impeachment was not merely a constitutional mechanism that allowed for Park's removal. It was a political economic process through which Korean citizens peacefully revolted against a structural capture of economic opportunities by the state-*chaebŏl* nexus.

Conclusion

This chapter has analyzed the nature of Park's impeachment process. Personalizing the candlelight protests is an analytical risk since it can overshadow the structural characteristics of Korea's political economy and

---

105 Dostal 2017, p. 486.
106 Acronym referring to Korea's three most prestigious universities: Seoul National University, Korea University, Yonsei University.
107 Author's interview, Seoul, April 2016.
108 Kim, H.-A. 2018.

the conditions that made such collusion possible. Considering the existing literature and its gaps, it was hypothesized that Park's impeachment was a political economic process through which citizens rejected a specific state-business configuration. Based on micro-sociological data collected on Korean citizens' perceptions of the country's political economic situation, I have shown that Park's impeachment process was not only about Park herself: it was also a class-based revolt against growing inequalities of opportunity and social polarization, epitomized by the structural power of the *chaebŏl* in contemporary Korea. Beyond Korea, such findings indicate that impeachment can serve as a form of political economic protest along with more traditional methods of protest for economic democracy.

There are, however, three obstacles to consolidate economic democracy in contemporary Korea that were not resolved by Park's impeachment. First of all, the Constitutional Court's decision to approve Park's impeachment could constitute what I call a 'legal fix:'[109] by removing Park from office, it seemingly appeased socio-economic tensions in a context of interdependent state-*chaebŏl* relations and growing inequalities of opportunity. The impeachment process has generated social relief by acknowledging, not only in moral terms, but also in legal terms, the crimes Park had engaged in. However, legal decisions do not resolve political crises. As Pérez-Liñán rightly notes, "impeachment may be the best institutional mechanism to channel the outbursts of public indignation, but it is often ineffective in preventing the episodes of corruption or abuse of power that create popular frustration in the first place."[110] The response to this revolt must therefore be political. This is particularly the case since by categorizing Park as a corrupted agent pitted against Korean capitalism and its competitive nature, the impeachment process does not effectively challenge the contemporary configuration of Korean capitalism, nor does it signal a shift in the state-capital-society relations.

Second, it seems that the candlelight protests were characterized by what I would call the 'illusion of classlessness.' The observers' narrative was that the protests gathered large segments of the Korean population who opposed Park's presidency, above socio-economic status or age, ideological commitment, or partisan affiliation. The apparent social consensus that characterized the protests is a welcome development but it should be taken for what it is: a temporary alliance against a president who came to

---

109 Paraphrasing Harvey, D. (2001). Globalization and the Spatial Fix. *Geographische revue*, 2.
110 Pérez-Liñán 2007, p. 13.

embody the current nature of Korean capitalism. It should not be read as a resolution of conflicts and should not be interpreted through a linear liberal narrative of a progressive national consensus promising positive and unchallenged change. Ironically, by their consensual and seemingly classless narrative, the protests can be read as a break from politics. The post-impeachment political landscape in Korea has already proven to be a return to the inherently conflictual nature of democratic politics.

Indeed, Moon's election took place in a virulently anti-*chaebŏl* context after Park's impeachment. Moon was hailed by his supporters and by liberal observers as a socially progressive politician who had promised to reduce the *chaebŏl*'s power over Korean society and to lead ambitious social reforms, such as increasing the minimum wage and limiting the maximum legal working time. His election as Time Magazine's 5th personality of the year in 2015 testified of the Moon fever that had followed his presidential ascendancy. However, since his election, Moon has been caught up by the confrontation of interests within Korean society. His social reforms have been less popular than expected. He has also come to realize, like Kim Dae-jung before him,[111] that under the currently dominant political paradigm, the Korean state is heavily dependent upon the *chaebŏl* as their economic output largely determines the economic stability of the country. The *chaebŏl* have notably appeared as necessary actors to advance Moon's strategy of rapprochement with North Korea.

Before Korea was internationally hailed for its management of the ongoing COVID-19 crisis, Moon has faced intense domestic criticism. Moon had chosen not to close Korea's borders to Chinese citizens to preserve Korea's privileged economic relationship with China (just in November 2019, 505,369 Chinese visitors had travelled to Korea[112]). In reaction to this controversial decision, more than a million Korean citizens had signed an online petition calling for Moon's impeachment claiming his inability to protect Korea from the virus. Impeachment claims therefore run the risk of being routinized to resolve the tensions arising from electoral democratic politics and oppose chief executives' decisions, regardless of the principle of majority rule. Despite such demands, Moon's Democratic Party (*Tŏburŏminjudang*) overwhelmingly won the legislative elections of April 2020. But the upcoming economic crisis will again bring to the fore

---

111 Kalinowski 2009, p. 288.
112 Data available at: Korea Tourism Organization. *Korea, Monthly Statistics of Tourism*, [online]. Available at: https://kto.visitkorea.or.kr/eng/tourismStatics /keyFacts/KoreaMonthlyStatistics/eng/inout/inout.kto [Accessed June 20, 2020].

debates surrounding the growing precariousness of labor and inequalities of access to socio-economic resources and opportunities.

References

Algan, Y., Beasley, E., Cohen, D., Foucault, M. and Peron, M. (2019). Qui sont les Gilets jaunes et leurs soutiens? [Who Are the Yellow Vests and Their Supporters ?] *Observatoire du Bien-etre du CEPREMAP et CEVIPOF*. Available at: https://www.sciencespo.fr/cevipof/sites/sciencespo.fr.cevipof/files/-Qui-sont-les-Gilets-jaunes-et-leurs-soutiens-1.pdf [Accessed January 28, 2020].

Amsden, A. (1989). *Asia's Next Giant: South Korea and Late Industrialisation*. New York: Oxford University Press.

Bréchon P. (2019). Le mouvement des 'gilets jaunes' ou le retour des valeurs matérialistes? [The Yellow Vests Movement: Return of Materialist Values?]. *Revue Politique et Parlementaire*, 1090, 113-120. Available at: https://www.revuepolitique.fr/le-mouvement-des-gilets-jaunes-ou-le-retour-des-valeurs-materialistes/ (Accessed January 28, 2020).

Bedeski, R. (2017). The Korean State and Candlelight Democracy: Paradigms and Evolution. *Journal of Contemporary Eastern Asia*, 16 (2), 82-92.

Black, C. L. Jr. (1998). *Impeachment: A Handbook*. New Haven: Yale University Press.

Carroll, T. (2014). Hong Kong's Pro-Democracy Movement is about Inequality: The Elite Knows It. *The Guardian*, July 28, 2014, [online]. Available at: https://www.theguardian.com/commentisfree/2014/jul/28/hong-kongs-pro-democracy-movement-is-about-inequality-the-elite-knows-it [Accessed February 6, 2020].

Cerny, P. G. (1997). Paradoxes of the Competition State: The Dynamics of Political Globalisation. *Government and Opposition*, 32 (2), 251-274.

Chang, H.-J. (2006). *The East Asian Development Experience: The Miracle, the Crisis and the Future*. Penang: Third World Network

Chang, K.-S. (2019). *Developmental Liberalism in South Korea: Formation, Degeneration, and Transnationalization*. Basingstoke: Palgrave Macmillan.

Chang, P. Y. (2018). Candlelight Protests in South Korea: The Legacies of Authoritarianism and Democratization. *Ehwa Journal of Social Sciences*, 34 (1), 5-18.

Choe, Y. (2018). Chaebol Affect: Emotional Capital and the Interiority of Wealth in Im Sang-soo's 'The Housemaid' and 'The Taste of Money'. *Cinema Journal*, 57 (4), 25-46.

Dent, C. M. (2018). East Asia's New Developmentalism: State Capacity, Climate Change and Low-Carbon Development. *Third World Quarterly*, 39 (6), 1191-1210.

Diamond, L. (1999). *Developing Democracy: Toward Consolidation*. Baltimore: Johns Hopkins University Press.

Diamond, L., and Kim, B. K. (2000). *Consolidating Democracy in South Korea*. Boulder: Lynne Rienner.

Dostal, J. M. (2017). South Korean Presidential Politics Turns Liberal: Transformative Change or Business as Usual? *The Political Quarterly*, 88 (3), 480-491.

Doucette, J. (2017). The Occult of Personality: Korea's Candlelight Protests and the Impeachment of Park Geun-hye. *The Journal of Asian Studies*, 76 (4), 851-860.

Gerhardt, M. J. (2019). *The Federal Impeachment Process: A Constitutional and Historical Analysis*. Chicago/London: University of Chicago Press.

Guichard, J. (2022). The Political Role of Courts in the Trials of South Korea's 2016-2017 Impeachment Scandal. In Dumin, J. (Ed.), *South Korea after the 2017 Impeachment: Implications for Politics, Society, and Democracy*. Baden-Baden: Nomos, 67-96.

Guilluy, C. (2016). *Le Crépuscule de la France d'en Haut [Twilight of the Elites: Prosperity, the Periphery, and the Future of France]*. Paris: Flammarion.

Harriss-White, B. and White G. (1996). Introduction: Liberalization and the New Corruption. *IDS Bulletin*, 27 (2), 1-5.

Harvey, D. (2001). Globalization and the "Spatial Fix". *Geographische revue*, 2.

Hee, M. and Yun, S. (2018). Selective Exposure and Political Polarization of Public Opinion on the Presidential Impeachment in South Korea: Facebook vs KakaoTalk. *Korea Observer*, 49 (1), 137-159.

Hirst, P. and Thompson, G. (1995). Globalization and the Future of the Nation State. *Economy and Society*, 24, 409-442.

Hopkin, J. (2002). States, Markets and Corruption: A Review of Some Recent Literature. *Review of International Political Economy*, 9 (3), 574-590.

Hundt, D. (2005). A Legitimate Paradox: Neo-Liberal Reform and the Return of the State in Korea. *Journal of Development Studies*, 41 (2), 242-260.

Im, H. B. (2006). Korean Democracy in an Era of Polarization. In *Co-sponsored conference of the Korean Political Science Association and Korean Sociological Association*.

Im, H. B. (2018). Globalization, Democracy and Social Polarization in South Korea. In Kim, Y. (Ed.), *Korea's Quest for Economic Democratization*. Basingstoke: Palgrave Mac Millan, 89-118.

Jellab, A. (2019). Gilet jaunes: les enjeux d'une mobilization. Les 'gilets jaunes' à l'épreuve de la démocratie et des injustices sociales [Gilets Jaunes: Issues Around a Mobilization. The 'Gilets jaunes' up against Social Injustice and the Democratic System]. *Futuribles*, 6 (433), 81-94.

Kada, N. (2003). The Role of Investigative Committees in the Presidential Impeachment Processes in Brazil and Colombia. *Legislative Studies Quarterly*, 28 (1), 29-54.

Kakakhel, M. N. (1978). The Theory of Impeachment in Islamic polity. *Islamic Studies*, 17 (2), 93-103.

Kalinowski, T. (2009). The Politics of Market Reforms: Korea's Path from Chaebol Republic to Market Democracy and Back. *Contemporary Politics*, 15 (3), 287-304.

Kalinowski, T. (2016). Trends and Mechanism of Corruption in South Korea. *The Pacific Review*, 49 (4), 625-645.

Kalinowski, T. and Park, M. (2016). South Korean Development Co-operation in Africa: The Legacy of a Developmental State. *Africa Spectrum*, 51 (3), 61-75.

Kang, S. (2001). *Globalization and Income Inequality in Korea: An Overview*. Available at: https://www.oecd.org/dev/2698445.pdf [Accessed February 6, 2020].

Kelly, R. (2016). South Korea's Most Bizarre Corruption Scandal Yet. *The Diplomat*, November 4, 2016. Available at: https://thediplomat.com/2016/11/south-koreas-most-bizarre-corruption-scandal-yet/ [Accessed January 19, 2020].

Kim, H. (2017). "Spoon Theory" and the Fall of a Populist Princess in Seoul. *The Journal of Asian Studies*, 76 (4), 839-849.

Kim, H.-A. (2018). Labor Polarization: Labor Aristocracy versus Irregular Workers in Post-developmental Korea. In Kim, Y. (Ed.), *Korea's Quest for Economic Democratization*. Basingstoke: Palgrave Macmillan, 119-140.

Kim, S. (2019). From Remonstrance to Impeachment: A Curious Case of "Confucian Constitutionalism" in South Korea. *Law and Social Inquiry*, 44 (3), 586-616.

Kim, Y. (2008). *Bureaucrats and Entrepreneurs: The State and the Chaebol in Korea*. Seoul: Jimoondang.

Kim, Y. (2018). Hell Joseon: Polarization and Social Contention in a Neo-liberal Age. In Kim, Y. (Ed.), *Korea's Quest for Economic Democratization*. Basingstoke: Palgrave Macmillan, 1-20.

Kim, Y. and Park, S. (2018). Emerging Cleavages in Korean Society: Region, Generation, Ideology and Class. In Kim, Y. (Ed.), *Korea's Quest for Economic Democratization*. Basingstoke: Palgrave Macmillan, 63-88.

Kim, Y.-T. (1999). Neoliberalism and the Decline of the Developmental State. *Journal of Contemporary Asia*, 29 (4), 441-460.

Kim, Y.-Y., Baek, S.-H. and Lee, S. S.-Y. (2018). Precarious Elderly Workers in Post-Industrial South Korea. *Journal of Contemporary Asia*, 48 (3), 465-484.

Koo, H. (2019). Rising Inequality and Shifting Class Boundaries in South Korea in the Neo-Liberal Era. *Journal of Contemporary Asia*, September 16, 2019, [online]. Available at: https://www.tandfonline.com/doi/abs/10.1080/00472336.2019.1663242 [Accessed January 20, 2020].

Korea Tourism Organization. *Korea, Monthly Statistics of Tourism*, [online]. Available at: https://kto.visitkorea.or.kr/eng/tourismStatics/keyFacts/KoreaMonthlyStatistics/eng/inout/inout.kto [Accessed June 20, 2020].

Kornbluh, P. (2019). Why Chileans Are Protesting for a New Socioeconomic Order. *The Nation*, December 10, 2019, [online]. Available at: https://www.thenation.com/article/archive/chile-protests-inequality-pinochet/ [Accessed February 6, 2020].

Kwon, O. Y. (2019). *Social Trust and Economic Development: The Case of South Korea*. Cheltenham: Edward Elgar Publishing.

Labovitz J. R. and Labovitz, M. (1978). *Presidential Impeachment*. New Haven: Yale University Press.

Langman, J. (2019). From Model to Muddle: Chile's Sad Slide Into Upheaval. *Foreign Policy*, November 23, 2019, [online]. Available at: https://foreignpolicy.com/2019/11/23/chile-upheaval-protests-model-muddle-free-market/ [Accessed February 6, 2020].

Lee, Y. (2015). The Birth of the Insecure Class in South Korea. *Globalizations*, 12 (2), 184-202.

Mosler, H. B. (2017). The Institution of Presidential Impeachment in South Korea, 1992-2017. *Verfassung und Recht in Übersee*, 50 (2), 111-134.

Na, E.Y. (2009). Oehwanwigi ihu kyech'ŭng-ŭi yanggŭkhwa: pyŏnhwadoen ilsang-gwa sobisaenghwal [The Gap between Social Stratification in the Aftermath of the 1997 Crisis: The Change of Living Conditions and Daily Life as a Consumer]. *Chosa Yŏn'gu [Research Study]*, 10 (1), 1-32.

Nugent, C. (2020). From Chile to Hong Kong, the World Saw a Lot of Protests in 2019. Here's Why That Trend Is Going to Continue. *Time*, January 16, 2020, [online]. Available at: https://time.com/5766422/protests-unrest-2019-2020/ [Accessed February 6, 2020].

Ohmae, K. (1995). *The End of the Nation State: The Rise of Regional Economies*. New York: Simon and Schuster.

Ortmann S. (2015). The Umbrella Movement in Hong Kong: From Economic Concerns to the Rejection of Materialism. *Kyoto Review of Southeast Asia*, 17.

Papuchon, A. and Duvoux, N. (2019). How to Measure Subjective Poverty in France – And What This Tells Us About the Anger of the Yellow Vests. *EUROPP LSE Blog*. Available at: https://ssrn.com/abstract=3312298 or http://dx.doi.org/10.2139/ssrn.3312298 [Accessed January 28, 2020].

Park, S. (2018). The Politics of Impeaching Shamanism: Regulating Religions in the Korean Public Sphere. *Journal of Church and State*, 60 (4), 636-660.

Pérez-Liñán, A. (2007). *Presidential Impeachment and the New Political Instability in Latin America*. Cambridge: Cambridge University Press.

Pirie, I. (2007). *The Korean Developmental State: From Dirigisme to Neoliberalism*. London: Routledge.

Pirie, I. (2018). Korea and Taiwan: The Crisis of Investment-Led Growth and the End of the Developmental State. *Journal of Contemporary Asia*, 48 (1), 133-158.

Schwak, J. (2016a). Branding South Korea in a Competitive World Order: Discourses and Dispositives in Neoliberal Governmentality. *Asian Studies Review*, 40 (3), 426-443.

Schwak, J. (2016b). L'inquiétant taux de suicide des personnes âgées en Corée du Sud [The Worrying Suicide Rate of the Elderly in South Korea]. *Korea Analysis*, 9, 24-28.

Schwak, J. (2019a). Dangerous Liaisons? State-Chaebol Cooperation and the Global Privatisation of Development. *Journal of Contemporary Asia*, 49 (1), 104-126.

Schwak, J. (2019b). Nothing New under the Sun: Korea's Developmental Promises and Neoliberal Illusions. *Third World Quarterly*, 41 (2), 302-320.

Shaw, M. (1997). The State of Globalization: Towards a Theory of State Transformation. *Review of International Political Economy*, 4 (3), 497-513.

Shifter, M. (2020). The Rebellion Against the Elites in Latin America. *The New York Times*, January 21, 2020, [online]. Available at: https://www.nytimes.com/2020/01/21/opinion/international-world/latin-america-elites-protests.html [Accessed February 6, 2020].

Shin, G. and Moon, R. J. (2017). South Korea After Impeachment. *Journal of Democracy*, 28 (4), 117-131.

Shin G.-H. and Shin D.-G (2007). Sodŭkpunp'o yanggŭkhwa-ŭi t'ŭksŏng-gwa kyŏngje, sahoejŏk yŏnghyang [Income Polarization and Its Social and Economic Impact]. *Han'gukkyŏngje-ŭi Punsŏk* [Korean Economy Analysis], 13 (2), 63-123.

Shin, S. (2020). The Rise and Fall of Park Geun-hye: The Perils of South Korea's Weak Party System. *The Pacific Review*, 33 (1), 153-183.

Starrs, S. (2013). American Economic Power Hasn't Declined – It Globalized! Summoning the Data and Taking Globalization Seriously. *International Studies Quarterly*, 57 (4), 817-830.

Suh, D. (2018). Democracy Disenchanted and Autocracy Glamorized in Korea. In Kim, Y. (Ed.), *Korea's Quest for Economic Democratization*. Basingstoke: Palgrave Macmillan, 41-62.

Sullivan, T. (1998). Impeachment Practice in the Era of Lethal Conflict. *Congress & the Presidency*, 25 (2), 117-128.

Theobald, R. (2002). Containing Corruption. *New Political Economy*, 7 (3), 435-449.

Thurbon, E. (2016). *Developmental Mindset: Revival of Financial Activism in South Korea*. Ithaca, NY: Cornell University Press.

Van Dijk, T. A. (2017). How Global Media Manipulated the Impeachment of Brazilian President Dilma Rousseff. *Discourse and Communication*, 11(2), 199-229.

Weiss, L. (1997). Globalization and the Myth of Powerless State. *New Left Review*, 225, 3-27.

Whitehead, L. (2002). *Democratization: Theory and Experience*. Oxford: Oxford University Press.

Woll, C. (2008). *Firm Interests*. Ithaca, NY: Cornell University Press.

Woo-Cumings, J.E. M. (1999). *The Developmental State*. Ithaca, NY: Cornell University Press.

Yang, M. (2018). *From Miracle to Mirage: The Making and Unmaking of the Korean Middle Class, 1960-2015*. Ithaca, NY: Cornell University Press.

Yeung, H. (2014). Governing the Market in a Globalising Era: Developmental states, Global Production Networks and Intra-Firm Dynamics in East Asia. *Review of International Political Economy*, 21 (1), 70-101.

You, J.-S. (2019). The Political Economy of Inequality and Capture in South Korea. In Park, C.-M. and Uslaner, E. M. (Eds.), *Inequality and Democratic Politics in East Asia*. Abingdon/New York, NY: Routledge.

Who Raised a Candle and Why?
Ascertaining Participation in the 2016-2017 Candlelight Protest in South Korea

Youngho Cho

Introduction

Over the last two decades, political scenes have been shifting "from formal politics to protest" around the world.[1] When citizens of Eastern Europe organized protests to express their dissatisfaction with the 2007-2010 economic recession and people in the Middle East and North Africa drove the 2010-2011 Arab uprisings, comparative scholars tended to attribute these mass protests to the political dysfunction of new democracies and authoritarian countries. However, the yellow vests movement in France demonstrates that protest has become a part of old democracies. Although specific triggers, forms, and causes of these global protests differ, there is one common feature across countries: Centrality of representative politics is in question and citizens are not hesitant to take direct actions that challenge representative elites.[2]

In line with this trend, several million citizens in South Korea (hereafter, Korea) raised candles and participated in anti-government protest every Saturday from late October 2016 to April 2017. With indignant reactions to scandals of President Park Geun-hye (*Pak Kŭn-hye*), these protesters forced legislators of the National Assembly to impeach Park, an act that was unanimously ruled as just by the Constitutional Court. The six months of candlelight protest (*ch'otpuljiphoe*) ended with her dramatic fall from president to prisoner.

---

1 Krastev, I. (2014). From Politics to Protest. *Journal of Democracy*, 25 (4), 5-19, p. 5.
2 According to the report of the Carnegie Endowment for International Peace (Carothers, T. and Youngs, R. (2015). *The Complexities of Global Protests*. Washington, DC: Carnegie Endowment for International Peace), major protests have occurred around the world with increasing frequency; 73 protests were counted between January 2010 and September 2015, and they were different in terms of triggers and motivations.

The 2016-2017 candlelight protest exhibited both differences from and similarities to other contemporary uprisings. For example, the candlelight protest differed from other recent examples (e.g., the electoral revolutions of Eastern Europe,[3] economic crisis-induced revolts of the Arab Spring,[4] Latin American social protests for the right to live against neoliberal reforms,[5] and popular protests stamped by government repression in semi-authoritarian countries[6]) in that the candlelight demonstration in Korea was not directly related to elections, economic recessions, and identities. Moreover, the candlelight protest was internationally isolated, unlike the popular uprisings of Eastern Europe and the Middle East, and it was not affected by democratic movements in other East Asian countries. Despite these differences, the candlelight protest is similar to contemporary examples of successful anti-government movements in the sense that several million Koreans participated in a series of street demonstrations and toppled incumbent president Park Geun-hye.

The candlelight protest provides a unique case to enrich our knowledge about recent mass uprisings in a comparative perspective. Because the candlelight protest was recorded as the largest in modern Korean history and a turning point of Korean politics, it enables research into individual participation in and meanings of the protest using representative survey methods.

By employing two unique survey datasets on the 2016-2017 candlelight participants, the study is purposed to expand knowledge of popular protest from the perspective of ordinary citizens. Why did millions of Koreans raise candles? What motivated them to take part in more than twenty Saturday anti-government rallies? What sustained such a solid and enduring coalition of diverse citizens? What are the meanings of the candlelight protest? How was the candlelight protest different from and similar to past successful protests in Korea?

---

3 Bunce, V. and Wolchik, S. (2011). *Defeating Authoritarian Leaders in Postcommunist Countries*. New York: Cambridge University Press.

4 Beissinger, M., Jamal, A., and Mazur, K. (2015). Explaining Divergent Revolutionary Coalitions. *Comparative Politics*, 48 (1), 1-21.

5 Arce, M. (2010). Parties and Social Protest in Latin America's Neoliberal Era. *Party Politics*, 16 (5), 669-686.

6 Aytaç, S. E., Schiumerini, L., and Stokes, S. (2017). Protests and Repression in New Democracies. *Perspectives on Politics*, 15 (1), 62-82.

These questions are important, but they are hard to answer without survey data about protest participants. Though there are exceptions,[7] comparative studies on popular protests have plenty of theoretical arguments and suffer a dearth of empirical analyses about protest participants. In particular, when a large number of citizens are massed on the streets, they tend to be described with such abstract terms as "people power" and "democratic uprising." For example, Hong-koo Lee *(Yi Hong-gu)*, the former prime minister of Korea, praised "South Korea as a beacon of Asian democracy,"[8] and Yascha Mounk stated that the candlelight protest "can serve as inspiration to defenders of liberal democracy around the world."[9] Ha-Joon Chang *(Chang Ha-chun)*, a famous Korean economist, described in *The New York Times* that "South Koreans worked a democratic miracle."[10]

Despite these observational interpretations, few studies have empirically examined why Korean protesters raised candles and what influences the protest has had on Korean democracy. As Mark Beissinger emphasized,[11] although recent popular uprisings result in successful political changes, participants and their motivations differ across countries and are more realistic than democratic and idealistic. This study provides systematic information about who participated in the candlelight protest and how they behaved differently in this unusual situation.

As I suggest through the case of the Korean protest, candlelight protesters were primarily motivated by outrage about Park Geun-hye. The analysis reveals that candlelight protesters centered on one overarching issue (the resignation of President Park Geun-hye), but they were not driven by such ideal factors as democratic causes. Overall, my in-depth

7 Beissinger, M. (2013). The Semblance of Democratic Revolution. *American Political Science Review*, 107 (3), 574-592; Beissinger et at. 2015; Kang, W. J. (2019). Determinants of Unaffiliated Citizen Protests. *Korea Journal*, 59 (1), 46-78; Rosenfeld, B. (2017). Reevaluating the Middle-Class Protest Paradigm. *American Political Science Review*, 111 (4), 637-652.

8 Lee, H.-K. (2017). South Korea as a Beacon of Asian Democracy. *East Asia Institute Column*, September 21, 2017, p. 1.

9 Mounk, Y. (2018). *People vs. Democracy: Why Our Freedom Is in Danger and How to Save It*. Cambridge: Harvard University Press, p. 185.

10 Chang, H.-J. (2017). South Koreans Worked a Democratic Miracle. Can They Do It Again? *The New York Times*, September 14, 2017. Available at: https://www.nytimes.com/2017/09/14/opinion/south-korea-social-mobility.html [Accessed April 3, 2021].

11 Beissinger 2013, p. 590.

case study suggests the protest will have a limited effect in deepening and stabilizing Korean democracy.

1. Background: Popular Protests and Korean Democracy

Since the 1948 founding of Korea, it has been understood among Koreans that popular uprisings lead to government change. Two successful movements have been stamped on the collective memory of Korean people: the April 1960 and the June 1987 movements. Outraged by severe fraud and intimidation during the presidential election, students were massed on streets to demand restoration of democracy in April 1960. As urban citizens and intellectuals joined the movement in reaction to the government's bloody suppression, the first president and civilian dictator, Rhee Syngman (*Yi Sŭng-man*), resigned and new elections were held.[12]

The next successful movement occurred in June 1987. Similar to the 1960 movement in the escalation process, a number of university students organized street protests and urban white-collar workers started to support them. Finally, in response to the unusual size and intensity of the anti-government coalition of students and middle-class citizens, Chun Doo-hwan (*Chŏn Tu-hwan*), the military dictator, promised to restore democratic elections and transfer government power in a peaceful way. This was a turning point of Korean politics to democratization. These two movements have been remembered among many Koreans as the incomplete revolution and the victory of democracy, respectively.[13]

Occurring three decades after the 1987 democratization, the 2016-2017 candlelight protest surprised scholars, politicians, and even millions of the participants themselves because they did not anticipate the likelihood of such a gigantic protest and the resulting dynamic political change. The candlelight protest seemed aberrant and extraordinary, like a sudden earthquake, because Korea has gradually democratized representative institutions such as elections, multi-party competition, and independent courts over the three decades since the 1987 transition.

In particular, Korea has expanded elections from national to local governments, and Korean parties represent a range of conservative and

---

12 Kim, C. (2017). *Youth for Nation: Culture and Protest in Cold War South Korea.* Manoa: University of Hawai'i Press, chapter 5.

13 Kim, S. H. (2000). *The Politics of Democratization in Korea: The Role of Civil Society.* Pittsburgh: University of Pittsburgh, pp. 2-4.

progressive groups. According to the modernization theory,[14] Korean democracy should be stable because its economy is highly modernized and not experiencing recession. Korea has also passed Huntington's two-turnover test of democratic consolidation in which Korean conservative parties lost power in 1997 and returned to power in 2007 in peaceful elections.[15] Nonetheless, millions of protest participants toppled President Park Geun-hye and completed government change via the vacancy election of May 2017. Given that Korea's population is 51 million, a protest with several million participants is simply enormous, far exceeding previous mass movements in modern Korean history.

Because the candlelight protest had a massive scale with substantive consequences, scholars and opinion leaders have attempted to characterize it. During the candlelight protest, for example, *Bloomberg* correspondent Sam Kim stated that "the wave of populism that fueled Brexit, the rise of Donald Trump and the fall of Italian leader Matteo Renzi has reached South Korea."[16] Sungmoon Kim interpreted the events of the 2016-2017 protest in a Confucian perspective, contending that "the Candlelight Revolution was strongly motivated by moral concerns closely affiliated with Korea's traditional Confucian political ideal."[17]

Most scholars, however, commonly express the candlelight protest as an effort of the masses to correct democracy marred by President Park Geun-hye and her government. Paul Chang described the candlelight protest as "a critical moment in the maturation of South Korean democracy."[18] Gi-Wook Shin and Rennie Moon stated that the candlelight protest is "a familiar pattern in Korean politics and that what took place indicates not a crisis of democracy, but a step forward."[19] These observations are

---

14 Lipset, S. M. (1960). *Political Man: The Social Bases of Politics*. Garden City: Doubleday, chapter 2.

15 Huntington, S. (1991). *The Third Wave: Democratization in the Late Twentieth Century*. Norman and London: University of Oklahoma Press, p. 267.

16 Kim, S. (2016). Brexit, Trump Tide of Populism Swamps South Korea President Park. *Bloomberg*, December 8, 2016. Available at: https://www.bloomberg.com/news/articles/2016-12-08/brexit-trump-tide-of-populism-swamps-south-korea-president-park [Accessed April 3, 2021].

17 Kim, S. (2018). Candlelight for Our Country's Right Name. *Religions*, 9 (11), 330, p. 17.

18 Chang, P. (2018). Candlelight Protests in South Korea. *Ewha Journal of Social Science*, 34 (1), 5-18, p. 5.

19 Shin, G.-W. and Moon, R. (2017). South Korea after Impeachment. *Journal of Democracy*, 28 (4), 117-131, p. 117.

in line with Fiori and Kim, who pointed out that "Korea is one of those examples of 'democratization by social movements.'"[20]

Despite these characterizations of the candlelight protest, two important questions remain to be answered. The first overarching question is whether the candlelight protest would improve the unstable nature of Korean democracy. The candlelight protest consequentially stopped deconsolidation of Korean democracy. However, underlying the protest is the failure of representative elites to check the wrongdoings of President Park Geun-hye.

Thus, the candlelight protest reveals one enduring problem of Korean democracy: feeble representative politics and hyper-active civil society. Given that modern democracy takes the form of representative government with the consent of the masses in elections, its politics is unavoidably a business of parties and elected representatives.[21] Since the democratic transition of 1987, Korean democracy has been unstable, characterized by an uneasy combination of dysfunctional parties and active citizens skeptical of viewing and accepting representative institutions. Thus, Sunhyuk Kim called Korean politics "contentious democracy"[22] and Yoonkyung Lee termed it "democracy without parties."[23] In some sense, the failure of representative politics is a cause of the candlelight protest.[24] In other words, the outbreak of the candlelight protest has again confirmed the mile-wide gap between ineffective representative institutions and resistant civil society.

Can the candlelight protest stabilize and deepen Korean democracy? If prior scholars' characterization of the candlelight protest as democratic is correct, the protest would be expected to make a contribution to the functioning of Korean democracy. This point is important because the candlelight protest was not a democracy protest[25] to end authoritarian

---

20 Fiori, A. and Kim, S. H. (2018). Civil Society and Democracy in South Korea. In Kim, Y. (Ed.), *Korea's Quest for Economic Democratization: Globalization, Polarization and Contention.* New York: Palgrave Macmillan, 141-170, p. 141.

21 Dahl, R. (1998). *On Democracy.* New Haven: Yale University Press.

22 Kim, S. H. (2012). 'Contentious Democacy' in South Korea. *Taiwan Journal of Democracy,* 8 (2), 51-61, p. 51.

23 Lee, Y. (2009). Democracy Without Parties? *Korea Observer,* 40 (1), 27-52, p. 27.

24 Shin, D. (2018). The Deconsolidation of Liberal Democracy in Korea: Exploring its Cultural Roots. *Korea Observer,* 49 (1), 107-136; Turner, M., Kwon, S.-H., and O'Donnell, M. (2018). Making Integrity Institutions Work in South Korea. *Asian Survey,* 58 (5), 898-919.

25 See Brancati, D. (2016). *Democracy Protests: Origins, Features and Significance.* New York: Cambridge University Press.

rule. A successful democratic movement to topple authoritarian governments results in open elections, multi-party competition, and expanded civil rights, which are necessary components of liberal and representative democracy. However, the candlelight protest was a reaction to politics after democratization. Popular protest long after democratization is likely to reflect dissatisfaction with how representative politics work.[26]

The second question to examine is why millions of Koreans raised candles, maintaining more than twenty Saturday anti-government rallies. Because prior studies offer observational interpretations of the candlelight protest without analyzing empirical data, only a few studies have examined this question. For example, Kang investigated motivations of the participants and found that social justice and democratic attitudes were the main reasons unaffiliated citizens joined the protest.[27] Nonetheless, little is known about the social background and political motivations of individual protesters. Without empirical research of the participants, it is difficult to ascertain the dynamic of the candlelight protest, which would indicate credible information about the direction and magnitude of reforms after the protest. Expectations and concerns have already been raised among scholars and politicians with regard to the future of Korean democracy after the candlelight protest.[28]

These two questions are related. If candlelight protesters were primarily motivated by strong democratic and reform orientations, the protest would be a political force to improve Korean democracy. This would be the expected effect of the candlelight protest on Korean democracy, which is implied among the recent accounts of prior scholars.[29] However, if individual participants in the protest were mainly driven by anti-Park Geun-hye sentiment, the dramatic events of 2016-2017 were just an effort to promote a government change by means other than regular elections. In this case, the implication of the candlelight protest would be limited in deepening Korean democracy.

Thus, existing scholarship offers a lack of systematic micro-level evidence on the background and motivations of protest participants. This is obviously due to a lack of appropriate empirical data. To advance the existing knowledge about the candlelight protest, I leverage detailed data on protest participants.

---

26 Norris, P. (2011). *Democratic Deficit: Critical Citizens Revisited.* New York: Cambridge University Press, chapter 1.

27 Kang 2019, p. 46.

28 Kim 2018; Shin 2018; Shin/Moon 2017; Turner et al. 2018.

29 Chang 2017; Lee 2017; Mounk 2018; Shin and Moon 2017.

2. The 2016-2017 Candlelight Protest and Survey Data

To investigate the underlying motivations of the protesters and characterize the meaning of the candlelight protest, this research employs two public opinion datasets: the field survey of the protest participants and the Sogang Public Opinion Survey (hereafter, SPOS). As Rosenfeld pointed out, "A major challenge of studying protest at the individual level is access to suitable data."[30] Because no survey is unbiased, I combined these two datasets to offer better information about the candlelight protest participants.

Figure 1 shows the number of participants during the candlelight protest, important watershed events, and the dates for the two surveys. The Organizing Committee for People's Candlelight Demonstration (*Pak Kŭn-hye chŏnggwŏn t'oejin pisanggungminhaengdong*) estimated the number of participants on the basis of information about the Wi-Fi signals of cellphones around Seoul Kwanghwamun Square. The candlelight protest suddenly escalated during November 2016 when political parties hesitated and failed to pass the impeachment of President Park Geun-hye. The protest on December 3, 2016, was the largest recorded in modern Korean history: 2.3 million citizens nationwide and 1.9 million in Seoul and the capital areas took to the streets and demanded the immediate impeachment and resignation of Park Geun-hye. Forced and shocked by the massive scale of this protest, the National Assembly passed the impeachment on December 9, 2016. After the impeachment, the candlelight protest declined and then rebounded as the Constitutional Court reviewed the impeachment case. More than 1 million protesters gathered before the final ruling of the Constitutional Court. The court unanimously ruled that Park Geun-hye violated the constitution and laws throughout her time in office and that her impeachment was just.[31] Finally, Park Geun-hye was arrested and imprisoned on March 31, 2017, and the vacancy election was scheduled on May 9, 2017.

---

30 Rosenfeld 2017, p. 641.
31 Shin and Moon 2017, pp. 118-119.

Figure 1. Number of the Candlelight Participants and Survey Dates

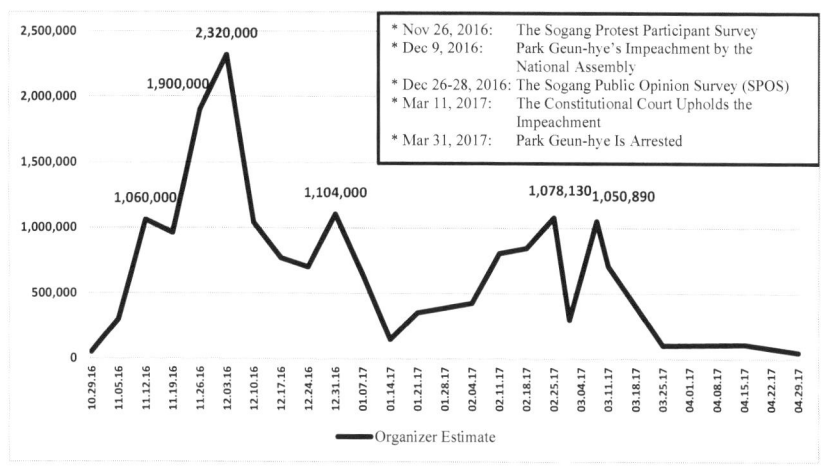

Source: Organizing Committee for People's Candlelight Demonstration

The first dataset is a field survey of the protest participants at the fifth Saturday protest on November 26, 2016. The Institute of Contemporary Politics (*Hyŏndaechŏngch'iyŏngguso*) at Sogang University (*Sŏgang taehakkyo*), Seoul, Korea,[32] hired about 50 graduate and undergraduate students majoring in political science and trained them through two formal sessions. The institute sent them to Seoul Kwanghwamun Square to survey participants from Seoul and the capital areas. The protest started at 1:00 PM and reached its peak around evening (6:00-10:00 PM) when the main event, a cultural performance, occurred and the march progressed toward the Blue House (*Ch'ŏngwadae*, the official residence and workplace of the Korean president). Thus, the interviewers first surveyed participants at representatively sampled posts of the square from 3:00-5:00 PM and then later surveyed those at subway stations and bus stops around the square from 8:00-10:30 PM. On the date of the field survey, the protest organizers estimated there were about 1.7 million participants in Seoul Kwanghwamun Square, and the surveyors interviewed 2,058 respondents about their socio-economic background and motivations. I excluded 615 participants under 19 years of age and non-residents of the capital areas (Seoul/Kyŏnggi/Inch'ŏn) in order to compare the results with the SPOS.

---

32 See the website: http://sips.re.kr/.

The second dataset for the present study was culled from the SPOS. The Institute of Contemporary Politics at Sogang University chose a nation-wide and representative sample of the 1,200 respondents and interviewed them via telephone and cell phone during December 26-28, 2016. The SPOS asked Korean citizens about three main themes: democracy, socio-economic issues, and candlelight protest and President Park Geun-hye.

Neither of these surveys was free from potential problems, which is an enduring issue in survey research. For example, the SPOS asked respondents whether they had recently participated in the candlelight protests: about 24% of them answered positively. The adult population of Korea is 42 million, and the survey indicates that about 10 million citizens participated in the candlelight revolution. Because the accumulated number of participants exceeded 10 million in the rally of December 31, this study retrospectively infers that the rate is somewhat biased toward participation. The field survey has a problem of representation. Although Seoul Kwanghwamun Square was a central and symbolic place where several million Koreans massed every Saturday during the 2016-2017 candlelight protest, the field survey is not a nationwide representative survey method. Rapid modernization of the last half century has resulted in substantial variation in socio-demographic background and political attitudes across regions as well as between capital and regional areas. Obviously, the field participant survey tends to emphasize characteristics of citizens in highly modernized Seoul and capital areas.

Despite these shortcomings, these surveys have one unique strength: They provide live and concrete information about public opinion and real participants during the culmination of the candlelight protest. These datasets together enable this research to compare participants and nonparticipants during the moment of the candlelight protest in terms of their different orientations toward the candlelight protest and Park Geun-hye and, thus, their different behaviors. Therefore, I expect that the research contributes to the existing knowledge of social movements and Korean democracy by analyzing both surveys together and ascertaining the nature of the candlelight protest.

3. Theories and Hypotheses

What connected protest participants in the collective candlelight rallies and what distinguished them from those who did not take a part? There is no shortage of theoretical explanations to identify these protest participants. Three theories stand out within the literature of democracy protest: modernization, partisan model, and redistribution.

First of all, within the literature of democratization, there is a long-standing tradition, rooted in modernization theory, that views democratic demand and change as the outcome of socio-economic changes and their derivative effects.[33] At the individual level, they include educational attainment and increasing income reflecting the rise of middle-class citizens. Indeed, many of the recent uprisings across developing and developed nations have by and large been driven by middle-class, educated, and urban citizens supportive of democracy and demanding participation in politics.[34] Moreover, the resource theory of political participation complements the modernization theory in democratic societies in that those with material, cognitive, and relational resources are more participatory in politics than are the have-nots.[35] Therefore, modernization theory expects one of the following hypotheses to be true about participants of the candlelight protest.

H1-1: Participants in the candlelight protest were college-educated, middle-class, and urban citizens

H1-2: Participants in the candlelight protest were motivated by democratic attitudes.

Second, political participation, both conventional and unconventional, is likely to follow political lines such as partisanship and political cleavages.[36] Specifically, political actors are not automatically passive in reflecting their interests; rather, they actively organize and reorganize social groups in the political dynamics of social resistance. Building on Schattschneider's famous statements such as "the political parties created democracy,"[37] the partisan theory of democracy protest presents the view that public demand for democratic change follows as existing political parties see opportunities

---

33 Inglehart, R. and Welzel, C. (2005). *Modernization, Cultural Change, and Democracy: The Human Development Sequence.* New York: Cambridge University Press; Lipset 1960.

34 Beissinger et al. 2015; Carothers and Youngs 2015; Rosenfeld 2017.

35 Dalton, R. (2014). *Citizen Politics: Public Opinion and Political Parties in Advanced Industrial Democracies.* Washington, DC: CQ Press.

36 Arce 2010; Kostelka, F. and Rovny, J. (2019). It's Not the Left: Ideology and Protest Participation in Old and New Democracies. *Comparative Political Studies*, 52 (11), 1677-1712.

37 Schattschneider, E. E. (1942). *Party Government.* New York: Farrar and Rinehart, p. 1.

within social movements to maximize their political interests and incumbent politicians mobilize supporters.[38] Empirically, Su showed from a cross-national analysis of 107 democracies that opposition parties were the primary agents of protest mobilization against incumbent governments during the 1990s and the 2000s.[39] Moreover, anti-government rallies tend to reflect political cleavages. Since the early 2000s, Korean politics has been shaped by two new cleavages of ideology and generation in addition to regional cleavage.[40] Because Park Geun-hye was born in Kyŏngsang and was a conservative president representing old generations, participants of the candlelight protest were likely to have opposite social backgrounds and political orientations reflecting dominant cleavages of Korean politics. If the partisan model is valid in the case of Korea, therefore, the model expects to find evidence consistent with the following hypotheses:

H2-1:   The main participants of the candlelight protest were opposition party supporters, young generations, and Chŏlla residents.

H2-2:   Participants in the candlelight protest were motivated by progressive ideology.

Finally, the redistribution model of democracy protest follows the Marxist tradition of class conflict and has been recently driven by formal theorists.[41] These scholars assume that democratization and regime choice are a matter of wealth redistribution among the wealthy, the middle class, and the poor classes and their different interests and strategies. According to this model, the median poor citizens have a strong preference for redistribution through democratic change because democracy is the only political system by which they can take political power, tax both the rich and upper middle classes, and redistribute economic wealth. Expecting this potential threat from the poor class for democracy and redistribution, the wealthy class supports authoritarianism, whereas the middle class is strategically

---

38 Dasgupta, A. and Ziblatt, D. (2015). How Did Britain Democratize? *Journal of Economic History*, 75 (1), 1-29; Teele, D. L. (2018). *Forging the Franchise: The Political Origins of the Women's Vote*. New York: Princeton University Press.

39 Su, Y.-P. (2015). Anti-Government Protests in Democracies. *Comparative Politics*, 47 (2), 149-167, p. 158.

40 Kim, H. M., Choi, J. Y., and Cho, J. (2008). Changing Cleavage Structure in New Democracies. *Electoral Studies*, 27 (1), 136-150, p. 136.

41 Boix, C. (2003). *Democracy and Redistribution*. Cambridge: Cambridge University Press; Acemoglu, D. and Robinson, J. (2006). *Economic Origins of Dictatorship and Democracy*. New York: Cambridge University Press.

ambiguous about regime choice. With regard to the 1987 democratic movement of Korea, Acemoglu and Robinson specifically posited that democracy arrived in Korea in the late 1980s "not because of the wishes or the actions of the middle class, but because of the effective protests, in the face of repression and sometimes violence, organized by students and workers."[42] On this basis, the redistributive theory expects one or both of the following hypotheses to be true about participation of the candlelight protest:

H3-1:   Main actors of the candlelight protest were disproportionately from the working class and the low-income group.

H3-2:   Participants in the candlelight protest were motivated by concerns with redistribution and inequality.

Overall, these theories provide plausible accounts of why social and political groups participated in the candlelight protest in Korea and enable us to draw meaningful inferences about the nature of the protest. The candlelight protest was so large we can take advantage of survey data about its participants and offer micro-level evidence about the strategic behavior of different groups during that unusual situation.

4. Empirical Results

The purpose of this study is to examine socio-economic and political characteristics of the candlelight protest participants and determine the nature of the protest in terms of Korean democracy. To this end, the study took two sequential steps in analyzing these data. First, I compared both of the field and public opinion surveys and show socio-demographic and ideological backgrounds of protest participants in Seoul and capital areas. Second, I statistically analyzed the SPOS to identify sources of participation because the SPOS is a nationwide and representative survey covering both participants and non-participants. Finally, I used SPSS statistics 22 for the following empirical analyses.

At the preliminary stage, I compared the candlelight protest participants and nonparticipants across the following eight variables representing the

---

42   Acemoglu, D. and Robinson, J. (2013). Middle Class Rising? *Whynationsfail.com*, July 2, 2013, [online]. Available at: http://whynationsfail.com/blog/2013/7/2/midd le-class-rising.html [Accessed April 3, 2021].

hypotheses detailed in the previous section: residence, gender, generation, education, occupation, family income, subjective class status, and ideology. Because Seoul Kwanghwamun Square was the most popular place for the candlelight protest and the field survey focused there, the first analysis is restricted to citizens in Seoul and capital areas.

Table 1. *Candlelight Participation by Socio-demographic and Political Categories in the Seoul and Capital Areas*

	Field Survey	SPOS	
	Percentage of the Protesters	Percentage of the Protesters	Average Participation in Each Group
Residence			
Seoul	53%	40%	40%
Kyŏnggi/Inch'ŏn	47	60	28
Gender			
Male	48	58	38
Female	52	42	27
Generation			
≤ 29	37	23	41
30-39	19	20	34
40-49	25	26	39
50-59	15	20	33
≥60	5	11	17
Education			
Below college	14	20	22
College or above	86	80	42
Occupation			
Professional and Office Employee	43	42	33
Labor Worker	3	6	28
Other occupations	33	41	22
Family Income (KRW)			
≤ 2,500,000	12	16	30
2,500,000-3,500,000	17	20	33
3,500,000-4,500,000	18	11	20
4,500,000-7,000,000	26	34	40
≥7,000,000	16	20	35
Subjective Class Status			
Low	44	38	32
Middle	46	51	35
High	10	10	25
Ideology			
Progressive	65	45	51
Middle	22	37	28
Conservative	10	17	24
Total	100	100	**Average** 33
(No. of observations)	(1443)	(193)	(593)

Table 1 summarizes the two surveys in Seoul and the capital areas and shows several notable patterns. Both the field survey and the SPOS, first, show that citizens of Seoul and capital areas were more participatory in the candlelight protest than the rest during December 2016. According to the Organizing Committee for People's Candlelight Demonstration, 1.7 million of the 1.9 million Koreans gathered on Seoul Kwangwhamun Square (see Figure 1). Moreover, the third column of Table 1 shows that the average participation rate in Seoul and capital areas was 33%, which was 9% higher than the national average (24%) and 18% higher than the average of the non-capital areas (15%). Seoul and Kyŏnggi/Inch'ŏn were 16% and 4% higher in the candlelight participation, respectively, than the national average. This suggests that citizens of Seoul and capital areas led the early escalation of the candlelight protest. Considering that Seoul and capital areas are the most modernized regions in Korea, this finding is supportive of the modernization theory (H1-1).

Second, the main protesters of the candlelight protest were citizens who were college educated, young, and male. Those with a college education were dominant in the Seoul square, and their participation was nearly twice that of citizens with a high school education or below (42% vs. 22%), which is in line with the modernization theory (H1-1). Active participation among young Koreans reflected generational cleavage, which is consistent with the partisan model (H2-1). The number and proportion of participants linearly decreased by generation from 41% of those in their 20s to 17% of those in their 60s and above. Because gender inequality is socially pervasive in Korea, women were more passive than men in this unusual situation.

Third, with regard to occupations, professional and office employees were the most dominant group, with 43% in the Seoul square. On the other hand, labor workers constituted a small number of protesters and their participation did not exceed that of professional and office employees, according to the SPOS. Moreover, subjective class status is negatively associated with candlelight participation, but family income has a positive relationship with participation. When these two patterns are combined, the main protesters were those who were dissatisfied with their social status and had resources to transform their discontent into political actions. Consistent with the micro-level evidence of recent popular uprisings,[43] citizens with more resources were more participatory than those with less resources, which is close to the modernization theory (H1-1) but deviates from the expectation of the redistributive model (H3-1).

---

43   Beissinger et al. 2015; Rosenfeld 2017.

Finally, it does appear the protest was escalated by progressive citizens. Table 1 positively confirms this pattern, which is consistent with cross-national evidence of the partisan model of social protest (H2-2).[44] About two thirds of the candlelight participants (65%) were identified as progressives, and their participation was about two times that of moderate and conservative groups participating in the SPOS. Nonetheless, given that Korean citizens have been ideologically divided since the early 2000s, it is remarkable that the SPOS found that 28% and 24% of the moderate and conservative groups, respectively, joined the candlelight protest. Why even conservative citizens raised candles against conservative President Park Geun-hye is an important question, and it will be discussed later in this article.

Taken together, these preliminary results suggest that these two datasets are not different in terms of protest participation across social groups. Thus, both the field survey and the SPOS can be used for further empirical analyses. Theoretically, the preliminary results are more supportive of the modernization and partisan theories of political participation than the redistribution model of democracy protest.[45] Candlelight participants are skewed toward young and college-educated office employees with upper levels of resources. As evident in the partisan model, the candlelight protest was pushed by those who are ideologically progressive. Whereas those with lower subjective class status were active in the candlelight protest, those with low financial and cognitive resources were weakly mobilized. Finally, labor workers were slightly more participatory (28%) than those of the reference groups.

The preliminary analysis points to the presence of varied participation across socio-demographic and political groups in the candlelight protest. Nonetheless, these findings are tentative because they are drawn from the basic information about candlelight protesters of Seoul and the capital areas provided in Table 1. Therefore, as a further test, I subjected these initial findings to multivariate regression analysis to determine the independent effects and relative influence of each on participation. Because I assumed that social groups are rational actors in the process of dramatic change, I tried to unpack which groups were the main participants in demanding political change and what factors motivated them.

Furthermore, to test the theoretical expectations detailed in the previous section in a rigorous manner, I included socio-demographic, partisanship, and political variables (see Appendices I and II for survey questions and

---

44 Arce 2010; Su 2015.
45 Dalton 2014; Inglehart and Welzel 2005.

descriptive statistics, respectively). First, following the partisan model of political cleavages, two regions (Kyŏngsang and Chŏlla) are included in the variables of socio-demographic backgrounds because Korean politics has been divided by regional rivalry between Chŏlla and Kyŏngsang since the 1987 democratic transition. Chŏlla province produced the former president Kim Dae-jung (*Kim Tae-jung*), who experienced brutal oppression by the Kyŏngsang-born military dictators (Park Chung-hee (*Pak Chŏng-hŭi*) and Chun Doo-hwan (*Chŏn Tu-hwan*)), thereby becoming a symbol of Korean democratization. Kyŏngsang was a home region for the two military dictators and the three conservative presidents (Roh Tae-woo (*No T'ae-u*), Lee Myung-bak (*Yi Myŏng-bak*), and Park Geun-hye). Given that Park Geun-hye was born in Kyŏngsang and she is a daughter of Park Chung-hee,[46] people of Chŏlla are expected to be more participatory than those in Kyŏngsang and other regions.

Second, as the partisan model suggests, I included citizens' support for three main parties: the ruling Saenuri Party (*Saenuridang*), the opposition Democratic Party (*Tŏburŏminjudang*), and the leftist Justice Party (*Chŏngŭidang*). Because the Saenuri Party is Park Geun-hye's party, I expected its supporters had been less participatory in the candlelight protest than those of the opposition Democratic and Justice Parties.

Finally, I added four motivational variables that might have affected the decision of individual Koreans to take a part in the candlelight protest: perceived salience of politics, democratic support, demand for direct democracy, and concern over inequality and redistribution. Whereas I retained ideology for the partisan model, I included the first three for the modernization theory of democratization and the last one for the redistribution model. According to the partisan model, participants were ideologically oriented toward progressive because Park Geun-hye was a conservative president and those progressive citizens opposed her, thereby demanding government change via both institutional and non-institutional methods. Modernization theorists posit that citizens join democracy protests because they are interested in politics and supportive of democracy over authoritarianism. Because the SPOS does not have a standard question for political interest, I used perceived salience of politics as a proxy variable. Extending modernization theory, moreover, Dalton contends that citizens in advanced countries become participatory and critical because they think

---

46 Joo, H.-M. (2017). A Return of 'The Strong Man's Daughter'. *Japanese Journal of Political Science*, 18 (2), 360-382, p. 360.

citizens' participation is necessary in government decision-making.[47] Finally, because the redistribution model contends that the main motivation of democracy protesters is redistribution and inequality, I included citizens' perceptions of these two social issues.[48]

Table 2. Empirical Result: Logistic Regression of Protest Participation [SPOS]

	Model 1		Model 2		Model 3	
	Standard-ized Coefficients	Odds Ratio	Standard-ized Coefficients	Odds Ratio	Standard-ized Coefficients	Odds Ratio
Socio-demographic Variables						
Male	0.194**	1.215	0.181**	1.199	0.230***	1.258
Generation	-0.193**	0.825	-0.205**	0.814	-0.144	0.866
College Education	0.228**	1.256	0.229**	1.257	0.152	1.164
Family Income	0.127	1.135	0.130	1.139	0.135	1.145
Subjective Class Status	-0.046	0.955	-0.053	0.948	-0.016	0.984
Capital Areas	0.399***	1.490	0.385***	1.470	0.421***	1.523
Chŏlla	-0.008	0.992	-0.019	0.981	-0.038	0.962
Kyŏngsang	-0.146	0.864	-0.142	0.868	-0.134	0.875
Professional and Office Employees	0.185**	1.204	0.187**	1.206	0.157**	1.170
Labor Workers	0.131*	1.140	0.132*	1.141	0.091	1.095
Partisanship Variables						
Saenuri Party Supporters			0.118	1.125	0.047	1.048
Democratic Party Supporters			0.175**	1.191	0.122	1.130
Justice Party Supporters			0.169**	1.184	0.151**	1.162
Motivational Variables						
Perceived Salience of Politics					0.188**	1.207
Ideology (Conservative-Progressive)					0.309***	1.362
Democratic Support					0.030	1.030
Demand for Direct Democracy					0.085	1.089
Perception of Redistribution and Inequality					0.228***	1.257
Observations	1103		1103		1026	
Pseudo R²	0.091		0.099		0.126	

Note: *$p \leq 0.10$; **$p \leq 0.05$; ***$p \leq 0.01$. Standard errors are not reported.

47 Dalton 2014; Norris 2011.
48 Acemoglu and Robinson 2006.

Table 2 displays the empirical results of the logistic regression of participation in the SPOS. I report the standardized coefficients and their odds ratios to clarify interpretation and comparison. According to model 1, the main social groups active in the protests were male, young, college-educated professional and office employees living in Seoul and the capital areas, which confirms the modernization theory (H1-1) and the partisan model (H2-1). On the other hand, the candlelight protests were not strong in Chŏlla and Kyŏngsang, which is not consistent with the partisan model of regional cleavage (H2-1). Unlike the characteristics displayed in Table 1, subjective class status and family income failed to reach statistical significance and their impacts were not strong. Finally, labor workers were more active than those of the other occupation groups, but the impact was not as strong as other variables, which is not supportive of the redistributive model in identifying participants in the candlelight protest.

In addition to the socio-demographic information about the main participant groups, which party supporters were active in the candlelight protest? The empirical results of model 2 are consistent with my theoretical expectation in that supporters of the two opposition parties were more participatory than those supportive of other minority parties and with no party affiliations (reference group), which confirms the partisan model (H2-1). Having preferences for the Democratic Party and Justice Party increased the odds of participation over non-participation by 19% and 18%, respectively. It is also interesting that supporters of the ruling Saenuri Party were not less participatory in the candlelight protest than those of the reference group, which indicate the ambiguity and complexity that those Saenuri Party supporters had toward the candlelight protest and President Park Geun-hye. When these findings are considered together, one can reasonably conclude that the candlelight protest was led by opposition party supporters. Thus, the candlelight protest was a social as well as a political movement.

What motivated individual participation of Korean citizens during the culmination of the candlelight protest? The upshot from model 3 is that the main players of the candlelight protest were progressive citizens (H2-2) and perceived politics as important. On the other hand, democratic support and demand for direct democracy failed to reach statistical significance and their effects were negligible, suggesting that participants and non-participants did not differ in these two motivational dimensions. This finding departs from the expectation of the modernization theory and it has substantial implications about the nature of the candlelight protest. Although democratic slogans and agitations were prevalent on the streets, the candlelight protest was driven more by realistic and partisan motivations than by idealistic and normative ones.

From model 3, it appears that candlelight protest participants had a more negative perception of redistribution and inequality in Korea than non-participants (H3-2). This result suggests that the candlelight protest reflected the worsening of social and economic inequality.[49] According to World Inequality Data,[50] since the 1997 financial crisis, the fiscal income share of the top 1% and top 10% has increased from 7% and 32%, respectively, in 1995 to 12% and 43%, respectively, in 2016.

Overall, the candlelight protest reflected the political cleavages of contemporary Korean politics and the dissatisfaction of urban middle class citizens with regard to politics and social inequality. As modernization theory suggests, individual participants in the candlelight protest were educated and attentive middleclass citizens living in the capital areas. Moreover, although the candlelight protest was described as the people's democratic revolution, the driving force behind this phenomenon included partisanship and ideology. In some sense, the candlelight protest was the political challenge of progressive and opposition party supporters against the conservative Park Geun-hye government. Moreover, in line with the redistribution model, concern about inequality and redistribution lay beneath individual participation of the candlelight protest. Nonetheless, this motivation factor was not exclusively supported by social actors such as the poor and labor workers; instead, the negative perception of redistribution and inequality were widely shared among college-educated and attentive citizens.[51]

Our results differ from the democratic description of the candlelight protest among recent scholars because I found no evidence that the underlying motivations of protest participants were democratic. This finding is

---

49 See also the chapter by Juliette Schwak in this volume.

50 See the website: https://wid.world/.

51 I ran model 3 in the three income groups and the two educational groups and found no difference across them. This suggests that most participants shared concern about inequality and redistribution, which differs from the expectation of the redistribution model in that the poor citizens see inequality as negative and demand redistribution via a protest. This makes sense in Korean politics given that rising inequality has been a political agenda of both progressive and conservative parties during the last decade. Although inequality and redistribution are issues of leftist parties, they are non-partisan issues running through attentive and middle-class citizens in Korea. For example, both Park Geun-hye and Moon Jae-in (*Mun Chae-in*) promised welfare programs to cope with rising inequality when they campaigned in the 2012 presidential election.

rather surprising because democratic narratives and slogans poured out in the Seoul square and Park Geun-hye's governance style was seen as authoritarian and closed like that of her father, Park Chung-hee. Thus, the democratic description of the candlelight protest is a partial and outcome-oriented interpretation.

If individual participation in the candlelight protest was not driven by democratic causes, what directly forced people onto the street? Although the SPOS did not have a question about Park Geun-hye, the field survey in Seoul Kwanghwamun Square asked participants about the biggest reason for their participation and whether they were willing to participate in the candlelight protest until the current political situation changed. Because the field survey was conducted in the early stage of the candlelight protest on November 26, the survey reveals how individual participants thought about Park Geun-hye and the candlelight protest.

Figure 2. Reasons for Individual Participation and Willingness for Further Participation [Field Survey]

A.   Reasons for Individual Participation

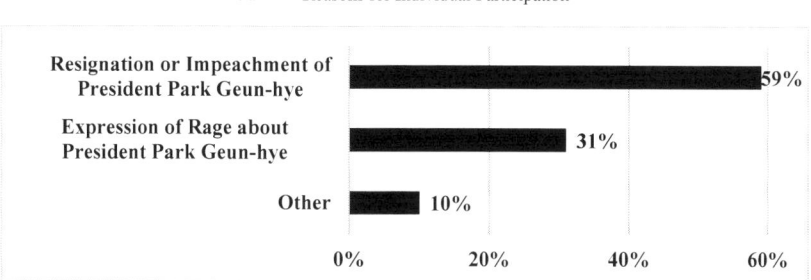

B.   Willingness for Further Participation

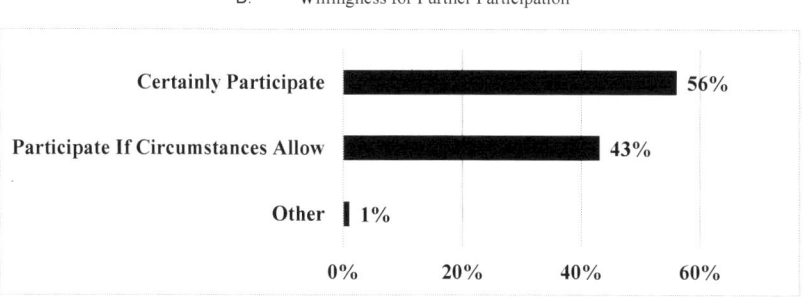

According to Figure 2, the most important reason for individual participation was resignation or impeachment of President Park Geun-hye (59%), and the second most popular reason was to express outrage about her (31%). Moreover, 99% of the participants showed willingness to continue their participation until the political situation changed. When these two results are considered together, most participants in the candlelight protest were directly and strongly motivated by Park Geun-hye.

During October and November of 2016, Korean mass media discovered that Park Geun-hye allowed Choi Soon-sil (*Ch'oe Sun-sil*), her personal confidante, who held no government position, to freely meddle in the formation and implementation of domestic and foreign policies, actions collectively called the "Choi-gate" scandal.[52] The president also enabled this confidante to enrich herself by forcing 53 companies to donate more than USD 69 million to the two foundations under her control. It was also reported that the Park Geun-hye government blacklisted about 10,000 political opponents and progressive artists critical of her presidency.[53] This series of media exposures infuriated and cemented the resolve of middle-class citizens and supporters of her opponent groups. It is also valid to state that her wrongdoings and corruption stimulated a minority of conservative and lower-class citizens to join the candlelight protest, as made clear in Table 1. There is credible evidence that the candlelight protest comprised a negative and political coalition against the Park Geun-hye government. Therefore, it is reasonable to conclude that outrage about Park Geun-hye was a main force behind the enduring and resolute coalition of the candlelight protest.

5. Further Discussion

I have revealed that the main participants in the candlelight protest were urban middle-class and progressive citizens who were motivated by realistic outrage about Park Geun-hye rather than normative causes such as democratic change. Although I have determined the social and political characteristics of the protest participants, my analysis raises four additional questions that are worth further discussion.

First of all, my analysis showed that a disproportionate number of protest participants were from the capital areas and that Kyŏnggi/Inch'ŏn

---

52 Shin and Moon 2017, p. 119.
53 Shin 2018, p. 108.

citizens were more actively engaged than those of Seoul. On the day of the field survey, 1.7 million of the total 1.9 million participants were from the capital areas (see Figure 1). Why were citizens of the capital areas far more engaged in the protest than those of other regions? Two answers could explain this outstanding pattern of the disproportionate participation of the capital areas. One is that the capital areas constitute the most modernized and advanced region in Korea; the other is that the Blue House, the presidential office of Park Geun-hye, is located at the center of Seoul. However, these two factors are only partially valid in accounting for the large proportion of participants from the capital areas.

Although our survey-based research could not answer this question, I suspect that the situational cause is the Sewol ferry (*Sewŏlho*) disaster. The Sewol ferry sunk on the morning of April 16, 2014, when the ferry headed from the capital areas to Cheju Island (also in Korea). In total, 339 passengers and crew members died in the disaster; what grieved ordinary Koreans was that 250 of the victims were high school students from Ansan city, which is near Seoul. Many Koreans criticized the captain and most of the crew for escaping from the ferry and abandoning passengers and the Korean coastguard for being hesitant and failing to save them, instead watching them drown in the sea. What angered residents of the capital areas most was that President Park Geun-hye did not take appropriate, immediate action to rescue the passengers; rather, she was responsible for delaying the rescue operations.[54] The victims (especially the high school students) were stamped in the minds of people living in the capital areas. The grief and sympathy eventually arose and spread among urban middle-class citizens in this region because they emphasize strong familism and are likely to have children.[55] The spiral of critical reactions escalated until the candlelight protest because Park Geun-hye kept her distance from the victims' families and hindered the formal investigation of the Sewol ferry disaster.

This account of the extraordinary protest participation of the capital area citizens is consistent with recent research examining popular uprisings in the Middle East and Eastern Europe.[56] According to these studies, unlike past revolutions such as those in Russia and China, recent popular

---

54 Choe, S.-H. (2015). Legacy of a South Korean Ferry Sinking. *The New York Times*, April 11, 2015. Available at: https://www.nytimes.com/2015/04/12/world/asia/legacy-of-south-korea-sewol-ferry-sinking.html [Accessed April 3, 2021].

55 Lie, J. (2015). The Wreck of the Sewol. *Georgetown Journal of International Affairs*, 16 (2), 111-121, p. 111.

56 Aytaç et al. 2017; Beissinger 2013; Beissinger et al. 2015; Rosenfeld 2017.

uprisings have been characterized by citizens' reactions to policies and strategies of incumbent government in the years leading up to those upheavals. In particular, as state institutions have been globalized and established in most countries over the last half century, wielding enormous influence on society and economy,[57] it is governments that provoke particular distributions of political dissatisfaction and shape opposition that mobilizes coalitions. In Korea, Saturday anti-government rallies lasting six months escalated and endured predominantly due to the participation of urban middle-class citizens of the capital areas who were angry with various wrongdoings of Park Geun-hye and her misconduct in the Sewol ferry disaster.[58]

A second question relates to the first: Is the candlelight protest similar to other contemporary upheavals? As stated in the introduction, the candlelight protest is not associated with international diffusion, democratic transition, elections, or economic recession. Nonetheless, two facts run across the candlelight protest and other successful uprisings that have resulted in government change. One is that governments determine social configurations and the strength of protest coalitions. Like protesters in other uprisings, most of the candlelight participants were outraged with the incumbent government leader, Park Geun-hye. The other is that protest participants in contemporary uprisings are not motivated by democratic causes but display ideological and political characteristics.[59] As reported in the prior section, I found no evidence to discriminate between the candlelight protest participants and non-participants in terms of democratic attitudes.

According to the partisan model of social protest, (un)balance of power between the ruling and opposition parties is known to have affected the

---

57 Geddes, B. (2011). What Causes Democratization. In Goodin, R. (Ed.), *Oxford Handbook of Political Science*. New York: Oxford University Press, 594-615; Goldstone, J. (2011). Understanding the Revolutions of 2011. *Foreign Affairs*, 90 (3), 8-16.

58 The field survey asked respondents to indicate their levels of anger at the Sewol ferry disaster and the Park Geun-hye and Choi Soon-sil scandal. Using a scale of 0 to 10, 83% of the respondents rated 8 and above on the Sewol ferry disaster and 92% did the same on the Park Geun-hye and Choi Soon-sil scandal. Although the Sewol ferry disaster occurred two and a half years before the candlelight protest, the survey shows that many participants in the protest had strong empathy for the victims of the disaster and shared outrage about Park Geun-hye. The survey also reported that the Park Geun-hye and Choi Soon-sil scandal directly infuriated the protest participants.

59 Beissinger 2013; Beissinger et al. 2015; Kostelka and Rovny 2019.

intensity and strength of recent social protests, especially in new democracies.[60] This finding is valid in the candlelight protest as well. In the 2016 legislative elections, the ruling Saenuri Party of Park Geun-hye lost 22% of its seats, thus losing the majority held before the elections and giving leading legislative status to the opposition Democratic Party. Moreover, the chronically low institutionalization and high fragmentation of Korean parties has hindered the consolidation of Korean democracy since the 1987 democratic transition,[61] and both the Saenuri Party and Park Geun-hye seemed to pour oil over the process culminating in the candlelight protest, solidly bonding a large number of urban middle-class and progressive partisan citizens. This interpretation of the candlelight protest is consistent with Brancati's conclusion that "democracy protests are also not spontaneous, but rather are carefully planned, typically by either political parties or civil society groups."[62]

The third question that needs to be answered is whether the candlelight protest differs from the previous successful movements of April 1960 and June 1987. Shin and Moon contend that the candlelight protest is "an integral part of Korea's political development for decades" like the successful 1960 and 1987 movements.[63] In what respect does this claim make sense? The candlelight protest did not differ from the two previous movements in terms of main participants and consequential results. Although there are no empirical studies on the participants in the 1960 and 1987 movements, it is well known in the modern history of Korea that urban middle-class citizens and professional/office employees joined the initial demonstrations of students to overthrow the Rhee Syngman and Chun Doo-hwan governments.[64] In this sense, the candlelight protest repeated the phenomenon of protest-led government change, which resulted in consequential democratization.

---

60 Su 2015.
61 See Croissant, A. and Völkel, P. (2012). Party System Types and Party System Institutionalization. *Party Politics*, 18 (2), 235-265; Hicken, A. and Kuhonta, E. (2015). *Party System Institutionalization in Asia: Democracies, Autocracies, and the Shadows of the Past*. New York: Cambridge University Press. For example, Hicken and Kuhonta (2015) showed that among eleven East Asian countries electoral volatility of Korea was the second lowest after Thailand. Croissant and Völkel (2012) compared 24 democracies of East Asia and Latin America and revealed that Korea tied with Guatemala for the lowest party system institutionalization.
62 Brancati 2016, p. 176.
63 Shin and Moon 2017, p. 118.
64 Kim 2000.

However, there is one difference between the latest candlelight protest and past successful democratic movements: Concern about social inequality played a key role in the mass mobilization of the candlelight protest.[65] In contrast, it was not a big factor in past uprisings because most people were poor in 1960 and Koreans experienced economic development with equity in 1987.

The final question is what influence the candlelight protest has on post-candlelight politics and democracy in Korea. In the literature of social movements, the larger a popular uprising, the greater the impacts on political change.[66] To date, it appears that the Democratic Party produced President Moon Jae-in *(Mun Chae-in)* on the vacancy election of 2017 and won a landslide victory in the recent April legislative election of 2020. Although there is a situational variable in which the Moon Jae-in government has coped well with the COVID-19 pandemic,[67] the fact that the Democratic Party gained 60% of the legislative seats reveals that the candlelight coalition of urban, college-educated, and middle-class voters in Seoul and capital areas are in line with the ruling Democratic Party and unfavorable about the United Future Party *(Miraet'onghaptang)*, which was Park Geun-hye's party. This government change and power shift are by and large consistent with the findings of this study because the candlelight protest was enormous in size and intensity and the main participants formed a coalition of opposition party supporters and urban middle-class citizens at that time.

However, it is still unclear what specific kinds of democratic change result from popular protests. Although it is a correct post hoc observation that the candlelight protest stopped the deconsolidation of Korean democracy under the Park Geun-hye government, can the protest lead to further democratic change? My analysis of the protest participants is negative regarding this question. It is because the predominant motivation for the candlelight protest was anti-Park Geun-hye sentiment. Our analysis showed that the candlelight protest was a negative coalition against Park Geun-hye and it lacked the substance for democratic change. In this respect, the candlelight protest should be described as a popular effort for government change by means other than elections.

---

65 Kang 2019.
66 Brancati 2016.
67 Choe, S.-H. (2020). In South Korea Vote, Virus Delivers Landslide Win to Governing Party. *The New York Times*, April 15, 2020. Available at: https://www.nytim es.com/2020/04/15/world/asia/south-korea-election.html [Accessed April 3, 2021].

6. Conclusion

Recently, popular uprisings and social protests have entered the central scene of politics around the world. The rise of social protests seems to be accompanied by problems of formal representative politics such as eroding political trust. This phenomenon is not restricted to developing and non-democratic countries but has also been observed in advanced countries. Despite the increasing number and scale of massive uprisings, there has been a lack of empirical studies on individual participation in the massive social protests, with some notable exceptions.[68] Because several million citizens participated in the candlelight protest and more than twenty Saturday anti-government rallies finally led to government change, the protest provides a unique case to investigate the backgrounds and motivations of the protest participants and expand current knowledge about the nature, causes, and consequences of recent mass uprisings.

Thus, the first contribution of this research is that I empirically identified the main configurations of participants in the candlelight protest and determined motivations driving their participation. Using the field survey of protesters and the nationwide SPOS, I found that main protest participants were college-educated and urban middle-class citizens, on the one hand, and opposition party supporters with progressive ideology, on the other. In addition, I showed that an overwhelming number of protest participants were residents of Seoul and the capital areas. It appears that those protest participants were predominantly driven by outrage about various misconducts of Park Geun-hye rather than for democratic reasons. Therefore, the candlelight protest was a negative and political coalition against Park Geun-hye rather than a positive one toward further democratic change.

Theoretically, this in-depth study of the candlelight protesters supports both modernization and partisan models and emphasizes a political explanation of recent mass uprisings. Although the political dynamics of protests varies across countries,[69] social configurations, and the strength of recent protests are determined by how governments treat (or mistreat) society and the economy in the years leading up to the popular uprisings.[70] The strength of popular uprisings is also influenced by the (un)balance

---

68 Beissinger 2013; Beissinger et al. 2015; Kang 2019; Rosenfeld 2017.
69 Brancati 2016; Carothers and Youngs 2015.
70 Beissinger 2013; Rosenfeld 2017.

of the ruling and opposition parties.[71] This reflects the fact that social movement has become political as state and democratic institutions have been globalized over the last half century.

Finally, what does the candlelight protest imply about Korean democracy after the protest? Because the candlelight protest was colossal in terms of size and duration, it has resulted in the end of democratic deconsolidation and enabled subsequent government change in 2017 and legislative power shift in 2020. However, my analysis suggests that describing the candlelight protest as democratic is post hoc and exaggerated because individual participants did not differ from non-participants in terms of democratic substance. The candlelight protest, which focused on a single issue, the impeachment of Park Geun-hye, indicates limitation in terms of further democratic change. This conclusion is also reasonable because the candlelight protest itself demonstrated the enduring problem of Korean democracy: hyper-civic activism in juxtaposition with weak representative institutions.[72] The systematic dissonance between them has remained intact even after the candlelight protest. In this respect, Korean democracy will be unstable unless Korean parties develop channels, networks, and linkages with various segments of civil society.

References

Acemoglu, D. and Robinson, J. (2006). *Economic Origins of Dictatorship and Democracy*. New York: Cambridge University Press.

Acemoglu, D. and Robinson, J. (2013). Middle Class Rising? *Whynationsfail.com*, July 2, 2013, [online]. Available at: http://whynationsfail.com/blog/2013/7/2/middle-class-rising.html [Accessed April 3, 2021].

Arce, M. (2010). Parties and Social Protest in Latin America's Neoliberal Era. *Party Politics*, 16 (5), 669-686.

Aytaç, S. E., Schiumerini, L., and Stokes, S. (2017). Protests and Repression in New Democracies. *Perspectives on Politics*, 15 (1), 62-82.

Beissinger, M. (2013). The Semblance of Democratic Revolution. *American Political Science Review*, 107 (3), 574-592.

Beissinger, M., Jamal, A., and Mazur, K. (2015). Explaining Divergent Revolutionary Coalitions. *Comparative Politics*, 48 (1), 1-21.

Boix, C. (2003). *Democracy and Redistribution*. Cambridge: Cambridge University Press.

---

71 Su 2015.
72 Kim 2012; Lee 2009.

Brancati, D. (2016). *Democracy Protests: Origins, Features and Significance*. New York: Cambridge University Press.

Bunce, V. and Wolchik, S. (2011). *Defeating Authoritarian Leaders in Postcommunist Countries*. New York: Cambridge University Press.

Carothers, T. and Youngs, R. (2015). *The Complexities of Global Protests*. Washington, DC: Carnegie Endowment for International Peace.

Chang, H.-J. (2017). South Koreans Worked a Democratic Miracle. Can They Do It Again? *The New York Times*, September 14, 2017. Available at: https://www.nyti mes.com/2017/09/14/opinion/south-korea-social-mobility.html [Accessed April 3, 2021].

Chang, P. (2018). Candlelight Protests in South Korea. *Ewha Journal of Social Science*, 34 (1), 5-18.

Choe, S.-H. (2015). Legacy of a South Korean Ferry Sinking. *The New York Times*, April 11, 2015. Available at: https://www.nytimes.com/2015/04/12/world/asia/le gacy-of-south-korea-sewol-ferry-sinking.html [Accessed April 3, 2021].

Choe, S.-H. (2020). In South Korea Vote, Virus Delivers Landslide Win to Governing Party. *The New York Times*, April 15, 2020. Available at: https://www.nytimes .com/2020/04/15/world/asia/south-korea-election.html [Accessed April 3, 2021].

Croissant, A. and Völkel, P. (2012). Party System Types and Party System Institutionalization. *Party Politics*, 18 (2), 235-265.

Dahl, R. (1998). *On Democracy*. New Haven: Yale University Press.

Dalton, R. (2014). *Citizen Politics: Public Opinion and Political Parties in Advanced Industrial Democracies*. Washington, DC: CQ Press.

Dasgupta, A. and Ziblatt, D. (2015). How Did Britain Democratize? *Journal of Economic History*, 75 (1), 1-29.

Fiori, A. and Kim, S. (2018). Civil Society and Democracy in South Korea. In Kim, Y. (Ed.), *Korea's Quest for Economic Democratization: Globalization, Polarization and Contention*. New York: Palgrave Macmillan, 141-170.

Geddes, B. (2011). What Causes Democratization. In Goodin, R. (Ed.), *Oxford Handbook of Political Science*. New York: Oxford University Press, 594-615.

Goldstone, J. (2011). Understanding the Revolutions of 2011. *Foreign Affairs*, 90 (3), 8-16.

Hicken, A. and Kuhonta, E. (2015). *Party System Institutionalization in Asia: Democracies, Autocracies, and the Shadows of the Past*. New York: Cambridge University Press.

Huntington, S. (1991). *The Third Wave: Democratization in the Late Twentieth Century*. Norman and London: University of Oklahoma Press.

Inglehart, R. and Welzel, C. (2005). *Modernization, Cultural Change, and Democracy: The Human Development Sequence*. New York: Cambridge University Press.

Joo, H.-M. (2017). A Return of 'The Strong Man's Daughter'. *Japanese Journal of Political Science*, 18 (2), 360-382.

Kang, W. J. (2019). Determinants of Unaffiliated Citizen Protests. *Korea Journal*, 59 (1), 46-78.

Kim, C. (2017). *Youth for Nation: Culture and Protest in Cold War South Korea.* Manoa: University of Hawai'i Press.

Kim, H. M., Choi, J. Y., and Cho, J. (2008). Changing Cleavage Structure in New Democracies. *Electoral Studies,* 27 (1), 136-150.

Kim, S. (2016). Brexit, Trump Tide of Populism Swamps South Korea President Park. *Bloomberg,* December 8, 2016. Available at: https://www.bloomberg.com/n ews/articles/2016-12-08/brexit-trump-tide-of-populism-swamps-south-korea-presi dent-park [Accessed April 3, 2021].

Kim, S. (2000). *The Politics of Democratization in Korea: The Role of Civil Society.* Pittsburgh: University of Pittsburgh.

Kim, S. (2012). 'Contentious Democracy' in South Korea. *Taiwan Journal of Democracy,* 8 (2), 51-61.

Kim, S. (2018). Candlelight for Our Country's Right Name. *Religions,* 9 (11), 330.

Kostelka, F. and Rovny, J. (2019). It's Not the Left: Ideology and Protest Participation in Old and New Democracies. *Comparative Political Studies,* 52 (11), 1677-1712.

Krastev, I. (2014). From Politics to Protest. *Journal of Democracy,* 25 (4), 5-19.

Lee, H.-K. (2017). South Korea as a Beacon of Asian Democracy. *East Asia Institute Column,* September 21, 2017.

Lee, Y. (2009). Democracy Without Parties? *Korea Observer,* 40 (1), 27-52.

Lie, J. (2015). The Wreck of the Sewol. *Georgetown Journal of International Affairs,* 16 (2), 111-121.

Lipset, S. M. (1960). *Political Man: The Social Bases of Politics.* Garden City: Doubleday.

Mounk, Y. (2018). *People vs. Democracy: Why Our Freedom Is in Danger and How to Save It.* Cambridge: Harvard University Press.

Norris, P. (2011). *Democratic Deficit: Critical Citizens Revisited.* New York: Cambridge University Press.

Rosenfeld, B. (2017). Reevaluating the Middle-Class Protest Paradigm. *American Political Science Review,* 111 (4), 637-652.

Schattschneider, E. E. (1942). *Party Government.* New York: Farrar and Rinehart.

Shin, D. (2018). The Deconsolidation of Liberal Democracy in Korea: Exploring its Cultural Roots. *Korea Observer,* 49 (1), 107-136.

Shin, G.-W. and Moon, R. (2017). South Korea after Impeachment. *Journal of Democracy,* 28 (4), 117-131.

Su, Y.-P. (2015). Anti-Government Protests in Democracies. *Comparative Politics,* 47 (2), 149-167.

Teele, D. L. (2018). *Forging the Franchise: The Political Origins of the Women's Vote.* New York: Princeton University Press.

Turner, M., Kwon, S.-H., and O'Donnell, M. (2018). Making Integrity Institutions Work in South Korea. *Asian Survey,* 58 (5), 898-919.

Appendix I. Main Survey Questions (The Sogang Public Opinion Survey, SPOS)

Perceived Salience of Politics (Composite Index)

Do you agree or disagree with the following statements?

1. Politics have an important influence on my life.
2. Politics plays a key role in development and state.

Democratic Support

Which of the following statements do you agree with most?

1. Democracy is always preferable to any other kind of government.
2. Under certain situations, a dictatorship is better than democracy.
3. It does not matter whether we have a democratic government or a dictatorship.

Demand for Direct Democracy

Do you agree or disgree with the following statement?

Referendums must be held to ask citizens' opinion when government determines an important policy.

Perception of Redistribution and Inequality (Composite Index)

Do you think that redistrbution of wealth is fair in our society?
How do you evaluate the gap between the rich and poor?

Appendix II. Descriptive Statistics (The Sogang Public Opinion Survey, SPOS)

	Observations	Min.	Max.	Mean	Standard Deviation
Participation in the Candlelight Protest	1199	0	1	0.24	0.43
Male	1200	0	1	0.50	0.50
Generation	1200	1	5	3.15	1.42
College Education	1192	0	1	0.67	0.47
Family Income	1119	1	5	2.85	1.44
Subjective Class Status	1185	1	3	1.71	0.68
Capital Areas	1200	0	1	0.50	0.50
Chŏlla	1200	0	1	0.10	0.30
Kyŏngsang	1200	0	1	0.26	0.44
Professional and Office Employees	1200	0	1	0.30	0.46
Labor Workers	1200	0	1	0.04	0.21
Saenuri Party Supporters	1200	0	1	0.10	0.30
Democratic Party Supporters	1200	0	1	0.28	0.45
Justice Party Supporters	1200	0	1	0.07	0.25
Political Interest	1200	0	2	1.58	0.64
Ideology (Conservative-Progressive)	1147	0	10	5.06	1.99
Democratic Support	1179	0	1	0.77	0.42
Demand for Direct Democracy	1178	1	4	3.27	0.75
Perception of Redistribution and Inequality	1183	3	8	6.64	1.07

South Korean Democratic Consolidation: Lessons from the 2017 Impeachment

Gabriel Jonsson

Introduction

In 2017, President Park Geun-hye (*Pak Kŭn-hye*) became the first president in South Korea (hereafter Korea except for quotations) to be impeached following nationwide candlelight demonstrations (*ch'otpuljiphoe*). The Constitutional Court suspended her from office owing to severe offences against criminal law and the constitution.

The impeachment raises many questions about the state of democracy in Korea. One of them is: What are the implications for democratic consolidation? Since in order to answer this question it is necessary to define what "democratic consolidation" is, well-known scholars' definitions are recorded in the first section and then applied in the empirical account. Among numerous definitions, the most relevant for this study were selected. In the next section, a brief review of whether democratic consolidation was reached or not following democratization in 1987 until 2014, when the author's book *Consolidation of Democracy in South Korea?* was published is made. Otherwise, developments in 2016-2017 cannot be properly evaluated. A few assessments by politicians and scholars from 2017, 2018 and 2019 of the implications of impeachment on democratic consolidation are presented and analyzed in far more detail to find out the impact. The study aims to enhance knowledge on this issue by critically evaluating the recorded assessments. The account includes opinions of a revision of the 1987 Constitution of the Republic of Korea since it will affect presidential power.

1. Theoretical Framework

On democratic consolidation Adam Przeworski (1991) writes:

> "Democracy is consolidated when under given political and economic conditions a particular system of institutions becomes the only game in town, when no one can imagine acting outside of the democratic

institutions, when all the losers want to do is to try again within the same institutions under which they have just lost."[1]

Hyug Baeg Im (2000) objects to Przeworski's minimalist conception that emphasizes a spontaneous and self-enforcing compliance with democratic norms and institutions: "Compliance constitutes the equilibrium of the decentralized strategies of all relevant political forces."[2] Instead, he regards the institutionalization of competition as a too narrow definition of democratic consolidation since it rests on Joseph Schumpeter's limited definition "Democracy means only that the people have the opportunity of accepting or refusing the men who are to rule them,"[3] that is equating democracy with elections. Democracy is a far more complex concept than regular electoral competition.

Im claims that in addition to the "procedural minimum" of regularly contested elections, "[...] a consolidated democracy needs guarantees of basic civil rights for citizens, accountability and responsiveness from its leaders, civilian control over the military, and Tocquevillian social democratization (that is the absence of extreme forms of social relations and the protection of citizens by law in social and economic relationships.)"[4] Also, "[i]n sum, one cannot consolidate democracy by simply institutionalizing electoral competition; one needs, more broadly, to stabilize, institutionalize, routinize, internalize, habituate, and legitimize democratic procedures and norms in political, social, economic, cultural, and legal arenas at both the elite and mass levels."[5]

Larry Diamond and his co-author Doh Chull Shin (2000) write that democracy to become consolidated must achieve deep, broad, and lasting legitimacy among political elites, politically significant parties and organizations, and the general public. At each level, actors must show a normative commitment to democracy as the best form of government and a behavioural commitment to follow the specific rules and procedures of the constitutional system. At its base, democratic consolidation involves

---

1 Quoted from Im, H. B. (2000). South Korean Democratic Consolidation in Comparative Perspective. In Diamond, L. and Kim, B.-K. (Eds.), *Consolidating Democracy in South Korea*. Boulder: Lynne Rienner Publishers, Inc., 21-52, pp. 22, 47: fn. 2.
2 Przeworski quoted from Im 2000, p. 22. Original quotation marks.
3 Schumpeter quoted from Fell, D. (2012). *Government and Politics in Taiwan*. London and New York: Routledge, pp. 29-30. Original quotation marks.
4 Im 2000, p. 23.
5 Ibid.

political leadership and institution building.[6] Together with Yun-han Chu (2001), they argue that consolidation of a democracy requires "broad and deep legitimation, such that all significant political actors, at both the elite and mass levels, believe that the democratic regime is the most right and appropriate for their society, better than any other realistic alternative they can imagine."[7]

Jean Grugel (2002) views democratic consolidation "[…] as the routinization and widespread acceptance of his [Przeworski's] definition of the democratic political system […]."[8] According to Samuel Huntington (1991), "[…] a democracy can be considered consolidated if it can survive two changes in ruling parties through post-transition elections," that is "the two turnover test."[9] It is an often cited definition and is the best measured criteria for consolidation.

According to Juan Linz (1990), a consolidated democratic government is one "[…] in which none of the major political actors, parties, or organized interests, forces, or institutions consider there is any alternative to democratic processes to gain power, no political institution or group has a claim to veto the action of democratically elected decision makers."[10] Hyug Baeg Im (2004) calls his definition "[…] standard criteria for negative consolidation."[11] In contrast, a positive concept of democratic consolidation assesses the degree of democratic consolidation by measuring how close the new liberal democracies come toward the achievement of full democratic rule. The question is: How much or to what extent did the country accomplish the 'second transition' from a democratic government to a democratic regime?

The positive concept of democratic consolidation investigates whether a new democracy moves forward by deepening democratic institutions, settling democratic governance, and ensuring quality democracy. In

---

6 Diamond, L. and Shin, D. C. (2000). Introduction: Institutional Reform and Democratic Consolidation in Korea. In Diamond, L. and Shin, D. C. (Eds.), *Institutional Reform and Democratic Consolidation in Korea*. Stanford University, Stanford: Hoover Institution Press, 1-41, pp. 18-19.

7 Chu, Y.-H., Diamond, L., and Shin, D. C. (2001). How People View Democracy: Halting Progress in Korea and Taiwan. *Journal of Democracy*, 12 (1), 122-136, p. 123. Original quotation marks.

8 Grugel quoted from Fell 2012, pp. 31, 263.

9 Huntington quoted from Fell 2012, pp. 30, 264.

10 Linz quoted from Im, H. B. (2004). Faltering Democratic Consolidation in South Korea: Democracy at the End of the 'three Kims' Era. *Democratization*, 11 (5), 579-597, pp. 181, 196: fn. 6. Original quotation marks.

11 Im 2004, p. 181.

other words, the concept focuses more on the quality of democracy than its survival. To call a new democracy a consolidated democracy, on the institutional level democratic governance in terms of high degrees of accountability, transparency, the rule of law, participation, representation, and stateness should be instituted in constitutional and representational systems and function as public governance of the administration, political parties, elections, the parliament, the judiciary, and civil society. On the behavioral and normative level, positive consolidation of a new democracy means, by Im quoting Larry Diamond (1999), "[...] broad and deep legitimation, such that all significant political actors, at both elite and mass levels, believe that the democratic regime is the best and most appropriate for their society, better than any other realistic alternative they can imagine."[12]

While agreeing with the above definition of a consolidated democratic government by Linz, Richard Gunther, Hans-Jürgen Puhle, and P. Nikiforos Diamandouros (1995) note "the absence of politically significant anti-system party or social movements" as the key indicator of democratic consolidation.[13] In a more comprehensive definition, Linz and Alfred Stepan (1996) point out three conditions that have to be fulfilled to consolidate democracy:

> "Behaviorally, no significant political group seriously attempts to overthrow the democratic regime; attitudinally, the overwhelming majority of people believe that any further political change must emerge within the parameters of democratic procedures; and constitutionally, all actors become habituated to the fact that political conflicts will be resolved according to established norms and that violations of these norms are likely to be both ineffective and costly."[14]

Linz and Stepan (1996) also write that unless a state exists, free and authoritative elections cannot be held, winners cannot exercise their power and citizens cannot have their rights effectively protected by a rule of law. They assert that "[...] democracy cannot be thought of as consolidated until a democratic transition has been brought to completion."[15] The comple-

---

12 Diamond quoted from Im 2004, pp. 182, 197: fn. 13. Original quotation marks.
13 Gunther, Puhle, and Diamandouros quoted from Im 2004, pp. 181, 196: fn. 7. Original quotation marks.
14 Linz and Stepan quoted from Im 2000, pp. 22, 47: fn. 4.
15 Linz, J. J. and Stepan, A. (1996). Toward Consolidated Democracies. *Journal of Democracy*, 7 (2), 14-33, p. 14.

tion of a democratic transition requires the holding of free and contested elections.

However, holding elections is not a sufficient condition for completion if the government subsequently formed is constrained in exerting power due to remaining authoritarian legacies. Additionally, "[…] no regime should be called a democracy unless its rulers govern democratically."[16] If elected governments violate the constitution and the rights of individuals and minorities, impinge upon the legislature's legitimate functions and thereby fail to rule within the bounds of a state of law, then they are not democracies. A "consolidated democracy" refers to a state in which democracy with its complex system of institutions, rules and patterned incentives and disincentives has become "the only game in town."[17] With consolidation, democracy becomes routinized and deeply internalized socially and institutionally as well as in political calculations to achieve success. Linz and Stepan point out that there is not only one type of consolidated democracy but many different types.

In addition to a functioning state, five other interrelated and mutually reinforcing conditions must be present, or be crafted, in order for a democracy to be consolidated:

- First, there must be space for the development of a free and active civil society, that is, self-organized and relatively autonomous groups, movements and individuals who attempt to articulate values, create associations, and promote their interests. Civil groups can include women's organizations, neighborhood associations, religious groupings, intellectual organizations, trade unions, entrepreneurial groups, and professional associations.
- Secondly, there should be a relatively autonomous political society. Political society refers to the space where political actors compete for the legitimate right to exercise control over public power and the state apparatus. Citizens have to develop an appreciation of the core institutions of a democratic society, that is, political parties, legislatures, elections, electoral rules, political leadership, and interparty alliances.
- Thirdly, all major political actors must nationwide be effectively subjected to a rule of law that protects individual and associational freedoms. There should be a strong consensus regarding the constitution and in particular a commitment to compelling procedures of governance that can be changed only by exceptional majorities. There must

---

16 Linz and Stepan 1996, p. 15.
17 Ibid. Original quotation marks.

be a clear hierarchy of laws that are interpreted by an independent judicial system and supported by a strong legal culture in civil society. A state of law is particularly crucial to consolidate democracy since it is the most important and routine way in which the elected government and the state administration operate under a network of laws, courts, semi-autonomous review, control agencies, and civil society norms that both check the state's illegal tendencies and embed the state in an interconnected web of mechanisms that require transparency and accountability.

- Fourthly, there must be a state bureaucracy that can be used by a democratic government to protect citizens' rights and deliver other basic services citizens demand by effectively exercising its claim to a monopoly of the legitimate use of force.
- Fifthly, there must be an institutionalized economic society to establish accepted norms, institutions, and regulations that mediate between the state and the market. The state also has to provide public goods in education, health, and transportation as well as implement such tasks as narrowing the scope of public ownership, that is, privatization.[18]

Aurel Croissant (2002) uses the concept "consolidation" also with regard to the party system. Consolidation on a macro level "[…] is achieved when the fragmentation and the degree of volatility between the parties are stable, and when the level of ideological polarization of the party system is low."[19] On a micro level, "consolidation is achieved when stable party structures have developed."[20] Indicators are the parties' age, their degree of internal cohesion and their degree of organizational stability and professionalism.[21] Similarly, John Peeley (2004) argues that, along with an active civil society and stable governing institutions, the institutionalization of a stable political party system is one of the critical elements of democratic consolidation.[22]

Clearly, there are many definitions among which particularly "the only game in town" will be applied in the following section. Given the com-

---

18 Linz and Stepan 1996, pp. 17-22.
19 Croissant, A. (2002). Strong Presidents, Weak Democracy? Presidents, Parliaments and Political Parties in South Korea. *Korea Observer*, 33 (1), 1-45, p. 10.
20 Ibid.
21 Ibid.
22 Bailey, D. (2010). Politics on the Peninsula: Democratic Consolidation and the Political Party System in South Korea. *Graduate Journal of Asia-Pacific Studies*, 7 (1) (2010), 32-48, p. 36.

plexity of a political system, presidential power, how institutions work and the role of political parties are also included in the analysis.

2. The Significance of the Impeachment of President Park Geun-hye

The author applied the above definitions in his book from 2014 and concluded that Korea had "[…] made great progress towards accomplishing democratic consolidation by fulfilling it in certain respects" but still had "[…] a long way to go to complete democratic consolidation by institutionalizing the political process."[23] Huntington's "two-turnover test" was accomplished with Lee Myung-bak's (*Yi Myŏng-bak*) victory in the 2007 presidential election but applying Przeworski's concept "the only game in town" to assess the degree of democratic consolidation is more difficult. For instance, the high fluidity of political parties due to political attachment to individuals, factionalism, and the weak organization makes it hard to assess what Przeworski's term "[…] a particular system of institutions […]" means.[24] However, when President Kim Young-sam (*Kim Yŏng-sam*) (1993-1998) by pursuing purges within the military secured civilian control over the military, democratic institutions became the only game in town but democratic procedures were not always followed. For example, unilateral voting took place a few times in the National Assembly after the 1987 revision of the constitution undermining democratic consolidation.

To in line with the opinion of Im (2000) create democratic consolidation by establishing democratic procedures and norms in political, social, economic, cultural, and legal arenas at all levels in society turned out to be very difficult. Explanations were the high power concentration to the president in a strictly hierarchical Confucian society idealizing the leader, weak political parties, remaining authoritarian legacies, inter-Korean tensions, the time aspect in introducing democracy, and that the presidents themselves to a large extent have shaped the political system. Regionalism, weak political parties, the legacy of authoritarian governments, and tense inter-Korean relations were the main obstacles to democratic consolidation. In contrast to the importance of political parties to work properly to reach democratic consolidation identified, personalization rather than institutionalization of politics contributed to create political quarrels. "Po-

---

23 Jonsson, G. (2014). *Consolidation of Democracy in South Korea?* Stockholm: Stockholm University, p. 116.
24 Ibid., p. 112.

litical parties were far from democratic or policy-oriented but the political tools of their leaders."[25] In brief, the difficulties to following democratization in 1987 also accomplish democratic consolidation should not be underestimated.[26]

Considering these characteristics of Korean politics, an important question to ask is whether the conclusions reached in 2014 have changed or not following the 2017 impeachment.[27] Park Geun-hye was elected president in December 2012 but was on December 9, 2016, charged by the National Assembly with a variety of offences against criminal law as well as the constitution and was suspended from office. Offences recorded by scholars Seonhwa Kim (2017) and Junhan Lee (2017) include a) entrusting a friend to make important decisions and appointments, b) abusing the presidential authority, c) infringing on press freedom, d) failing to appear or act following the 2014 Sewol ferry (*Sewŏlho*) tragedy in which more than 300 people, mostly school children, died, e) demanding bribes from prominent *chaebŏl*, and f) preparing unlawful action against political opponents.[28]

---

25 Jonsson 2014, p. 113.

26 Ibid., pp. 112-116.

27 On March 12, 2004, a motion to impeach President Roh Moo-hyun (*No Mu-hyŏn*) was passed in the National Assembly since he prior to the parliamentary elections by appealing for support to his Uri Party (*Uridang*) had violated the constitution. He had also refused to publicly apologize for his conduct. Other reasons were illegal funds and bribes involving his allies, the president's reckless remarks and the proposal in October 2003 to hold a referendum on his leadership in violation of the constitution. His presidency was immediately suspended. The impeachment was highly unpopular. On May 14, the Constitutional Court restored the status quo by dismissing the impeachment, although the president had violated the required impartiality during elections but the violation was not serious enough to remove him from office. The verdict was widely accepted by the Korean public. From Jonsson 2014, pp. 82-83.

28 Jonsson 2014, p. 109; Kim, S. (2017). Reforming South Korea's 'Imperial Presidency'. *Policy Brief*, 205, October 10, 2017. Stockholm: Institute for Security and Development Policy, p. 2; Lee, J. (2017). Pak Kŭn-hye kukhoe t'anhaeg-ŭi yŏksajŏk ŭimi-wa Han'guk chŏngch'i-e kwanhan hamŭi [The Historical Significance of the National Assembly's Impeachment of Pak Kŭn-hye and Its Implications for South Korean Politics]. In *T'anhaek soch'uan kagyŏl 1 chunyŏn t'oronhoe: Pak Kŭn-hye kukhoe t'anhaeg-ŭi chŏngch'isajŏk ŭimi-wa Han'guk chŏngch'i-ŭi sidaejŏk kwaje [Debate Forum on the First Anniversary of the Approval of the Proposal for Impeachment: The Significance for the Political History of the Impeachment by the National Assembly of Pak Kŭn-hye and The Present Tasks for South Korean Politics]*. n. p.: Tŏmirae yŏn'guso [Korea Institute for the Future], Tŏburŏminjudang [Democratic Party], Member of Parliament U Sang-ho, 11-34, pp. 26-27, 29. The author

After the Constitutional Court on March 10, 2017, unanimously had approved impeachment dismissing president Park Geun-hye as the first president from office law scholar Jongcheol Kim made the first to the author known assessment of its significance. He argues that the Constitutional Court through the decision set a new milestone in the country's history of constitutional democracy by clearly setting the constitutional and legal standard to which government officials, including the president, should adhere. Such standards include that the president's acts should be open and transparent to the extent that they can be assessed by the people and the National Assembly. The case represented the maturity of constitutional democracy. The impeachment decision was monumental since it confirmed that the Constitutional Court is an important coordinator of the system. At the same time, the turmoil surrounding the impeachment made it clear that the democratic order established through the 1987 Constitution of the Republic of Korea needed to be strengthened by reforming the Prosecutor's Office, the judiciary, the election law, and the political party law. Such reforms relate to his point that how to eradicate corruption remained as a challenge to citizens after impeachment.[29]

Doh Chull Shin (2017) makes a more negative assessment of the impeachment by writing that fully consolidated liberal democracy broke down. In spite of their wealth and education, Koreans preferred paternalistic autocracy to liberal democracy since the political and social legacies of Confucianism are deeply embedded in society encouraging "[...] leaders to play an autocratic or commanding role and their subordinates to play a deferential or submissive role."[30] He well illuminates how the Confucian culture affected abuse of presidential authority recorded above:

---

has not found any exact answer to how the steps leading to impeachment took place but has come to know two plausible explanations. One is that the president did not understand that her acts could be detected. The other is that a certain circle of top people all knew what she was doing but did not intervene. They may have feared for their position. Nonetheless, several people were basically complicit in allowing her to misuse power.

29 Kim, J. (2017). The Impeachment of South Korean President Park Geun-Hye: Constitution, Politics and Democracy. *East Asia Foundation Policy Debates*, 67, March 21, 2017, pp. 1-3.

30 Shin, D. C. (2017). *President Park Geun-hye and the Deconsolidation of Liberal Democracy in South Korea: Exploring its Cultural Roots President Park Geun-hye and the Deconsolidation of Liberal Democracy in South Korea: Exploring its Cultural Roots.* UC Irvine, Center for the Study of Democracy Working Paper, July 14, 2017. Available at: https://escholarship.org/uc/item/1t68c47v [Accessed April 7, 2021], p. 3.

"More so than any of her predecessors, President Park Geun-hye likened herself to a virtuous and wise ruler of ancient Confucian Korea, and placed herself above the law. Envisioning herself as a reigning queen, she refused to open the policymaking process especially to those with opposing views, while demanding allegiance from the government officials who worked closely with her. Those officials and many others inside and outside her government remained merely her allegiant subordinates. The end results were the resurgence of autocratic politics and the deconsolidation of liberal democracy in Korea."[31]

However, as we will see, opinions on the impact of impeachment are diverse. On December 8, 2017, a debate forum was held on the first anniversary of the National Assembly's approval of impeachment of President Park Geun-hye. Positive assessments were made by participants from the ruling Democratic Party *(Tŏburŏminjudang)*. Party representative Choo Mi-ae *(Ch'u Mi-ae)* argues that the impeachment was the first step to recover the collapsed constitutional order and the beginning of a long march to restore the damage made on democracy. Impeachment would have been impossible without the nationwide candlelight demonstrations.[32]

Floor representative U Wŏn-sik points out that the impeachment of an incumbent president was indeed a misfortune in Korea's constitutional history but it was resolved through protection of the constitutional order. By approving impeachment, the horizons of Korean democracy and rule of law have been further widened. In fact, the core principles of democracy that the citizens are the owners of the country and that no power can stand above the people were reconfirmed. The principle that power rests with the people was realized through procedures decided by the constitution and legislation. Especially the National Assembly played with popular support the leading role to overcome the national crisis in a peaceful and legal way. The approval of impeachment is a symbol that Korean democracy is solid and healthy. The event will also be remembered forever as an im-

---

31 Shin 2017, p. 14.
32 Ch'u, M.-A. (2017). Ch'uksa [Congratulation Address]. In *T'anhaek soch'uan kagyŏl 1 chunyŏn t'oronhoe: Pak Kŭn-hye kukhoe t'anhaeg-ŭi chŏngch'isajŏk ŭimi-wa Han'guk chŏngch'i-ŭi sidaejŏk kwaje [Debate Forum on the First Anniversary of the Approval of the Proposal for Impeachment: The Significance for the Political History of the Impeachment by the National Assembly of Pak Kŭn-hye and The Present Tasks for South Korean Politics]*. n. p.: Tŏmirae yŏn'guso [Korea Institute for the Future], Tŏburŏminjudang [Democratic Party], Member of Parliament U Sang-ho, 4-5, p. 4.

portant milestone in parliamentary democracy.[33] Member of parliament U Sang-ho concurs with Choo's opinion that impeachment would have been impossible without the nationwide candlelight demonstrations. Through impeachment, democracy has been revived. The National Assembly reconfirmed that power rests with the people by exerting its power based on the constitution and legislation.[34]

In a positive and the most comprehensive assessment of the approval of impeachment known to the author, Lee (2017) agrees with the opinions of the members of the Democratic Party on the importance of the National Assembly. It sincerely implemented its task to decide on impeachment on the basis of the Constitution of the Republic of Korea, Article 65, and the National Assembly Law, Chapter 11. Both documents contain provisions on how to impeach the president if the constitution or the law have been broken.[35] He enumerates ten significant points regarding the impeachment of Park Geun-hye:

- First, the National Assembly legally implemented its task to restrain the executive power in accordance with the constitution.
- Second, the National Assembly acted on the candlelight demonstrators' demand for the resignation of President Park Geun-hye in accordance with constitutional procedures and the processes of representative democracy.
- Third, since 234 members of parliament voted for impeachment, 56 against and nine abstained or cast non-valid notes and the total number of members from the opposition and independents was 172, also

---

33 U, W.-S. (2017). Ch'uksa [Congratulation Address]. In *T'anhaek soch'uan kagyŏl 1 chunyŏn t'oronhoe: Pak Kŭn-hye kukhoe t'anhaeg-ŭi chŏngch'isajŏk ŭimi-wa Han'guk chŏngch'i-ŭi sidaejŏk kwaje [Debate Forum on the First Anniversary of the Approval of the Proposal for Impeachment: The Significance for the Political History of the Impeachment by the National Assembly of Pak Kŭn-hye and The Present Tasks for South Korean Politics].* n. p.: Tŏmirae yŏn'guso [Korea Institute for the Future], Tŏburŏminjudang [Democratic Party], Member of Parliament U Sang-ho, 6-7, p. 6.

34 U, S.-H. (2017). Insamal [Greeting]. In *T'anhaek soch'uan kagyŏl 1 chunyŏn t'oronhoe: Pak Kŭn-hye kukhoe t'anhaeg-ŭi chŏngch'isajŏk ŭimi-wa Han'guk chŏngch'i-ŭi sidaejŏk kwaje [Debate Forum on the First Anniversary of the Approval of the Proposal for Impeachment: The Significance for the Political History of the Impeachment by the National Assembly of Pak Kŭn-hye and The Present Tasks for South Korean Politics].* n. p.: Tŏmirae yŏn'guso [Korea Institute for the Future], Tŏburŏminjudang [Democratic Party], Member of Parliament U Sang-ho, 8-9, p. 8.

35 Lee 2017, pp. 25-26.

62 members from the ruling Saenuri Party *(Saenuridang)* supported impeachment.

- Fourth, when impeachment was approved, the number of votes substantially exceeded the minimum number of 200 members reconfirming that also members from the Saenuri Party supported impeachment.
- Fifth, the ongoing Park Geun-hye-Choi Soon-sil *(Ch'oe Sun-sil)*-gate greatly changed the public opinion and enlarged the candlelight demonstrations, implying that her approval rate and leadership had dropped greatly.
- Sixth, the Park Geun-hye-Choi Soon-sil-gate was so severe that it evoked resentment among the whole population. The nationwide candlelight demonstrations demanding the president's resignation affected politics to the extent that there was no other alternative than to vote on impeachment and to approve it.
- Seventh, also the Constitutional Court systematically followed the constitution and the Constitutional Court Act in judging on impeachment.
- Eighth, the impeachment of President Park Geun-hye was a historical event that took place 30 years after democratization in 1987. The most democratic constitutional order was paradoxically adopted to judge against the president who had most severely violated democratic procedures.
- Ninth, since after the impeachment a peaceful and fair presidential election was held on May 9, 2017, the meaning of one of the definitions of democracy "democratic election is the only game in town" became clear. Lee argues that this suggests that Korea had accomplished a mature democracy or, differently expressed, democratic consolidation.
- Tenth, when the 1960 April Revolution occurred President Syngman Rhee *(Yi Sŭng-man)* had gone in exile before the opposition parties and the National Assembly had begun to work properly. The 1987 June Democratization Movement led to the June 29 Declaration that was followed by a revision of the constitution based on a grand political compromise and the holding of presidential elections. In comparison, the candlelight demonstrations ended with the Constitutional Court's decision on impeachment that was followed by presidential elections.[36]

In a comprehensive evaluation of the significance of the popular protests in 2016, sociologist Kim Yun-t'ae (2017) argues that by accomplishing

---

36 Lee 2017, pp. 30-31.

more than two shifts of political power since the democratization movement in 1987, democratic consolidation had been reached in accordance with the two-turnover test. However, such limits of democracy as a) abuses of power and graft, b) restrictions of popular fundamental rights, and c) the rise of socio-economic inequality were continuously appearing.[37] Notably, the first two points concur with points b and c by Seonhwa Kim (2017) and Lee (2017) on Park Geun-hye's impeachment identified above.

Although the popular candlelight demonstrations beginning in October 2016 were set off by the Park Geun-hye-Choi Soon-sil-gate and the National Pension-Samsung corruption scandal, the structural reasons behind them pointed out by Kim Yun-t'ae (2017) were a) breaches of such election promises as economic democratization and the creation of a welfare state, b) intervention of the National Intelligence Service in the 2012 presidential elections, c) the Sewol ferry disaster, and d) dissatisfaction with the government-business collusion. The peaks of the protests were the approval of impeachment in December 2016 followed by the verdict by the Constitutional Court in March 2017. At the same time, the six-month non-violent popular movement wrote new history through the honorary bloodless protests that followed constitutional procedures.[38]

The 2016 demonstrations showed new characteristics as a non-violent movement led by citizens who cooperated with political parties. Civil society was becoming more active than the political parties. During six months, there were 17 million participants in unprecedented long lasting, nationwide, and large-scale demonstrations. The candlelight demonstrations was a diverse popular movement led on one hand by high school and university students and organized movements such as the Korean Confederation of Trade Unions. On the other hand, actors were media such as the newspaper *Hankyoreh*, non-mainstream broadcasting stations and citizens from diverse classes. The age span was great from teenagers to people above 70 years of age. The demonstrations ended with

---

37 Kim, Y.-T. (2017). Simin hyŏngmyŏng-ŭi dilemma: 2016 nyŏn ch'oppul hyŏngmyŏng-ŭi yŏksajŏk ŭi ŭi-wa saeroun kwaje [The Dilemma of the Citizens' Revolution: The Historical Significance of and New Tasks for the 2016 Candlelight Revolution]. In *T'anhaek soch'uan kagyŏl 1 chunyŏn t'oronhoe: Pak Kŭn-hye kukhoe t'anhaeg-ŭi chŏngchi'sajŏk ŭimi-wa Han'guk chŏngch'i-ŭi sidaejŏk kwaje [Debate Forum on the First Anniversary of the Approval of the Proposal for Impeachment: The Significance for the Political History of the Impeachment by the National Assembly of Pak Kŭn-hye and The Present Tasks for South Korean Politics]*. n. p.: Tŏmirae yŏn'guso [Korea Institute for the Future], Tŏburŏminjudang [Democratic Party], Member of Parliament U Sang-ho, 49-56, pp. 49, 51.

38 Kim, Y.-T. 2017, p. 52.

impeachment and an early presidential election. Since there was a change of government in accordance with constitutional procedures, democracy showed stability and durability. Initially, the candlelight demonstrations were led by civil society organizations whereas the political parties were passive or followed events. However, when demonstrations expanded and popular support grew the parties worked in the National Assembly for impeachment. Since the parties were active, negative opinions about them in the candlelight demonstrations diminished. Consequently, in the 2017 presidential elections voting turnout rate was high, as was support for the new government.

The candlelight demonstrations accomplished impeachment and a change of government, but did not essentially change society. They could not affect many social characteristics. In fact, there was no change at all in the composition of the National Assembly, where the government was in minority and too weak to raise reforms. At the same time, popular dissatisfaction with the inability to exert influence on government policies was rising. In order to resolve the dilemmas of the popular protests there are a few urgent tasks to overcome that all match with the broad definitions of democratic consolidation such as those of Linz and Stepan (1996), Im (2000, 2004), and Diamond and Shin (2000):

- First, deep-rooted evils have to be cleared up and rule of law established. Deep-rooted evils include a) rigged elections and b) abuse of power and graft, as already pointed out above. Resolving such issues correspond with rule of law that was damaged by the Park Geun-hye-Choi Soon-sil-gate.
- Second, socio-economic reforms in order to accomplish a) economic democratization, b) a welfare state and c) social justice and equality are needed. Such issues were the structural reasons behind the popular protests in 2016-2017.
- Third, governance in terms of the state, supranational organizations, regional organizations and the administrative network in which civil society participates needs to be strengthened. Instead of one-sided decision-making by the government, civil society must become involved in discussions and consultations.
- Fourth, for an institutionalization of the success of the popular protests, a revision of the 1987 Constitution that would reduce excessive power of the imperial president and strengthen the power of the National Assembly is needed. A reorganization of election districts to allow broader political representation is also needed. The current

electoral system gives the larger parties a disproportionate number of seats in the National Assembly.[39]

Seonwha Kim (2017) writes that the impeachment gave renewed impetus to the issue of constitutional reform. She argues that if the constitution would be revised, the most important issue is decentralization of powers through the dispersion of presidential power and of centralized government. Critics argue that the constitution does not grant a provision for an adequate division of power, with a lack of proper mechanisms to check and balance a strong executive. Deficiencies include a) the tendency of the president to control the National Assembly through the authoritarian party system, b) the absence of a fully impartial judiciary since its appointees are nominated by the president, c) the inefficiency of congressional investigative powers and that of the prosecutor and, finally, d) the lack of a properly functioning board of audit and inspection. The body is supposedly independent and has the task to scrutinize government acts but it remains under the president.[40] Jongcheol Kim (2017) concurs with her opinion by writing: "Regarding the Constitution itself, groundbreaking decentralization is necessary in order to disperse the risks of a centralized political system. However, a parliamentary system or semi-presidential system will not easily gain public support, because it can intensify the decay of power and weaken people's sovereignty."[41]

Other [non-specified] observers referred to by Seonwha Kim (2017) argue that the constitution leaves room for interpretation, allowing presidential power to be restrained and a balance maintained between constitutional institutions. In 2017, the ruling Democratic Party advocated the maintenance of the current presidential system but with substantial checks and balances as well as to change the current single five-year term to a four-year, two-term presidency to make the president more accountable to the public at re-election. The opposition Liberty Korea Party *(Chayuhan'guktang)* favored a semi-presidential system dividing administrative functions between the president elected by the people and the

---

39 Kim, S. 2017, p. 2; Kim, Y.-T. 2017, pp. 52-56. Kim Yun-t'ae consistently writes "revolution" *(hyŏngmyŏng)* in front of "citizens" *(simin)* and "candlelight" *(ch'otpul)* which the author finds inappropriate since it was not a question of introducing a new social order, as often is the case when revolutions occur. Instead, "demonstrations" and "protests" are used as synonyms for the popular movement. Kim does not rank the importance of the urgent tasks but also the author writes "first" etc. for the sake of convenience.

40 Kim, S. 2017, pp. 1-2.

41 Kim, J. 2017, p. 1.

prime minister elected by the National Assembly. Such a system would make the administration more responsible to the legislative. Both models for constitutional revision necessitate a parliament with substantial supervisory power over the executive.[42]

In 2018, political scientist Erik Mobrand made a positive assessment of the state of democracy by writing: "On the other hand, developments in 2016-2017 proved that South Korea's democracy is among the most resilient in the world. When political institutions failed to prevent the corruption of an insulated elite, ordinary citizens intervened."[43] In a more general comment about the political system, he writes: "What is most impressive about South Korea's democracy is not the formal institutional arrangement but informal engagement by citizens."[44] Finally, he writes: "Having the example of the Candlelight Movement reminds people – and those in government – that mass action can change the course of politics dramatically."[45]

In 2019, scholars Jung Pak and Paul Park more cautiously assessed the state of Korean democracy by writing: "The candlelight movement was emblematic of a culture of protest in South Korean society and it reflects the weakness of its representative democracy and lingering suspicion of governments that are linked to the country's history of military regimes."[46] Thus, the protests "showcased Korea's vibrant civil society" but also "exposed the lingering weakness of the country's political institutions and the shortcomings of this 30-year-old liberal democracy."[47] They conclude with a rather gloomy assessment:

> "South Korea has come a long way in establishing a democratic system, but unless the country tackles the weaknesses of its democratic institutions and the way the government engages with the public to educate and empower its citizens, another mass protest like the candlelight movement is likely to reoccur."[48]

---

42 Kim, S. 2017, p. 2.
43 Mobrand, E. (2018). Democracy is More than a Political System: Lessons from South Korea's Democratic Transformation. *The Asan Forum*, 7 (4) (July-August), 1-19, p. 2.
44 Mobrand 2018, p. 11.
45 Ibid., p. 14.
46 Pak, J. and Park, P. (2019). Liberal Democracy in South Korea. Policy Brief. *Foreign Policy at Brookings*, February 26, 2019, p. 1.
47 Ibid., p. 2.
48 Ibid., p. 9.

In the latest to the author known assessment of impeachment, political scientist Soon-ok Shin (2020) points out that the scandal leading to the president's resignation revealed sharp impediments in the process towards democratic consolidation. As other researchers, she points out that one was the political party system that suffered from chronic structural weaknesses. The short life span of political parties was indicative of the system's inherent volatility. The longest standing party was the conservative Grand National Party *(Hannaradang)* that existed from 1997-2012. Political parties had evolved to reflect three characteristics: regionalism, personality-driven party politics, and factionalism.[49]

Conclusions

Democracy in Korea has been resilient while showing many weaknesses that need to be overcome to accomplish democratic consolidation. Until 2014 progress had been made through the accomplishment of the "two-turnover test" and the "only game in town" but when applying broader definitions of democratic consolidation such as those of Linz and Stepan (1996), Im (2000, 2004), and Diamond and Shin (2000), many obstacles remained.

Popular protests played a crucial role in impeachment of President Park Geun-hye in 2016-2017 following her severe offences against criminal law and the constitution. There were no uncertainties regarding the validity of the impeachment. Assessments of the 2017 impeachment identified are, generally speaking, positive. Observers emphasize that the process leading to impeachment took place in accordance with democratic procedures strengthening democracy. Critics argue that the strong influence of Confucianism caused a breakdown of liberal democracy leading to deconsolidation and that political parties remained weak. Political behavior did not change during the Park Geun-hye government reflecting the strong impact of Confucianism on politics that remained an obstacle to democratic consolidation. Considering main characteristics of democratic consolidation identified, democracy remained the only game in town but presidential power was excessive and the party system needed to be institutionalized. The National Assembly played the leading role in impeachment but there was a need for institutional reforms to enhance democratic consolidation.

---

49 Shin, S.-O. (2020). The Rise and Fall of Park Geun-hye: The Perils of South Korea's Weak Party System. *The Pacific Review*, 33 (1), 153-183, p. 157.

Also other evaluations on the impact of impeachment on democratic consolidation and the state of Korean democracy imply, if the broader definitions identified are applied, that the situation has not changed since 2017. Assessments confirm that democracy is "the only game in town" reconfirming that democratic consolidation has been reached but only from a narrow point of view. Democratic consolidation in a broader sense has not yet been accomplished since obstacles identified in 2014 remain. Only time will tell whether Korea will accomplish full democratic consolidation. It also remains to be seen whether a revision of the 1987 Constitution of the Republic of Korea will affect democratic consolidation.

References

Bailey, D. (2010). Politics on the Peninsula: Democratic Consolidation and the Political Party System in South Korea. *Graduate Journal of Asia-Pacific Studies, 7* (1) (2010), 32-48.

Ch'u, M.-A. (2017). Ch'uksa [Congratulation Address]. In *T'anhaek soch'uan kagyŏl 1 chunyŏn t'oronhoe: Pak Kŭn-hye kukhoe t'anhaeg-ŭi chŏngch'isajŏk ŭimi-wa Han'guk chŏngch'i-ŭi sidaejŏk kwaje [Debate Forum on the First Anniversary of the Approval of the Proposal for Impeachment: The Significance for the Political History of the Impeachment by the National Assembly of Pak Kŭn-hye and The Present Tasks for South Korean Politics].* n. p.: Tŏmirae yŏn'guso [Korea Institute for the Future], Tŏburŏminjudang [Democratic Party], Member of Parliament U Sang-ho, 4-5.

Chu, Y.-H., Diamond, L., and Shin, D. C. (2001). How People View Democracy: Halting Progress in Korea and Taiwan. *Journal of Democracy, 12* (1), 122-136.

Croissant, A. (2002). Strong Presidents, Weak Democracy? Presidents, Parliaments and Political Parties in South Korea. *Korea Observer, 33* (1), 1-45.

Diamond, L. and Shin, D. C. (2000). Introduction: Institutional Reform and Democratic Consolidation in Korea. In Diamond, L. and Shin, D. C. (Eds.), *Institutional Reform and Democratic Consolidation in Korea.* Stanford University, Stanford: Hoover Institution Press, 1-41.

Fell, D. (2012). *Government and Politics in Taiwan.* London and New York: Routledge.

Im, H. B. (2000). South Korean Democratic Consolidation in Comparative Perspective. In Diamond, L. and Kim, B.-K. (Eds.), *Consolidating Democracy in South Korea.* Boulder: Lynne Rienner Publishers, Inc., 21-52.

Im, H. B. (2004). Faltering Democratic Consolidation in South Korea: Democracy at the End of the 'three Kims' Era. *Democratization, 11* (5), 579-597.

Jonsson, G. (2014). *Consolidation of Democracy in South Korea?* Stockholm: Stockholm University.

Kim, J. (2017). The Impeachment of South Korean President Park Geun-Hye: Constitution, Politics and Democracy. *East Asia Foundation Policy Debates*, 67, March 21, 2017.

Kim, S. (2017). Reforming South Korea's 'Imperial Presidency'. *Policy Brief*, 205, October 10, 2017. Stockholm: Institute for Security and Development Policy.

Kim, Y.-T. (2017). Simin hyŏngmyŏng-ŭi dilemma: 2016 nyŏn ch'oppul hyŏngmyŏng-ŭi yŏksajŏk ŭi ŭi-wa saeroun kwaje [The Dilemma of the Citizens' Revolution: The Historical Significance of and New Tasks for the 2016 Candlelight Revolution]. In *T'anhaek soch'uan kagyŏl 1 chunyŏn t'oronhoe: Pak Kŭn-hye kukhoe t'anhaeg-ŭi chŏngchi'sajŏk ŭimi-wa Han'guk chŏngch'i-ŭi sidaejŏk kwaje [Debate Forum on the First Anniversary of the Approval of the Proposal for Impeachment: The Significance for the Political History of the Impeachment by the National Assembly of Pak Kŭn-hye and The Present Tasks for South Korean Politics].* n. p.: Tŏmirae yŏn'guso [Korea Institute for the Future], Tŏburŏminjudang [Democratic Party], Member of Parliament U Sang-ho, 49-56.

Lee, J. (2017). Pak Kŭn-hye kukhoe t'anhaeg-ŭi yŏksajŏk ŭimi-wa Han'guk chŏngch'i-i kwanhan hamŭi [The Historical Significance of the National Assembly's Impeachment of Pak Kŭn-hye and Its Implications for South Korean Politics]. In *T'anhaek soch'uan kagyŏl 1 chunyŏn t'oronhoe: Pak Kŭn-hye kukhoe t'anhaeg-ŭi chŏngchi'sajŏk ŭimi-wa Han'guk chŏngch'i-ŭi sidaejŏk kwaje [Debate Forum on the First Anniversary of the Approval of the Proposal for Impeachment: The Significance for the Political History of the Impeachment by the National Assembly of Pak Kŭn-hye and The Present Tasks for South Korean Politics].* n. p.: Tŏmirae yŏn'guso [Korea Institute for the Future], Tŏburŏminjudang [Democratic Party], Member of Parliament U Sang-ho, 11-34.

Linz, J. J. and Stepan, A. (1996). Toward Consolidated Democracies. *Journal of Democracy*, 7 (2), 14-33.

Mobrand, E. (2018). Democracy Is More Than a Political System: Lessons from South Korea's Democratic Transformation. *The Asan Forum*, 7 (4) (July-August), 1-19.

Pak, J. and Park, P. (2019). Liberal Democracy in South Korea. Policy Brief. *Foreign Policy at Brookings*, February 26, 2019.

Shin, D. C. (2017). *President Park Geun-hye and the Deconsolidation of Liberal Democracy in South Korea: Exploring its Cultural Roots President Park Geun-hye and the Deconsolidation of Liberal Democracy in South Korea: Exploring its Cultural Roots.* UC Irvine, Center for the Study of Democracy Working Paper, July 14, 2017. Available at: https://escholarship.org/uc/item/1t68c47v [Accessed April 7, 2021].

Shin, S.-O. (2020). The Rise and Fall of Park Geun-hye: The Perils of South Korea's Weak Party System. *The Pacific Review*, 33 (1), 153-183.

U, S.-H. (2017). Insamal [Greeting]. In *T'anhaek soch'uan kagyŏl 1 chunyŏn t'oronhoe: Pak Kŭn-hye kukhoe t'anhaeg-ŭi chŏngchi'sajŏk ŭimi-wa Han'guk chŏngch'i-ŭi sidaejŏk kwaje [Debate Forum on the First Anniversary of the Approval of the Proposal for Impeachment: The Significance for the Political History of the Impeachment by the National Assembly of Pak Kŭn-hye and The Present Tasks for South Korean Politics].* n. p.: Tŏmirae yŏn'guso [Korea Institute for the Future], Tŏburŏminjudang [Democratic Party], Member of Parliament U Sang-ho, 8-9.

U, W.-S. (2017). Ch'uksa [Congratulation Address]. In *T'anhaek soch'uan kagyŏl 1 chunyŏn t'oronhoe: Pak Kŭn-hye kukhoe t'anhaeg-ŭi chŏngchi'sajŏk ŭimi-wa Han'guk chŏngch'i-ŭi sidaejŏk kwaje. [Debate Forum on the First Anniversary of the Approval of the Proposal for Impeachment: The Significance for the Political History of the Impeachment by the National Assembly of Pak Kŭn-hye and The Present Tasks for South Korean Politics].* n. p.: Tŏmirae yŏn'guso [Korea Institute for the Future], Tŏburŏminjudang [Democratic Party], Member of Parliament U Sang-ho, 6-7.

Contributors

Dr. Youngho Cho is a political scientist and Associate Professor at the Department of Political Science at Sogang University, Seoul/Korea. His research interests center around the empirical investigation of public attitudes and political culture in democratization processes.

Julia Dumin is a researcher and PhD candidate at the Department of Philosophy and Political Science at TU Dortmund University, Germany. Her research centers on democratization processes, with a regional focus on Korea.

Dr. Justine Guichard is a political scientist and Associate Professor of Korean Studies at Université de Paris, France. Her research focuses on the study of contemporary Korean law and society.

Dr. Hannes B. Mosler is Professor for Korean politics and society at the University of Duisburg-Essen, Germany, where he is affiliated with the Institute for East Asian Studies (IN-EAST) and the Institute for Political Science (IfP). He studied at the University of Bremen, Humboldt University of Berlin, and Seoul National University, where he earned his PhD in political science. His research interests include political systems, comparative (constitutional) law, civic education, memory politics, and institutional change in East Asia, particularly Korea.

Dr. Gabriel Jonsson is Associate Professor of Korean Studies at the Department of Asian and Middle Eastern Studies at Stockholm University, Sweden. He received his PhD in Korean Studies at Stockholm University in 1996. His research focuses on modern South Korean politics, inter-Korean relations, and the two Koreas' relations with the UN. He is a regular visitor to South Korea.

Dr. Juliette Schwak is Assistant Professor in International Relations and Political Science at Franklin University Switzerland, Lugano/Switzerland. She is a political economist whose research focuses on South Korea. She has published on South Korea's nation branding and development assistance policies.